FROM DATA
TO DATABASE

ASPECTS OF
INFORMATION TECHNOLOGY

This series is aimed primarily at final year undergraduate and postgraduate students of Electronics and Computer Science, and provides an introduction to research topics in Information Technology which are currently being translated into teaching course material. The series aims to build bridges between foundation material covered in the first two years of undergraduate courses and the major research topics now attracting interest within the field of IT.

The format of the series is deliberately different from that of typical research reference works within the fields of interest. Depth of coverage is restricted in favour of providing a readable and comprehensible introduction to each topic, and to keep costs within the requirements for a course textbook. Nevertheless, each book provides a comprehensive overview and introduction to its subject, aimed at conveying the key elements in an attractive and clear fashion.

Each chapter is terminated by a summary itemizing the key points contained within, and problems and exercises are provided where appropriate to enable the student to test his knowledge. For the serious student, each book contains a comprehensive further reading list of texts and key reference papers covering the field, as well as giving an indication of those journals which publish within the area.

Series editors: **A C Downton**   *University of Essex*
                       R D Dowsing   *University of East Anglia*

FROM DATA TO DATABASE

D. S. Bowers
Lecturer in the School of Information Systems
University of East Anglia

 Van Nostrand Reinhold (UK) Co. Ltd

First published in 1988 by
Van Nostrand Reinhold (UK) Co. Ltd.
Molly Millars Lane, Wokingham, Berkshire, England

Typeset in 10/12 pt Times by
Columns of Reading Limited

Printed in Great Britain
at the University Printing House, Oxford

British Library Cataloguing in Publication Data
Bowers, D. S.
    From data to database.
    1. Database management   2. File organisation
    (Computer Science)
    I. Title
    005.74   QA76.9.D3

ISBN 0 442 31792 1

CONTENTS

PREFACE

Databases have been a part of computing for nearly three decades. They are concerned with storing large quantities of data which are shared between a number of applications. It is the sharing of data which distinguishes database systems from traditional file processing systems, and inevitably introduces some complications.

In order for such systems to be effective, and not to be tailored for one of the applications to the detriment of the others, the requirements of all of the applications must be carefully analysed and designed. This process is essentially one of modelling, at various levels of abstraction, those parts of the real world which are to be encapsulated in the database system. The target is to produce a complete definition of all of the information which is required by the organization for which the database is being constructed.

Thus, the most important part of designing a database application is deciding what data must be stored in order to satisfy all the applications. To be more precise, the most important task is the design of the **conceptual schema** for the database. This process has two distinct phases. The first, termed **data analysis** in this text, is concerned with discovering what data must be represented; the second, **data modelling**, addresses the problems of how the data will actually be represented.

Chapter 2 introduces some of the concepts which form the foundation for data analysis, which is developed in Chapter 3. Data modelling is discussed in Chapter 4, with Chapter 5 expanding on some details of the design process. Chapter 6 provides an overview of current and recent research in the data modelling field, and Chapter 7 introduces a number of implementation issues which must also be considered for real applications of database systems.

This book is intended for second or final year students of computing science or related disciplines who have already acquired an appreciation of traditional file processing techniques. Rather than concentrating on how to implement a database using a particular database management system, the text attempts instead to abstract the underlying ideas, presenting existing systems as instances of those concepts.

I am indebted to Roy Dowsing for his continued support and advice during the preparation of this book. Many of my colleagues have made helpful comments on the content of the various chapters, and their assistance is gratefully acknowledged.

1

WHY DATABASE?

Data processing is by no means exclusive to the computer age. Since the dawn of time, man has kept a record of his possessions, whether they were wives, sheep, cattle or coins. He has recorded this information, using at first cave wall-paintings, and then developing to use clay tablets, papyrus scrolls, paper, and now computers. There is nothing new about storing data for future use.

Databases are concerned with storing and processing data on computers. In some senses, they are little more than fancy filing systems, whose structure is just a little bit more complicated than that of the traditional file organizations. Perhaps there is nothing new about databases any more than there is about data processing.

This simplistic view is belied by the impact which databases have had in the data processing field. Databases are not **just** fancy new file structures. They bring with them a whole new way of thinking about data and what should be done with it. New activities, known as **data analysis** and **data modelling** have emerged to become the dominant components of applications design. Security and integrity features, which were hitherto appended to filing systems as afterthoughts, come built into database management systems. Perhaps of greatest significance, there is an emphasis on making the data available to the user, rather than protecting the computer and the data which it stores with ranks of white-coated 'priests' who are the only ones permitted to address the mighty machine.

Whilst not all of these changes are attributable solely to the development of database systems, the contribution made by databases has been by no means insignificant. The aim of this text is to explore some of the concepts behind the database approach, and to develop an understanding of the processes involved in designing a database application. This chapter starts by considering why the database approach is preferable to the traditional file processing approach.

1.1 THE FILE PROCESSING APPROACH

In a file processing environment, all of the data required for an application would be stored in a single file, or possibly in a set of files. If there were multiple applications, each would have its own file of data. Thus, for the three applications depicted in Fig. 1.1, each would be based on a single data file. Each application is just one of the tasks involved in running a large orchestra, namely, paying the musicians, scheduling rehearsals, and cataloguing music.

Further consideration of these tasks, however, might suggest that they each require some input from data held for one of the other applications. For example, the payroll system might take into account details of the performances in which a particular musician has taken part. Scheduling rehearsals may well depend not just on the details of the performance, but also on which musicians are available, and perhaps the number of rehearsals would depend on the music to be performed.

In general, given three distinct data files, it might be anticipated that there would be applications which would require data either from just

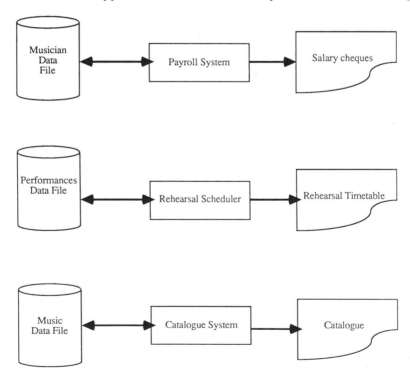

Fig. 1.1 Three file processing applications.

one file, or from any two. In a file processing environment, each application which uses a particular file must have a copy of the physical interface to the file. Thus, in Fig. 1.2, which depicts a more general situation, each line between an application and a file implies the existence of a physical interface.

If the number of files increases to, say, four, as in Fig. 1.3, and applications are generated which use data from one, two or three files, the number of interfaces increases rapidly. In fact, Fig. 1.3 contains no fewer than 42 interfaces. Such a situation might reasonably be termed an **interface explosion**.

Whilst the sheer number of interfaces may not itself be daunting, the problem is that they must all be kept in step. If, for some reason, the primary user of a data file suddenly requires the format of the file to be changed, then all the other applications which use that file must be changed also. It may be that, as far as the other applications are concerned, there is no logical difference between the old and new interfaces, since the same logical data items are being used; however, the fact remains that, because they interface with a physical file structure, they must be changed.

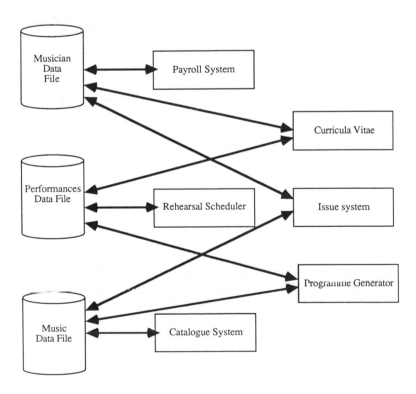

Fig. 1.2   Sharing data between applications.

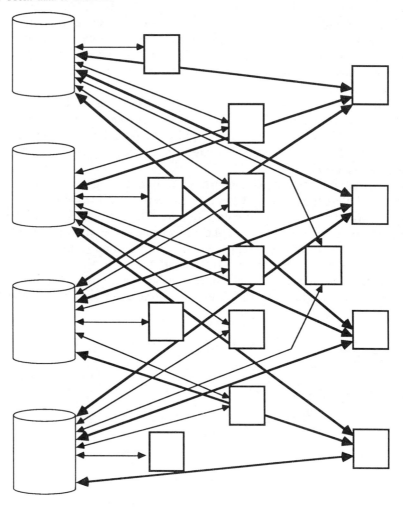

Fig. 1.3 Interface explosion.

An attempt might be made to overcome this problem by replicating some of the data. Figure 1.4 depicts a schematic arrangement in which three 'compound' data files are constructed. Each file contains its own 'native' data, together with **copies** of a fraction of the 'native' data for each of the other two files. The copied data is that which is used by some application which uses mainly the native data but also some of the data from each of the other two files. The compound file would then be used both by applications which address only the native data, and also by those which use the particular combination of native and replicated data which

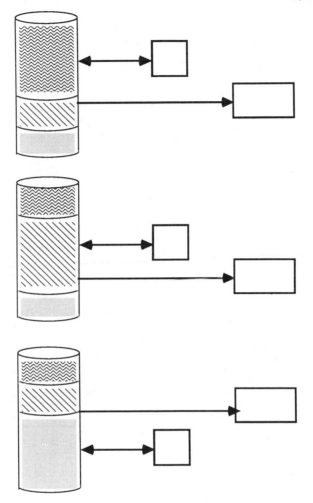

Fig. 1.4   Replicated data.

make up that file. The number of interfaces is drastically reduced to one per application.

However, Fig. 1.4 shows the 'compound' applications only **reading** data from the file. The situation becomes a little more complicated again if the 'compound' application needs to **update** data, particularly the replicated data. If the replicated data is updated, then it must also not only be updated, in step, in the file for which it is native, but also in any other file in which it is replicated. Thus, the updating application needs to know, not only how to access the replicated data, but also where and how it is

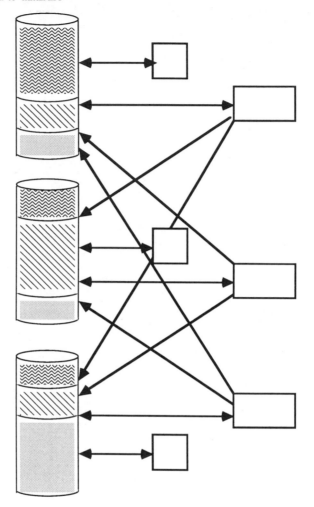

Fig. 1.5 Updates with replicated data.

replicated in other files. The position is indicated by Fig. 1.5, in which it is apparent that an interface explosion has occurred again.

It should be apparent that allowing different applications to share data in a traditional file processing environment can cause considerable problems, simply because of the number of interfaces required.

1.2 THE DATABASE APPROACH

One of the fundamental features of the database approach is that it allows data to be shared between different applications. The general architecture

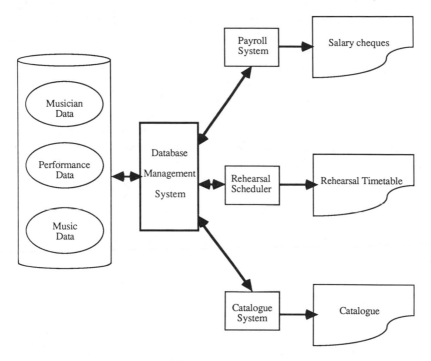

Fig. 1.6   Three database applications.

of a database system to support the applications of Fig. 1.1 would be as shown in Fig. 1.6. Instead of three separate physical files, all the data is **integrated** into one physical file, or a set of related files. The sets of data are separated only logically within the database. All access to the data is performed through a **database management system** (DBMS), a piece of software which understands and manipulates the logical data structures in the file.

Since all the applications interface only with the database management system, they require only a single interface. Further, that interface can be at a **logical** rather than a physical level. It is not necessary for any application to know how a particular data item is stored, as long as the database management system can provide the data in the form required by the application. If, for example, the data item is an integer, it matters nothing to the application if the value is actually stored in binary or character format, as long as it is supplied to the application in the format it requires. This property of needing to know nothing about the physical storage of the data is termed **data independence**.

An additional benefit of the interface between an application and the DBMS being logical rather than physical is that, should it be necessary to introduce a new field within any physical record, the application need know nothing about it. The interface between the application and the

DBMS need not be altered; the DBMS must simply map the application's requests onto the revised storage structure.

Unlike the replication approach to multiple applications, there need be no duplication of data within a database. Hence, there need be no problem of maintaining consistency between duplicate values.

Finally, since the number of interfaces is minimized, the task of adding new applications is eased considerably. Indeed, many database management systems incorporate some form of direct **user interface**, so that the data may be accessed directly without needing to write a lengthy program in some applications language.

1.2.1 Advantages of the database approach

It is common to summarize the advantages of adopting the database approach rather than a file processing approach as follows:

a Data is readily shared between applications, thus eliminating duplication and the problems of maintaining consistency between duplicate values.
b New requests, or one-of-a-kind requests, can more easily be implemented, because the logical interface with the DBMS is simpler than a set of physical interfaces.
c The applications programs are independent of the stored data. If the storage format changes, there is no need to alter the applications program, since they communicate with the DBMS in logical rather than physical terms.
d It can be argued that a single database management system for an integrated database allows for better management of data, since it is effectively in one place under the control of one set of people, namely those who implement the database.
e Finally, the integration, or sharing of data between applications, puts sophisticated programming within reach of all users of the database.

1.2.2 Disadvantages of the database approach

It would be unfair to pretend that database systems do not have their disadvantages as well:

a Both the database management system itself and any extra hardware which might be needed to support the system can be expensive. There may also be higher operating costs. However, these may well be offset by considerably greater productivity.
b A database management system is much more complex than a file

processing system. In particular, recovery from failure states may be more difficult. Indeed, a database system may be more vulnerable to failure than a file processing system, because there can be so many more interactions between different applications. A further problem is that the organization for whom the system is installed has put all their eggs in a single basket – the database.

The balance between the advantages and the disadvantages of the database approach depends on the particular environment for which a database is being considered, and on the complexity of the applications. Nevertheless, much of the material which is discussed in the remainder of this book is relevant regardless of whether or not a large integrated database is to be constructed.

1.3 ANSI/SPARC ARCHITECTURE

It is appropriate at this point to introduce the concept of a **three-level architecture**, proposed for databases by the Standards Planning and Requirements Committee (SPARC) of the American National Standards Committee on Computers and Information Processing (ANSI/X3). The SPARC established a Study Group on Data Base Management Systems in 1972. The study group produced a major interim report in 1975, and a final report in 1978.

The study group had been considering the areas, if any, of database technology for which standardization might be appropriate. The essence of their conclusions was that the only area in which standards would be appropriate would be the **interfaces** between the various components of a database management system. Although the generalized architecture proposed by the study group was rather detailed, it was basically one in which the number of potential interfaces was kept to a minimum by dividing the database architecture into three distinct layers. At each level in the architecture, the database was to be described at a different level of abstraction, with clearly defined interfaces between the layers. The overall architecture is summarized in Fig. 1.7.

The proposed architecture recognized that a database system is concerned with modelling three principal components:

a the physical representation of the data;
b the concepts represented by the data; and
c the subsets of data required by each individual user.

Each of these components is independent of the other. For example, it is of no consequence to any given user how a data item is represented physically, on disk, tape or anywhere else. Nor does it matter to any user

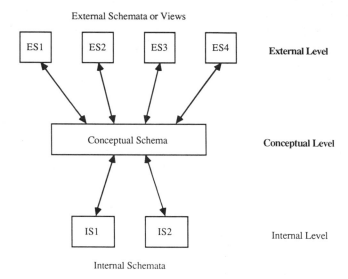

Fig. 1.7   ANSI/SPARC architecture.

what data are included in the database for the benefit of other users. Also, the concepts represented in the database can – indeed, should – be described independently of the manner in which the data is to be stored and of the particular demands which will be placed on the database by the users.

Hence, the 'standard' architecture proposed by the study group is centred around a **conceptual schema**, which is a single expression of the totality of operational data required by the enterprise for whom the database is constructed. The conceptual schema should include every item of data which is used by any application which has access to the database. The description should be implementation-independent, in the sense that the information which is stored should not change if some file is re-formatted, so that it follows that the conceptual schema should include no internal details such as physical data formats. The conceptual schema is, then, a **logical** description of the data in the database.

Physical details are confined to the **internal schema** (plural, *internal schemata*), of which there may be one or many. Each describes how particular data items are mapped onto physical storage devices. Should a particular internal schema change, for whatever reason, the effective mapping to the conceptual schema must remain effectively unchanged; that is, the conceptual schema must be completely independent of the internal schemata.

Finally, each user will access, rather than the entire conceptual schema, some subset of that schema. An **external schema** can contain not only a subset of the data items present in the conceptual schema, but also data items which are **derived** from underlying data present at the conceptual level. There can, in principle, be several such external schemata, perhaps one for each application or user which accesses the database. Each external schema is independent of every other, since each interfaces only with the conceptual schema. Should the conceptual schema change – perhaps because of the introduction of additional data items in the conceptual schema – the external schema should remain unchanged. External schemata can also be termed (**user**) **views** or **sub-schemata**.

2

ELEMENTS OF DATA

The primary purpose of a database system is to store data. Those data will rarely be simple in structure, nor are they likely to be small in quantity, and often they will be of a sensitive nature, requiring elaborate security protection mechanisms. Further, it is probable that much will depend on the stored data, so that it will be necessary to preserve their accuracy and consistency at all times. Any well designed file processing system should match up to the foregoing requirements. However, the fundamental feature of a database system which distinguishes it from any other file management system is that a database is built around the concept of **shared data**.

This sharing is more than the use of one or more of the data files by a number of distinct applications programs. If that were the case, then the 'interface explosion' of the last chapter would reduce to a trivial replication task, since each application would address a given file in an identical manner. Rather, it is likely to be the **concepts** embodied within the data which are shared, with particular details within the data being relevant only to specific applications.

For example, Fig. 2.1 depicts some data which might be required by three applications in a hypothetical college environment. The class scheduling application is concerned with the construction of a teaching timetable. For this, it needs to have access to information about which courses are to be taught, how many students are enrolled for each, which courses must not be scheduled simultaneously (in order to avoid clashes both for students and for lecturers), how many classes per week are required for each course, how they should be distributed through the week, and which type of teaching facilities will be required for each class. This collection of information is contained within the top 'balloon' of Fig. 2.1.

The student grading system is concerned with the classification of the

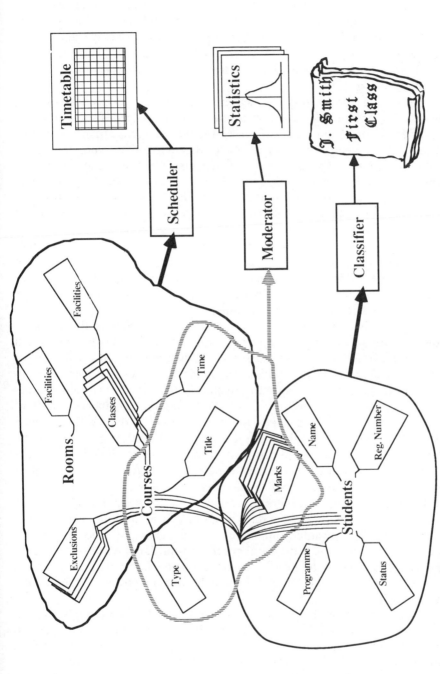

Fig. 2.1 Data sharing in the college database. Each application requires access to only a subset of the data, but the subsets overlap.

students' results given the marks obtained in each of the courses. Hence, it will need not only the marks for each student, and the rules for their combination, but also the students' full names and registration numbers (to ensure that the results are credited to the correct students) and details of the degree programmes for which they are registered and the stages which they have reached. The information for the 'classifier' is also depicted in Fig. 2.1.

The course moderating application, which is concerned with the distribution of marks awarded on particular courses, needs some, but not all, of the information used by each of the two previous applications. For each course, it needs information such as the course title, type, number of students enrolled and, perhaps, total teaching time. For each student it needs the marks he/she was awarded on each course in the year being considered. The dotted balloon in Fig. 2.1 encloses this information.

It is clear that there is considerable overlap in the data requirements of these three applications. However, the overlap is by no means complete. The course moderating program does not need access to the data concerning teaching facilities required, or other courses which must not clash, or the distribution of teaching sessions through the week. It does not require details of marks awarded to individual students in previous years either, nor their personal details.

As far as this application is concerned, there are merely things called *courses* with which sets of objects (*students*) are associated, and which association results in a set of *marks* whose distribution is the sole item of interest. The fact that the students have names, or dates of birth, is of no more consequence to this application than is the fact that certain courses have particular teaching requirements to the student classification system. Although the application needs to share part of its data with the class scheduler, and part with the student classifier, it neither needs all of the data for either of these applications, nor does it share all of its own data with either. Each of the three applications appears to require a **subset** of some overall pool of data which, in essence, represents the 'real world', and the subsets can, in general, overlap in an arbitrary manner.

However, the sharing of the data is not merely a question of subsetting, or of omitting unwanted information. For example, the moderator application requires just the total teaching time for the course, whereas the scheduler needs to know the requirement for individual teaching sessions. Whilst the first can clearly be derived from the second, it is not a subset of it.

A slightly more subtle example is the number of students registered on each course, required by the scheduler. This information could be derived from the fact that certain students were expecting (eventually) to be awarded a mark on particular courses, which is information that should be available to the classifier.

If these three applications are to be supported by a single database of information which is shared between them, then the data to be stored are not simply that there are students who are awarded a set of marks (to support the classifier), and that there are courses with certain teaching requirements (to support the scheduler). Instead, information needs to be stored about various **concepts**, some of which are required by just one of the applications, and some by more than one. A description of a set of concepts which could support the three applications might be as follows:

a   There is a set of things called courses, which have titles, which need certain teaching facilities, and which require a number of activities known as teaching sessions each week, each activity having a length and requiring to be separated from the other such activities by a minimum period. The teaching sessions for certain of the courses may not coincide.

b   There is another set of things, called students, which have names, and each is identified by a unique registration number. Each student is registered for a degree programme, which has a title and a duration, and the student is at a particular stage within the programme.

c   Each student is registered for a number of courses, and is awarded a mark for each course for which he is registered. Some of the courses are those currently being scheduled; others have been taught in previous years.

Given this description of the set of concepts, it would be trivial to generate three subsets which could each support one of the three applications in the example. Clearly, this process could be extended to cover the whole range of data processing activities within the college, with each application being supported by one of a set of overlapping subsets of a single set of concepts.

The **conceptual schema** of a database, as proposed in the ANSI/SPARC architecture, is the complete set of concepts which it is required should be represented in the database. Each subset of those concepts, required by a single application, forms a **user view** or **external schema**. The derivation of the conceptual schema and the views is the process of **data analysis**. It is a process of abstraction, in which it is not the detailed processing requirements of the applications which are paramount, but, rather, the concepts which the data used by the applications actually describe. The objective is to derive a conceptual model of the real world which specifies which data are to be included, in order to support the data processing activities of the enterprise in question. The form in which the data are to be stored should not be restricted by the processing requirements of particular applications, but should reflect the characteristics of the data themselves. Thus, it is necessary to identify the **concepts** about which it is needed to store information, and to determine the **characteristics** of those data.

Data analysis is probably the most important stage in the implementation of any database system. Whilst there are ample opportunities for errors elsewhere in the implementation, an error in the data analysis can cause complete failure of the system. If the data analysis is wrong, then either it is not possible to store data about some concept required by some application, or the conceptual model does not cater correctly for the characteristics of some concept or concepts. Either way, the system is a failure, and correcting the error is likely to be both difficult and costly.

2.1 FUNDAMENTALS

The concepts which comprise a conceptual model are that there exist some **things** which have certain **properties**, and which may be **related** in some way – or ways – to other things. The data represent specific **facts** about the things.

The existence of any thing is independent of the presence, or, rather, the absence, of any facts about it. Whether or not a goal is scored in a game of football does not depend on whether it is known who scored it. Provided that the ball, in play, has crossed the goal-line between the posts, then a goal has been scored – even if nobody saw the ball being kicked. The goal has still been scored even if nobody noted the time at which the ball crossed the line, and nobody knew which teams were playing.

Whilst the existence of the goal may not be particularly interesting unless it is known by whom and against which team it was scored at what time in which match, it exists nevertheless. The time, context and scorer are facts about a goal which exists in its own right, rather than the goal existing as a result of the facts being known. The goal is termed an **entity** (Entity: a thing's existence as opposed to its qualities: Concise Oxford Dictionary), and the facts about the goal are its **attributes** (Fig. 2.2).

Entities, then, are things. In the data analysis context, entities are things about which information is to be recorded. The things may be **objects**, such as a person or a car; or **events**, such as a birth or a goal being scored; or **activities**, such as the production of oil from a particular well or the playing of a football match; or **associations**, such as the fact that a particular man is married to a particular woman, or that a student Joe Smith is following a course in data analysis.

However, whatever the 'things', they are of interest only if there **could** be facts to be recorded about them; that is, if there could be some attribute values associated with particular entities which could be recorded and used in some application. Note that the attribute values need not be known for the entity to be of interest. What is required is

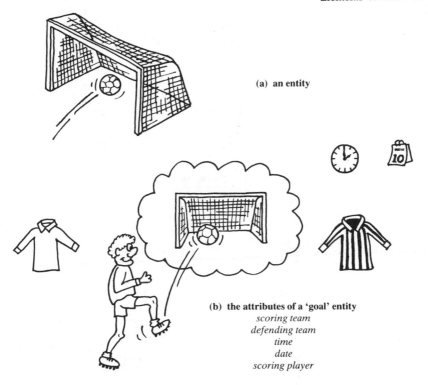

(a) an entity

(b) the attributes of a 'goal' entity
scoring team
defending team
time
date
scoring player

Fig. 2.2   The distinction between an entity and its attributes. (a) An entity; (b) the attributes of a *goal* entity: *scoring team, defending team, time, date, scoring player.*

that it should be possible to list facts which **could** be of use in some application.

At this point, it is useful to distinguish between the concepts of the **type** of an entity and an **instance** of that entity type. The distinction is analogous to that between data type and instance in programming languages. A *man* is an entity: it is a 'thing' which exists. A *man* has properties which include name, age and address. Joe Smith, aged 39, who lives at 29 High Street, Newtown, is a *man*. So is Fred Brown, aged 26, of 13 High Rise Flats, Downton. Both Joe Smith and Fred Brown, since they exist (for the sake of argument, at least) are entities. Clearly, insofar as they are described by the properties name, age and address, then Joe Smith and Fred Brown are entities of the same **type**. They are each examples of an underlying concept of what is meant by *man* (Fig. 2.3).

Thus, although it is correct to say that a man is an entity, what is important is that *man* represents the concept of an **entity type**, of which there may be many **instances**. Each instance is of the same form, having the same properties, or attributes. Even if Fred Brown is temporarily homeless, having moved out of his flat, he is still a *man*, and an instance

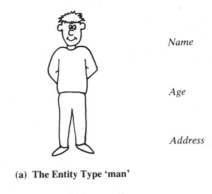

Name

Age

Address

(a) The Entity Type 'man'

Fred Brown

26

*13, High Rise Flats
Downton*

Joe Smith

39

*29, High Street
Newtown*

(b) Two INSTANCES of the Entity Type 'man'

Fig. 2.3 Entity type versus entity instance.

of the entity type *man*, despite the fact that he currently has no address: the address attribute value is **missing** or **null**.

Further, the entity type, which is merely a concept, can exist in the absence of any instances. The entity type *marriage*, which represents an association between two instances of the entity type *person*, can exist even if, within the scope of people of interest to the database, there are not currently any marriages.

Given an entity type for which there are multiple occurrences, such as *man*, with Joe Smith and Fred Brown, it is normally possible to know 'which one' any entity (instance) is: which car, which person, which goal, which oil production stream, or which marriage. This fact is the **identity** of the entity, and the attribute representing this fact is the entity **identifier**.

Sometimes, the identifier is a single attribute value. For example, most cars in use are identified by a unique registration number. However, many entities – even apparently simple objects – are identified by a combination of attribute values. People, for example, are often 'identified' by forename and surname – a combination of two attribute values. It may even be necessary, in order to distinguish between two Joe Smiths, to combine the names with, say, date-of-birth. Alternatively, some artificial code-like attribute value might be available – such as National Health Service registration number, which might be adequate as an identifier for UK residents.

In the case of entities which are associations between two or more entities, the identifier of the association will often simply be the combination of the identifiers of the entities involved in the association. The marriage between two people could be identified by their two names taken together, or, if two John Smiths were each likely to marry a Freda Brown, perhaps their NHS registration number could be used instead. Of course, even this might not suffice for certain well-publicized film stars for whom marriage is not a once-only affair!

The identifiers of entities which are activities or events will often include a time element, although this may be subsumed into an ordinal attribute, such as a sequence number. A goal, for example, could be identified by time and scorer, or, for prolific goal scorers, by such as 'the ninth goal by Bloggs in the match against X'. Similarly, the identification of an oil production stream might include date and time of the start of production, or alternatively, the sequence number of the stream for the well.

The idea of identity is important in data analysis. Clearly, it is of little use recording information about a set of entities if it is not possible to distinguish between them, or to say which attribute value corresponds to which entity. Nevertheless, it is not essential that the value of the identifier be known for an entity to exist, but merely for there to be an attribute, or combination of attributes, whose values(s), **if known**, would identify the entity. If the values of the identifying attributes are not known for some particular entity, that does not cause the entity not to exist. A man who walks into a police station having forgotten his name and address, and carrying no other means of identification, is, nevertheless, still a man, and should enjoy all the rights and privileges of being man. The fact that he is suffering from amnesia merely makes identifying him a little tedious; he can – in principle – survive perfectly well without ever again knowing his 'real' identity.

It is worth noting that several of the identifiers discussed above embody the identifiers of other entities, which may themselves be complex. The reference to other entities may be implicit to the entity in question – as in the case of a marriage – or may be necessary to provide some sort of context. For example, the identifier of a goal would have to include either that of the match in which it was scored, or that of its scorer, in order to indicate the context in which the events occurred. Such a context is a particular example of a **relationship** between two entity instances. A goal is related to the match in which it is scored, just as it is related to the player who scores it. Often, it is desirable to be able to represent such 'real–world' relationships, but, as with the 'things' and 'facts' which comprise the conceptual model, what is required is some abstraction of the relationship.

To pursue the goal example, what is of interest is that any instance of the *goal* entity type will be related to an instance of the *match* entity type, representing the match in which the goal was scored. That is, there is a relationship between the *goal* entity type and the *match* entity type, in which instances of the two entity types may partake. For example, the goal scored after 14 minutes by player Joe Brown was scored within a particular match – between Joe Brown's team and their opponents – which was held on a certain date. Conversely, that same match may be related, not only to Joe Brown's goal, but also, perhaps, to the goal scored by Joe's team-mate, Fred Smith, and also each of the three goals scored by the opposing team. The fact that a particular *goal* is related to a particular *match* is an example, or instance, of this possible relationship. As with entities themselves, it is possible to distinguish between the **relationship type** and an **instance** of that relationship type.

A relationship type is an expression of the concept that an instance of one entity type may participate in a relationship with an instance of another (or possibly the same) entity type. Just as with entities, the existence of an instance of the relationship (type) is not essential for the relationship type to be an appropriate component of the conceptual model. After all, even if no goals are scored in any of the matches of a football league, that neither precludes the possibility of goals being scored, nor implies that the fact of any goal being scored would not be of interest.

Whilst some relationship types may be treated as entity types, having properties which are represented by attribute values, it is more often simply the fact that the relationship type exists which is of interest; the only properties involved are those of the participating entities. For example, a marriage, which is a relationship between two instances of the *person* entity type, also has properties of its own, such as *date* and *place of registration*. Hence, the marriage is usually regarded as an instance of a *marriage* entity type rather than of a *marriage* relationship type. Further, the marriage entity may participate in other relationship types – for example, with the instances of the *person* entity type who acted as witnesses.

On the other hand, the relationships between a goal and the match in which it is scored, and between the goal and the player who scored it, are simply relationships. They have no special properties of their own which are not merely properties of one or other of the entities involved, and they would not normally be regarded as entities in their own right.

There are, however, a few properties of relationship **types** which are important. One such property is the **degree** of the relationship. The degree of a relationship type is the number of instances of each of the participating entity types which can partake in a single instance of the relationship type. The basic choice for each of the entity types is whether an instance of the relationship type will involve one instance of the entity type or many instances. Even if many instances of the entity type can be involved, it is still possible for some instances of the relationship type to involve just one instance of the entity type, since one is just a special case of many.

The *goal–match* relationship always involves only one instance of a *match*, but may involve several instances of the *goal* entity. The relationship is said to be **one-to-many** $(1:N)$ between *match* and *goal*. Other possibilities for the degree of a relationship are clearly **one-to-one** $(1:1)$ and **many-to-many** $(M:N)$. A *marriage* is an example of a one-to-one relationship, albeit more likely to be regarded as an entity, whereas the relationship between *students* and *courses* is likely to be many-to-many, since any student may register for more than one course, and any course will be taken by more than one student. These concepts are illustrated in Fig. 2.4.

Note carefully the distinction between type and instance in the definition of a relationship type. The fact that the *match–goal* relationship is one-to-many is not to say that only one *match* can be related to *goals*, but that, given a **specific instance** of a *goal*, that *goal* can be (is) related to exactly one *match*. Conversely, the '$1:N$' label does not imply that more than one goal is scored in a particular match, but merely that the number of goals is not fixed.

Indeed, it is perfectly possible for there to be no goals at all scored in a particular match. This is reflected in the **optionality** of the relationship type. This particular relationship is **optional** from the point of view of *matches*, but **non-optional** or **mandatory** from the point of view of any *goal*. That is, a *match* need not have any *goals*, but a *goal* must have been scored in a *match*. Thus, the relationship type is characterized not only by the degree of participation of each entity type, but also by the optionality of its participation.

A further property of a relationship type is the **roles** which are being played by the participating entity types. Consider a wicket falling in a cricket match. That entity type, as shown in Fig. 2.5, is related to three distinct instances of the *player* entity type: the batsman who is 'out', the bowler who delivered the ball, and the player who actually caught or stumped the batsman, as appropriate. Those three relationship types are all between the entity types *wicket* and *player*, but they signify different roles, and should be represented as three separate relationships, rather than being combined into a single many-to-many relationship. In fact, two of the relationships are mandatory (batsman and bowler), but the third is optional, since a player can also be out 'leg before wicket', for example.

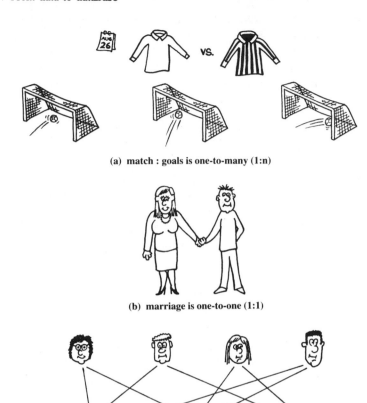

(a) match : goals is one-to-many (1:n)

(b) marriage is one-to-one (1:1)

(c) students to courses is many-to-many (m:n)

Fig. 2.4　The degree of relationships (illustrated by instance).

Fig. 2.5　Three roles — batsman, bowler and catcher.

2.2 DATA STRUCTURE DIAGRAMS

A convenient shorthand notation for a conceptual model is a **data structure diagram**. This is a graphical representation of the elements of a conceptual model, namely, entity types, attributes and relationship types. There are a number of conventions in use, some of which represent adaptations of the basic graphical form to suit particular approaches to data analysis; however, most embody the same fundamental features which have been discussed in this chapter.

Firstly, the fundamental building block of any conceptual model is, of course, the entity type. This is represented by the **name** of the entity type enclosed in a box (Fig. 2.6(a)). Attributes of an entity type are represented by the **names** of the attributes, not enclosed in any box, but joined by a line to the entity box (Fig. 2.6(b)). The attribute, or combination of attributes, whose value identifies a particular instance of the entity type is underlined. Where there are two or more alternative identifiers, which is quite likely if the identifiers are composite, one such candidate identifier is normally chosen arbitrarily; the idea of showing the identifier in the data structure diagram is merely to reassure the data analyst that there is at least one possible identifier for each entity type. Where the entity type possesses **no** attributes of its own which can serve as an identifier, such as is the case with the *goal* entity type, then it will normally be identified by its relationship to other (identifiable) entity types.

The relationship types themselves are shown as lines between entity type boxes, with the characteristics of the lines indicating the degree and optionality of the relationship types. Where many (that is, more than one) instances of an entity type can participate in a single instance of a relationship type, then a crow's-foot is drawn on the line representing the relationship type where it joins to the box of the entity type in question. Thus, three possible degrees of relationship types are represented, as in Fig. 2.6(c).

If a relationship type is between two, or more, instances of the same entity type, then both ends of the line representing the relationship type are connected to the same box, as in Fig. 2.6(d). Such relationship types are termed **involuted** or **recursive**.

Optionality in a relationship is indicated as in Fig. 2.6(e), by dotting of the relationship type line at the end **nearest** to the entity box whose participation in the relationship type is optional. If participation of both entity types is optional, then the line is completely dotted; if participation of both is mandatory, then the line is solid.

Where it is required that the **role** represented by a relationship type is recorded, then the name of the role is attached to the line representing the relationship type, usually by writing the name along the line. The

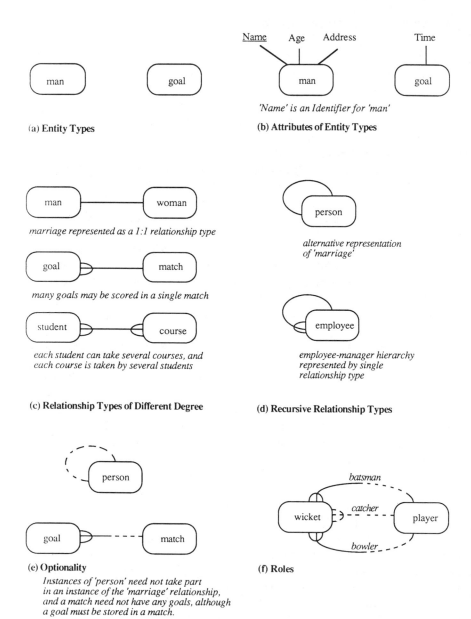

(a) Entity Types

(b) Attributes of Entity Types

'Name' is an Identifier for 'man'

marriage represented as a 1:1 relationship type

many goals may be scored in a single match

each student can take several courses, and each course is taken by several students

(c) Relationship Types of Different Degree

alternative representation of 'marriage'

employee-manager hierarchy represented by single relationship type

(d) Recursive Relationship Types

(e) Optionality

Instances of 'person' need not take part in an instance of the 'marriage' relationship, and a match need not have any goals, although a goal must be stored in a match.

(f) Roles

Fig. 2.6 Data structure diagram conventions.

three roles between *wicket* and *player*, for example, are shown in Fig. 2.6(f).

Finally, it is common to **abstract** the information to be represented to a level of detail which is useful. Thus, when drawing a diagram to represent the relationship types which exist between entity types, it is common practice to omit the representation either of all the attributes of the entity types, or of all the **non-identifying** attributes, depending on the particular stage of the design process for which the diagram is to be used.

Although there are a number of alternative diagrammatic schemes in use, some of which are illustrated in Fig. 2.7, the principal differences between these and that used in this book is in the way in which relationships are shown, rather than any difference in expressive power.

SUMMARY
Chapter 2

Database systems store data, which represent **facts** about **things**. Often, databases support a **variety** of applications which **share** some or all of the data. **Data analysis** is the process of **abstracting** the **concepts** involved in the data. The total collection of concepts comprises a **conceptual model**.

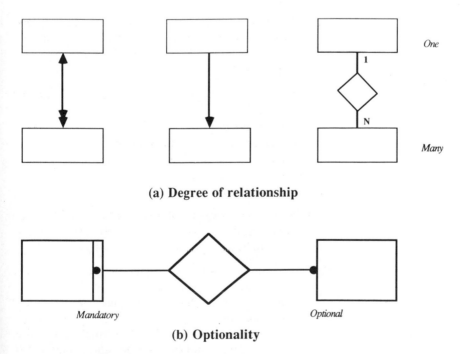

(a) Degree of relationship

Mandatory   *Optional*

(b) Optionality

Fig. 2.7   Alternative conventions.

Entities are things which exist, and about which there is information to be stored. The properties of, or facts about, entities are represented by **attributes** whose values may or may not be known. There will normally be one attribute, or a combination of attributes, whose value can **identify** an **instance** of particular **entity type**.

There will be certain **relationship types** between entity types. These will be characterized by **degree** (one-to-one, one-to-many or many-to-many), **optionality** and **role**.

For both entities and relationships, there is an important distinction between **type** and **instance**.

PROBLEMS
Chapter 2

P2.1 State whether each of the following is
  a an entity or an attribute;
  b a type or an instance:
    student, John Smith, 67%, goal, 'database systems', Manchester United, player, course, 3.41 p.m., age.

P2.2 Find **two** examples of each of object, activity and association entity types from within the examples of this chapter. What is the identifier of each entity type?

P2.3 What is the degree of each of the following relationships:
  a husband to wife;
  b student to degree programme;
  c child to parent;
  d player to team;
  e student to course?

P2.4 Why is the degree of the relationship between *player* and *wicket*, discussed in this chapter, many-to-many and not one-to-many?

P2.5 Draw a data structure diagram for each of the following:
  a a *man*, who has name, age, address and occupation;
  b a *woman*, who also has the attributes name, age, address and occupation, and is married to one man;

c as (b), only allowing either *man* or *woman* not to partake in the relationship;

d a *man* and *woman*, related as in **c**, and possibly having a number of children.

3

DATA ANALYSIS

Having established in the last chapter the basic concepts which form the components of a database system, the next stage is to address the process of deducing those concepts for a particular application.

This process, which is known as **data analysis**, usually starts with some form of **system description**. A system description is a verbal description of the system which is to be represented, as supplied by the prospective user(s) of the database or constructed by the systems analysis team. In general, the system description will comprise a set of overlapping **views** of the data to be manipulated, perhaps related specifically to an overall global view, or, more likely, completely independent.

The degree of refinement of the system description can vary considerably. Clearly, the preparation of the description is an exercise in systems analysis, and, as such, is beyond the scope of this text: the process of data analysis is the first stage of implementation, and can start only when there is in existence some form of system description.

Fortunately, the techniques which are to be considered in this chapter should succeed whatever the sophistication of the system description. Indeed, where the description is incomplete, the techniques should make it become apparent which questions need to be asked to elucidate the structure. However, it should be emphasized that the techniques can lead only to a description of the **structure** of the underlying data, and will not necessarily relate to the **processing requirements** of the application. Such questions, which can impinge critically on the efficiency of the eventual implementation, are the province of **functional analysis** and other standard systems analysis tools.

3.1 SYSTEMS DESCRIPTIONS

An example of a system description has been seen already in the previous chapter: the descriptions of the set of concepts required to support the three college applications. This description is reproduced in Table 3.1(a), but with the specific requirements of the three applications separated. Table 3.1(b) presents a rather less formal description of the systems involved in a publishing firm. It is clear that the first description, that of the college system, gives rather more detail than the second, of the publishing concern. However, each is an adequate starting point for the process of data analysis, as will be demonstrated in the following discussion.

Table 3.1
Systems descriptions

---

a College database

Scheduler   There is a set of things called courses, which have titles and types,which need certain teaching facilities, and which require a number of activities known as teaching sessions each week, each activity having a length and requiring to be separated from other such activities by a minimum period. The teaching sessions for certain of the courses may not coincide. There is another set of things called rooms which have numbers, can accommodate a certain number of people, and which are capable of being used with certain teaching facilities. Each teaching session must be in a room large enough to accommodate all those registered for the course, and no room may be used for more than one teaching session simultaneously.

Classifier   There is a set of things, called students, which have names, and each is identified by a unique registration number. Each student is registered for a degree programme, which has a title and a duration. Each student is also registered for a number of courses, and is awarded a mark for each course for which he is registered. Some of the courses are those currently being scheduled; others have been taught in previous years. There is a set of rules using which the marks obtained by the students on all of their courses are combined to give an overall degree classification.

Moderator   For each of the courses, which have titles and types, and for which a certain amount of teaching time is allocated, a certain number of students are enrolled, and a set of marks are obtained.

Table 3.1 *continued*

b Publishing database

A publishing company produces a number of specialist journals and papers. The company employs general editors who each take sole responsibility for editing one or more publications. Each author reports to one editor, but may submit copy for the publications of other editors. Authors are specialists in certain subjects, and it is company policy to try to keep more than one specialist for each subject.

A database is required to represent the above data, providing views appropriate for the payroll, publications and indexing divisions of the company.

3.2 TOP-DOWN ANALYSIS – THE ENTITY-RELATIONSHIP (E/R) APPROACH

The first technique to be investigated is that known as the 'entity-relationship' (E/R) approach, or alternatively – to distinguish it from the alternative method discussed below, and by analogy with other areas of computing science – 'top-down' analysis.

As the name suggests, the principal objectives are to identify first the entity types, and then the relationships between them in the system which is being studied. This technique is propounded by several authors in this field under various guises; indeed some authors claim that the E/R approach is the **only** feasible technique. However, it will be seen that, as with all techniques, it both has its strengths and suffers from weaknesses. Like all techniques, it should be regarded as one of a number of skills which form part of the analyst's armoury, rather than as a panacea for all evils.

In the previous chapter, it was shown that entities could be objects, events, activities or associations, and these are represented in the system description as **nouns** or **noun-phrases**. Hence, the first stage in the E/R approach is simply to deduce the entities by searching the system description for nouns or noun-phrases.

Some care must be taken, however, since attribute types will also appear in the system description as nouns. For example, in the first lines of Table 3.1(a), not only is 'course' a noun, but so also are 'title' and 'type'. However, whilst a *course* may well be an entity type which has an existence in its own right, a *title* and a *type* are more likely to be qualities of an entity than to have separate existences. When searching for entity types, therefore, it is necessary to exclude those nouns which are merely

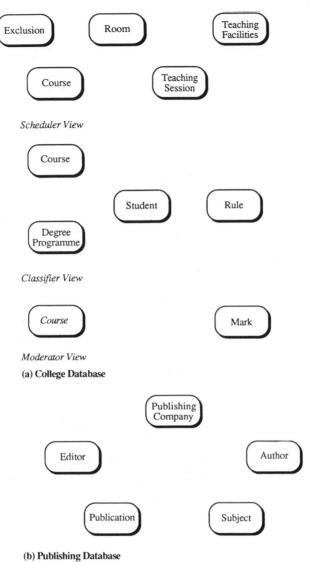

Fig. 3.1 Entity types for (a) college and (b) publishing databases.

qualities of other objects. Since such a selection relies, to a certain extent, on judgement, there may be no unique set of entities deducible from a given system description. However, successive iterations of the data analysis process should lead to the choice of entities which are at least adequate for the system required.

In the case of the scheduler view of the college database, the entity types selected are *course, room, teaching session, teaching facility* and *exclusion*. The last entity type is a conceptual entity type representing the

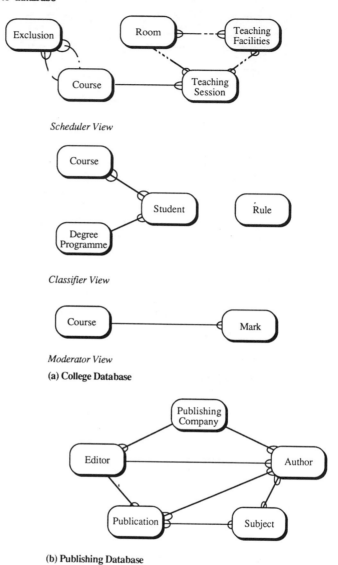

Scheduler View

Classifier View

Moderator View

(a) College Database

(b) Publishing Database

Fig. 3.2 Relationships deduced for (a) college and (b) publishing databases.

association between courses whose teaching sessions may not coincide. The remaining nouns in the description – *title*, *type*, *length*, *separation*, *number* and *capacity (of a room)* are taken to be attributes of the various entity types.

The entities deduced for the two complete system descriptions of Table 3.1 are shown in Fig. 3.1. At this stage there is an obvious difference between the two sets – apart from the rather obvious fact that they refer to different real-world systems. The 'college' description comprises distinct descriptions of each of three views, from which three (over-lapping) sets of entities can be deduced. The 'publishing' description, however, gives a single, global, description, and merely states that three views are required, rather than specifying them independently; hence, the result at this stage is a single set of entities. This superficial difference will, of course, be reconciled at a later stage.

Relationships in the system description are represented by phrases such as 'has', 'is composed of', 'require a number of', or similar. Hence, the next stage is to search for such phrases in the description, paying particular attention to the **degree** and **optionality** of the relationships represented by the phrases.

It is worth noting that there may be more than one relationship between any two entity types, representing different **roles**. Also, with this technique, only binary relationships, that is, relationships between two entity types, or between (sets of) two instances of a single entity type, can be captured in the data structure. Ternary, or higher-order, relationships must be represented as an **association** entity type. These points are discussed further in a later section.

The relationships deduced from the descriptions of Table 3.1 are shown in Fig. 3.2. It may be argued that the system description does not, in fact, justify the many-to-many relationship between *student* and *course* in the classifier view, since there is no indication of how many students are registered for any given course. Whilst it might be reasonable to assume that the relationship is, indeed, many-to-many rather than one-to-many, such assumptions must never be made without checking with the originators of the system description.

A similar case arises with the relationship between *author* and *subject* in the publishing firm's database. Here, the problem is one of imprecision in the English language: the description does not make it clear whether each author is a specialist in just one subject, or a specialist in one or more subjects. Again, no decision should be made without reference to the writers of the specification.

Great care must be taken that all the relationships which are either explicit or implicit in the description are detected. It would, in principle, be possible to check each pair of entities for a possible relationship between them, but this is likely to be a daunting task for a 'real' system comprising perhaps hundreds of entities. However, it would be unwise not to perform some such check, and the scope is often left to the data analyst, drawing upon his experience of similar systems! Fortunately, such problems often become apparent when considering the **applications** of the system, and, in particular, the **processing requirements** for the system. If a required relationship is missing, this will usually become apparent because some required operation will not be feasible. For example, omitting the relationship between *author* and *subject* for the publishing database would make it rather difficult to determine which

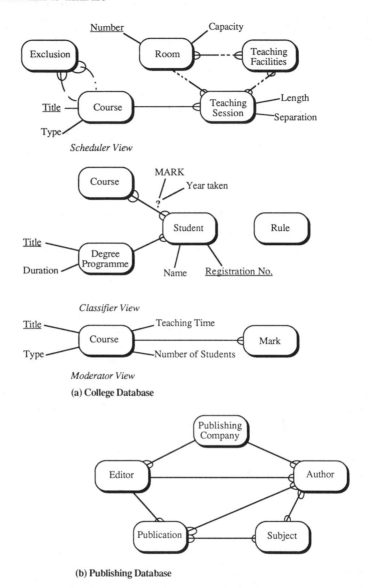

Fig. 3.3 Data structure diagrams for (a) college and (b) publishing databases.

authors were specialists in a given subject; it would be possible only to discover which authors had contributed to publications whose range of subjects included the one in question. This is, in fact, an example of a **connection trap**, which is discussed in more detail in a later section.

The third principal component of the data structure is the set of attributes for the entities: these, too can be deduced readily from the system description, being the **properties** of the entities. Figure 3.3 shows the complete data structures, comprising entities, attributes and relationships, deduced from the system descriptions of Table 3.1. The difference in the level of detail included in the two descriptions is reflected in the level of detail present in the data structure diagrams. Clearly, the data structure for the publishing enterprise would be woefully inadequate as it stands, and additional information would have to be sought from the user.

When deducing the attributes for the system, it is not uncommon for it to become apparent that one or more entity types have been omitted from the original selection. In the classifier view of the college database, the presence of the *mark* and *year taken* attributes, which are associated with the many-to-many relationship between *course* and *student*, underlines the omission of an association entity type *course registration* in place of that relationship. Thus, the data structure for the classifier view would, more properly, be as shown in Fig. 3.4.

It is at this stage that it is possible to **combine** the three structures derived for the distinct views required for the college database. Clearly, several of the entities are common to two, or all three, of the views, as are some of the relationships. However, there are also some which occur in only one of the views, and others which appear to be slightly different in the different views. The **conceptual schema** is a synthesis of all of the separate view structures, incorporating all the features of each, as shown in Fig. 3.5.

The linking entity type for the three views of the college database is clearly *course*. However, not all of the attributes of the *course* entity type are common to all three views. Indeed, some are, in fact, derived from attributes of other entity types which are not included in a particular view. Provided that the appropriate entity types themselves exist in the

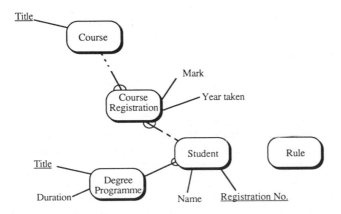

Fig. 3.4   Modified classifier view.

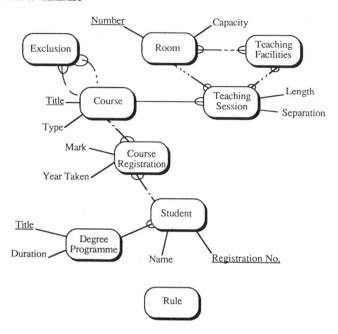

Fig. 3.5 Conceptual schema for college database.

conceptual schema, such derived attributes, such as *teaching time* and *number of students*, should not appear in the conceptual schema.

Where the attributes which occur in the views are, in fact, derived from other attributes, or entities or relationships, which do not occur in the view, then it is necessary to record the **derivation rules** using which the derived values are to be generated. The convention adopted in this text is that the derived attributes are **parenthesized** in the diagram for the complete conceptual schema, but appear as ordinary attributes in the structures for the views, with an accompanying note indicating the derivation rule. Thus, for example, the derived attributes of the *course* entity in the classifier view would be indicated as in Fig. 3.6.

Having deduced as many entity types, relationship types and attribute types from the system description as is possible, it is necessary then to check that an **identifier** exists for each entity type. Often, an attribute specified in the system description can serve this purpose, but this is by no means always the case. The discussion in the previous chapter showed that it may sometimes be necessary to combine two or more attribute values to form an identifier. Alternatively, it may be necessary to 'invent' a new attribute which can be used to identify instances of the entity type. This new attribute could merely be one which has been omitted from the original description, or it could be a special **surrogate**, some code-like item specially invented for the purpose. Naturally, it is not possible for

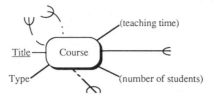

$$number\ of\ students = COUNT\ of\ course\ registrations\ for\ this\ course$$
$$with\ 'year\ taken' = this\ year$$
$$teaching\ time \qquad = SUM\ of\ length\ of\ teaching\ sessions\ for\ this\ course$$

Fig. 3.6   Derived attribute values.

the data analyst simply to invent the new attribute type – (s)he must confirm again with the user or systems analyst that the new attribute is appropriate; however, at least (s)he will know what question to ask!

Further complications can arise in that the attributes which are regarded in the 'real world' as identifiers may not actually be so; this problem was discussed in Chapter 2.

In the college database, the *teaching session* entity is one for which a composite identifier will be required – giving the context for the individual teaching session, and the *course* entity is one for which it is likely that a surrogate identifier will be required, since *title* may not be

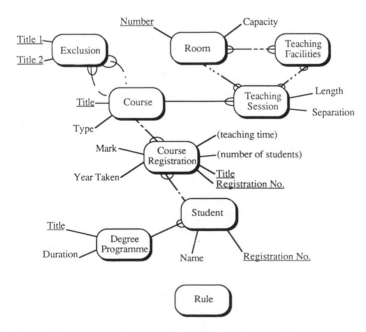

Fig. 3.7   Complete conceptual schema for college database.

Payroll View

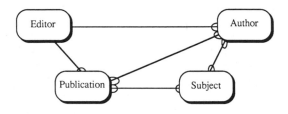

Publications View

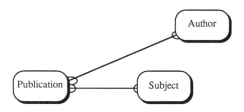

Indexing View

Fig. 3.8   Data structures for publishing database views.

unique between years, for example. These assumptions would, of course, need to be verified with the user. A complete conceptual schema for the college database, including all the identifiers, is shown in Fig. 3.7.

Since the system description for the publishing firm did not include separate definitions for the three views specified, it is necessary, having completed the construction of the conceptual schema, to define the required views in terms of the conceptual schema. It is quite likely that considerable consultation with the user will be required, although it should be possible for the data analyst to make reasonable suggestions for the views. The principal technique is to note that only those entities which are relevant to the application should normally be included in the view. Thus, the entities appearing in the three required views of the publishing database could be as in Fig. 3.8. For those entities, only those attributes and relationships which are used in the application should be included in the view, apart from their identifiers, which should always appear.

3.3 BOTTOM-UP ANALYSIS – THE DETERMINACY APPROACH

The two principal disadvantages of the E/R or 'top-down' approach are that:

a not all entity types are represented by nouns or noun-phrases – for example, association entity types, which will appear as relationship types, often 'many-to-many';

b not all nouns and noun-phrases in the description will correspond to entities which are actually required in the conceptual model.

The problem of relationships concealing association entity types should be fairly obvious from the preceding section, but the second point may require a little more explanation. Essentially, for most entities, it is necessary to record both attribute values and the fact that the entity participates in certain relationships with other entities. However, for some entities, the participation in relationships is the only information which is required. For example, an entity type *qualification* can be related to another entity type, *employee*. The information which is likely to be of interest is that certain employees have certain qualifications; that is, that a particular instance of the *qualification* entity type is associated with a certain (number of) instance(s) of the *employee* entity type. The existence of *qualifications* in their own right is not likely to be relevant to the organization, and there may be no other information about any particular *qualification* which is needed in the database.

In such cases, the only information which is required is the identifier of the entity, and that only in whatever structure is used to represent the relationship. However, since these **single attribute** entities are represented in the system description by nouns in the same way as all the other entities, they will be treated in the same way in the E/R approach, and appear in the conceptual schema as **superfluous entity types**.

The **bottom-up** technique discussed in this section, although having a number of different disadvantages, does go some way towards solving these two difficulties. The fundamental concept of the bottom-up approach is that entities are things about which information is stored; thus, given a particular instance of an entity type, then all the values of its

Programme	Title
	Duration
Student	Name
	Registration Number
Course	Year taken
	Mark
Rules	

Fig. 3.9 Data items for classifier view.

attributes, and the identities of all the other entities to which it is related, are determined. Therefore, entities can be found – within the data description – as those things which **determine** the values of others.

The procedure, then, is to list all the data items to which the system description refers, and to consider the relationships between them. Those which determine the values of others will represent entities, and any whose values are merely determined by other items can only be attributes.

To simplify the process, it is possible to disregard relationships between data items which are 'obviously' code-like, and to consider only 'real-world objects', but the definitions of 'obviously' and 'real-world object' can be a little risky. For example, an employee number might appear to be an 'obvious' code, but there might, in fact, be different types of employee number, characterized by, say, number of digits, pattern of digits (is it the first two or the last two digits which indicate the employee's division) and whether or not non-numeric characters are included – all attributes of the entity type *employee number*.

Taking the college example, Fig. 3.9 lists the data items mentioned in the system description for the classifier application. Figure 3.10 shows the relationships between the data items, using an arrowhead to show which data item has its value determined by the other: thus, a one-to-one relationship is represented by a line with an arrowhead at each end, a many-to-many by a line with no arrowheads, and a one-to-many by a line with a single arrowhead at the 'one' end. For example, in the relationship between *student* and *programme*, which is one-to-many, the value of the *programme* data item is determined by that of the *student* data item. In contrast, in the many-to-many relationship between *student* and *course*, neither determines the value of the other.

It should be noted that the data items, *year taken*, *mark* and *rule* do not appear to fit in with the rest of the data items. The first two are not determined by any of the existing data items, but by an association entity type which has not been specified at this stage. *Rule* is connected to nothing because there are no actual data items concerned with it.

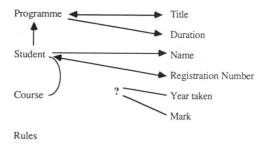

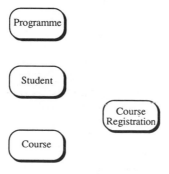

Fig. 3.10   Relationships in classifier view.

Considering the relationships between the data items, those whose value determines that of another are entities. Thus, taking first the one-to-many relationships, this gives a list of some of the entity types in the system.

Other entity types may be determined by considering the many-to-many relationships. Here, **both** participating data items are considered to be entities, **as is the relationship itself,** that is, the **association** of the two entity types. The many-to-many relationship is then replaced by two one-to-many relationships between the two data items and their association. Thus, for example, the relationship between *student* and *course*, which is many-to-many, requires that both *student* and *course* are taken to be entity types (which they are in any case because both determine the values of other data items), and also that the association between *student* and *course* is also an entity type. It happens that this association entity type then has attributes – the mark obtained by the student on the course, and the year in which (s)he took it – but this is not always the case. The entity types deduced in this process are shown in Fig. 3.11.

Finally, the one-to-one relationships can be considered. In most cases,

Fig. 3.11   Entities deduced using bottom-up analysis.

this type of relationship will be between an entity type and its identifier, and it will be the only relationship in which the identifier determines the value of anything. Occasionally, however, both of the data items will have been deemed to be entities because they either determine the values of other data items, or they participate in many-to-many relationships. In such a case, then there is a mapping between two entity types, and it is sensible to check that such a mapping really exists, and that it is not merely a case of a single entity type being represented by different data items. Such mappings do exist, but they are not common. For example, there might be a single examination paper associated with each course, but that is not included in the system description. It should be noted that the requirement is for one of the data items not to determine values of another, not for it not to be a real-world object. This point is discussed further below.

There may be some data items which are still not connected to any others even after the introduction of entity types for many-to-many relationships. One example is the *rules* data item which appears to be completely separate from the rest of the view. If such a data item is indeed required as part of the view, then it must be recorded as a free standing entity type.

Having determined which data items correspond to entity types, and having already classified the relationship types, it is then a simple step to construct an outline data structure diagram, as in Fig. 3.12. It is usually at this stage that the **optionality** of the relationships will be considered although it could clearly be introduced at an earlier stage if desired; the drawback is that it could add considerable complexity to a diagram such as Fig. 3.9, which is already rather crowded.

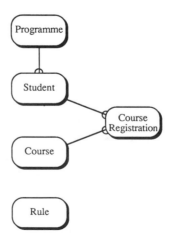

Fig. 3.12   Outline data structure from bottom-up analysis.

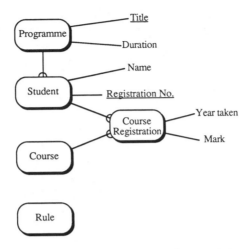

Fig. 3.13   Data structure diagram for classifier view.

Given the data structure diagram, the attributes – those data items whose values are determined, but which do not determine – can be added, and identifiers selected for those entities which do not have a one-to-one relationship with a non-entity data item. Fig. 3.13 shows the completed data structure diagram for the college database. It will be noted that it is essentially identical to that deduced when using top-down analysis (Fig. 3.3) with the exception that the association entity type *course registration* has appeared automatically. As with the structure of Fig. 3.3, the *course* and *rule* entity types have no identifier, and appropriate attributes would have to added to the structure to serve this function.

The procedure of combining the views, or deriving views from the conceptual schema, is as for the top-down approach.

3.4   COMPLEMENTARITY OF APPROACHES

Clearly, both the E/R (top-down) and the determinacy (bottom-up) approaches to data analysis suffer from problems. The former is liable to introduce more object entity types than might actually be necessary, whilst at the same time missing association entity types. The latter is much more long-winded, and tends to hide the overall picture behind a purely mechanistic technique. Nevertheless, the two techniques produce final schemata which are broadly similar, and, indeed, the two approaches are to a considerable degree complementary.

The bottom-up approach can be somewhat easier to use if, at the stage of writing down the complete list of data items, some 'top-down' knowledge is applied as to which are likely to correspond to entities and which are likely to be attributes, allowing the data items to be separated physically into two lists (as in Fig. 3.9) of probable entities and probable attributes. From the discussion above about superfluous entity types, it can be seen that the list of probable entities may well include some which are superfluous, but nevertheless the complexity of the search for determinacies is reduced somewhat.

Similarly, the top-down approach can be enhanced by use of the knowledge that only those nouns/noun-phrases about which some information is to be kept – apart from their identifiers – need be considered as entities; others may often be treated as attributes of other entities. (Note that this point is discussed further under the 'relation synthesis' technique in Chapter 4.)

Again, the 'hidden' association entity types, which are implicit in many-to-many relationships, can be brought out in top-down analysis by the application of bottom-up knowledge.

Finally, each technique can be complemented by the application of the other as a final stage. Given a schema derived by top-down analysis, are there any data items which determine other values, and should therefore be entities, but are not; or, given a schema derived 'bottom-up', are there any obviously real-world objects which are not entities – and if so, why are they not entities?

Hence, perhaps the most successful approach is to combine the two techniques, and to apply first one and then the other, as seems most appropriate to the problem in hand. Such an approach, which is likely to be iterative, could be described as 'sideways' – but the name does not matter. What does matter is an understanding of the techniques involved, and an appreciation that they can be complementary.

Such differences as do arise between the schemata resulting from the two techniques are concerned mainly with the **boundary** of the **universe of discourse** (or 'universe of data'). That is, given that the enterprise for which the data structure is to be deduced is not the whole of reality, the question arises, where is the boundary of the system?

Given that the system has a boundary, then any real-world object can be either **within** the boundary, **outside** the boundary, or **on** the boundary. In the first case, the object should appear as an entity type about which there is information to be kept; in the second case, the system can make no reference to the object at all, so it will not appear; but in the third, when the real-world object is **on** the boundary of the system, then other entity types which are within the system may be related to it, but there will not be any specific information to be kept about the object; hence it will usually appear as an **attribute** of some entity type(s) which are within the system.

Consider, as an example, the system description in Table 3.2, which is for part of a music database. The data structure which is deduced from this description, using the bottom-up technique, is shown in Fig. 3.14. It can be seen that several real-world objects appear, not as entities, but as attributes either of *performance* or of *work*. This is simply because these objects – *composer*, *orchestra*, *hall* and *conductor* – are referenced only in connection with either *work* or *performance*; they are on the boundary of the universe of discourse, and have no attributes of their own, excepting for their identifiers. Although *soloist* is also on the boundary of the universe of discourse, it appears as an entity in its own right because it is involved in a many-to-many relationship with performance.

Table 3.2

Performances

Performances are of particular works, which have titles, catalogue numbers, and were written by particular composers. Different types of work require different sizes of orchestra, and different numbers of solo instruments. The performances, which take place on certain dates in various halls, are given by various orchestras, always under the direction of a conductor, but not necessarily always the same one, and involve varying numbers of soloists.

Should any of these objects have other attribute values associated with them (for example, *instrument* for *soloist* then they would be within the system boundary, and would be represented as entities; in that particular example, of course, *instrument* would become a real-world object which, being on the boundary of the system, would appear only as an attribute.

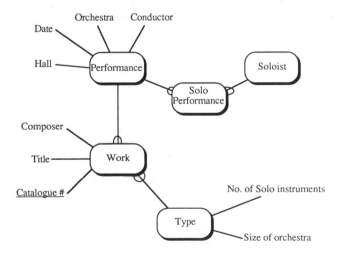

Fig. 3.14   Data structure deduced for *performances* using bottom-up analysis.

Alternatively, if it were required that the existence of all instances of a real-world object should be recorded (such as a list of all recognized conductors, whether or not they had conducted performances recorded in the database, for example) then that object would be within the system boundary, because information in addition to its identifier (namely, its existence) would be required.

In general, as the system boundary expands (as it does inevitably as a result of interaction with the user!) real-world objects tend to appear first as attributes, and then as entities in their own right.

3.5 MORE COMPLEX STRUCTURES

The music example of the previous section provides an example of three rather more complex data structures. The first is that of different roles being represented by a small **set** of relationships between two entity types. The set of relationships is not apparent from the data structure, because *composer*, *conductor* and *soloist* are all treated as separate object types, and, were they to be regarded as entity types, they would also be separate in that respect. However, it is not uncommon for a composer to conduct a performance of his own work, perhaps one in which he is a soloist, thus fulfilling three roles with respect to the performance.

The multiplicity of roles would be more evident if, instead of the separate relationships to the three distinct object types, there were three relationships between the *performance* entity and a *musician* entity, the latter including all composers, soloists and conductors. Still the distinct roles would be clear, but it is possible that they would be masked behind a single 'many-to-many' relationship. In fact, that 'many-to-many' would, properly, be a 'many-to-few', where the 'few' corresponded to the number of roles in which *musicians* could be related to *performances*. (This ignores, of course, the possibility of a variable number of soloists, or of having no conductor, but those are side-issues to the main argument.)

Thus, when considering a many-to-many relationship to discover whether it conceals an association entity type, it is necessary to bear in mind the possibility that, if the 'size' of the 'many' in one direction is small and denumerable, then the 'many-to-many' relationship may, in fact, be representing a number of simpler relationships which correspond to different roles.

A further structure is also evident in the *musician* object type. Although it is fair to assume that soloists, composers and conductors are all *musicians*, it would probably cause considerable offence to assert that they were all equivalent! In fact, the object types *soloist*, *composer* and *conductor* can be regarded as **sub-types** of the object type *musician*. **Sub-**

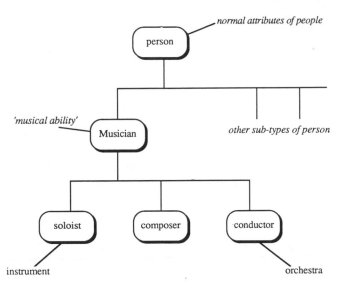

Fig. 3.15 Sub-types.

types are essentially subsets of the object type which have some, but not all, of the attributes and relationships of the parent type. A sub-type may also have additional attributes or relationships which are specific to the sub-type. For example, all musicians, whether they are conductors, soloists or composers, are people, and would be expected to have all the normal attributes of people; they would all be expected to have some attributes which define them as being 'musical'; but soloists would have a solo instrument, and conductors might be appointed to a particular orchestra. In point of fact, it can be seen that the object type *musician* is, in fact a sub-type of the object type *person*; the recursion is obvious. A diagrammatic convention for representing sub-types is shown in Fig. 3.15.

As far as data analysis is concerned, it is usually helpful to recognize sub-types when they arise. In bottom-up analysis, they will appear as separate entity types which appear to have some attributes and relationships in common, whereas in top-down analysis they will become apparent more directly as sets of instances of an entity type which are distinguished by having extra attributes or relationships.

The third additional structure which is implicit in the music example is an example of a relationship which is higher order than binary. The entity type *performance* conceals an association between *conductor*, *work*, *orchestra* and *solo performance*. In the absence of additional attributes for performance, the association entity type might not be recognized. However, an attempt to represent the association as a set of binary many-to-many relationships would result in a **connection trap** known as a complex fan trap, which is discussed in the next section.

3.6 CONNECTION TRAPS

Connection trap is the term used when a data structure appears to mirror the 'real world', but, in fact, shows the relationships between entity types without always being able to represent those same relationships between the instances of those entity types. The basic forms which arise are the **chasm trap**, where the link between two entity instances relies on there being a third related to both; the **fan trap**, where three entity types are related, but it is not possible to represent single-valued relationships between instances of two of them; and the **complex fan trap**, which involves a number of association entity types (or many-to-many relationships). It should be emphasized that these connection traps are not features of the real world, but arise from the way in which the data analysis is effected.

The **chasm trap**, in its general form, arises when three entity types are related to each other by one-to-many relationships as in Fig. 3.16(a). If the structure is represented in either of the forms of Fig. 3.16(b), it might be expected that there would be implicit in the structure a relationship between entity types A and C (or B); however, reference to the instance diagram of Fig. 3.16(c) reveals that this may not be the case. If, therefore, there is a real-world relationship between A and C (or B), then it is necessary to reintroduce the additional relationship from the original data structure. Alternatively, it is sometimes possible to eliminate the chasm trap by reconfiguring the 'simplified' structure, but this possibility depends on which relationships in the structure are optional.

If the chasm trap is to be detected, it is necessary to consider very carefully any structure of either of the forms in Fig. 3.16(b), to ensure that a chasm trap is not lurking unsuspected. Particular attention needs to be paid to the optionality of the relationships involved.

The **fan trap** can also arise when three entity types are related to each other, but their relationships are represented by a linear structure, such as that in Fig. 3.17(a). This time, however, optionality is irrelevant: it is never possible to represent a connection between instances of entity types A and C, as is shown by the instance diagram in Fig. 3.17(b). Once again, the trap can be resolved only by either introducing an extra relationship, or, if the underlying structure is appropriate, recasting the structure, as in Fig. 3.17(c).

Complex fan traps arise when three or more entity types are related in a cyclic manner by many-to-many relationships, as in Fig. 3.18(a). The standard example of such a structure is that involving *suppliers* who supply a number of *parts* to a number of *customers*, where each *customer* uses more than one *part* and more than one *supplier* for any given part, etc. Another example arises in the music example above: there is such a cyclic relationship structure between *work*, *conductor*, *orchestra* and *soloist*.

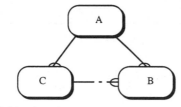

(a) underlying data structure

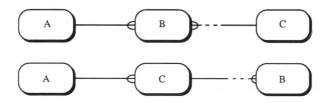

(b) 'simplified' data structure containing chasm traps

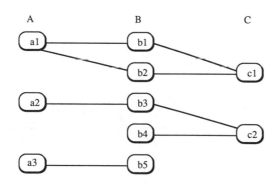

(c) instance diagram demonstrating chasm trap

Fig. 3.16   Chasm trap.

If the many-to-many relationships are decomposed, that is, the association entity types are introduced between each pair of the original entity types, as in Fig. 3.18(b), it is immediately clear that there are fan traps at each corner of the structure. (A moment's thought should convince the reader that the potential chasm traps do not arise, since they are introduced solely as a decomposition of the many-to-many relationships, and involve no optionality.)

As in the music example of the previous section, the resolution of this particular problem is brought about by introducing an additional entity type representing the higher-order relationship between the set of entity types which, in fact, was being mis-represented by the set of binary many-

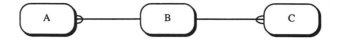

(a) Data Structure containing Fan Trap

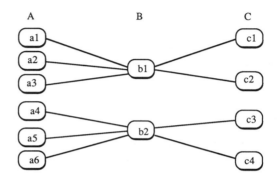

(b) Instance Diagram showing lack of unique connection between entities A and C

(c) Recast data structure avoiding fan trap

Fig. 3.17   Fan trap.

to-many relationships. In the music example, this new entity type is *performance*; in the supplier/customer/parts example, the new entity type is usually *shipment*, being a supply of certain parts by a certain supplier for a particular customer. The general solution is shown in Fig. 3.18(c).

Unfortunately, this new entity type may not solve all of the problems. In particular, it is no longer possible to represent an instance of one of the simple binary relationships in the absence of an instance of the new entity type. Hence, it may occasionally be necessary to retain one or more of the original binary relationships.

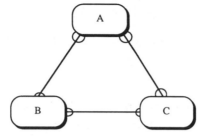

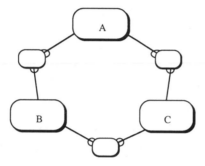

(a) Data Structure with Complex Fan Trap

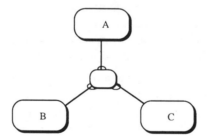

(b) Resolution of many-to-many relationships

(c) Resolution of Complex Fan Trap

Fig. 3.18   Complex fan trap.

3.7   OTHER TECHNIQUES

Two data analysis techniques – the entity relationship approach, and bottom-up analysis – have been presented in this chapter. It has been shown that these two are to some considerable extent complementary, and it has been emphasized that they are by no means the only techniques which will lead to a satisfactory logical design for a database. Indeed, much interest has been directed recently to the process of data analysis, and a number of new techniques have been proposed, some of which are discussed briefly in Chapter 6.

Perhaps a more realistic attitude for those faced with the problem of actually having to do something, rather than designing more 'elegant' ways of solving the problems, is to recognize that no one procedure can necessarily solve all of the problems, so it is prudent to be aware of several, and to have a thorough understanding of perhaps two or three techniques which can be applied as circumstances direct. Often, experience gained using one technique will help to overcome the shortcomings of another, as has been illustrated by the complementarity of the top-down and bottom-up approaches described in this chapter.

SUMMARY
Chapter 3

The starting point for the process of data analysis is a (set of) **system description**(s). The objective of data analysis is to deduce from the system description(s) the **entity types**, **relationship types** and **attributes** which comprise the **data structure** of the system, and to generate a **data structure diagram** which depicts graphically the elements of the **conceptual schema**. Where separate descriptions are given for a number of **views** of the system, it will be necessary to combine the resulting data structure diagrams to form the conceptual schema. Alternatively, if a single description is given, it may be necessary to deduce which subsets of the data structure are required by each view.

The **entity-relationship** (E/R) or **top-down** approach consists, essentially, of identifying the entity, relationship and attribute types **by inspection** from the system description. The **determinacy** or **bottom-up** approach deduces the entities and attributes from the **determinacies** implicit in the system description. Neither technique is infallible; each has problems, but they are **complementary**.

A real-world object may appear as an entity or as an attribute depending on whether it falls within or on the boundary of the **universe of discourse**. Entity types may have **sub-types** which have their own set of attributes and relationships in addition to those of the entity type. Many-to-few relationships between entity types often correspond to a set of **roles**.

The structure of the conceptual schema must be checked for **connection traps** – **fan**, **chasm** or **complex**

fan. Any connection traps which are present must be resolved either by introducing additional relationships, or by recasting the data structure.

Although two particular techniques have been presented in this text, in general the data analyst should be prepared to use a **variety** of techniques, rather than relying on a single (new?) technique to solve all the problems (s)he encounters.

PROBLEMS
Chapter 3

P3.1 A gramophone record database holds information about a number of records. A record consists of a number of tracks, each containing a recording of a performance of a particular work. Works are written by composers, and are played by orchestras under various conductors, often with soloists, on particular dates. Records are to be played at specific speeds, are released by one of a number of publishers, and have unique catalogue numbers.

    a Use an entity-relationship (top-down) approach to derive a data model for the gramophone record database outlined above.

    b Derive an alternative data model for the gramophone record database using a bottom-up approach.

    c Compare the two data models derived above.

How are they similar? How do the differences between them arise?

Which approach seems to be more appropriate in this case? Why?

Is there a unique model for the database?

P3.2 An employment agency offers a service in which the skills of prospective applicants are matched against the skills, or combination of skills, required for available jobs. Similar types of jobs may be offered by a number of employers, and any employer may offer more than one job. Each job is given a unique job number when it is entered into the system, and, in addition to the title of the job, a range of salaries and the length of time for which the job is available (e.g. one summer, three years, permanent) are recorded. Applicants are given unique applicant numbers, and a brief job history may be recorded giving job titles, salaries and dates, in addition to name, address and age. The information on jobs and applicants is to be recorded in a database, together with the date(s), if any, on which a particular applicant is matched to a particular job, and whether or not the match is successful (i.e. whether or not the applicant actually gets the job).

Abstract a data structure from the above enterprise description.

P3.3 A company records information on its fleet of vehicles and the employees who are permitted to drive them. The database is used by three groups of people: the department managers, the finance division and the services department.

For the department managers, each vehicle has a unique registration number and each driver a unique employee number. Drivers may be authorized to drive a number of vehicles, and any vehicle may be used by a number of drivers. Vehicles are allocated to departments within the company, although they may be used by drivers in other departments. Some classes of vehicle require specialist driver qualifications (e.g. HGV). There are occasional accidents which may lead to the vehicle being written off and/or the driver being disqualified from driving some or all classes of vehicle.

For the finance division, each vehicle, identified again by registration number, has a current and a replacement value, must be taxed on a certain date, and was bought on a certain date. For accounting purposes, the allocation of vehicles to departments is also required. Finally, details are recorded of any insurance claims associated with accidents, or repair costs if no insurance claim arose.

The service department is responsible for giving regular services to each vehicle. There are different types of service corresponding to different mileage values for each class of vehicle, with a short description documenting each type of service. Where vehicles have been involved in accidents, details of repairs effected are recorded.

   a Abstract from the descriptions given above:
      i a data structure which could be used as the basis for the company database;
      ii three subsets or 'views' of the data structure which could satisfy the requirements of three groups of users.

     Pay particular attention to the membership classes of the relationships in the data structure, and check for connection traps and superfluous entity types.

   b How does the data analysis change if drivers and vehicles may be shared between departments, but the fact that a given employee may drive a particular vehicle for one department does not mean that he/she can necessarily drive that vehicle for another department?

P3.4 A university research group publishes an analysis of all journal papers relating to a particular area of chemistry, namely reaction kinetics. Each paper may have one or more authors, and may discuss one or more reactions, but may appear in only one journal. Journals are identified by title, volume and issue number, and each issue contains many papers. Each paper contains a series of references to other papers. Authors can, and usually do, contribute to a large number of papers appearing in a variety of journals.

In order to reduce the work involved in preparing their analysis, the research group wishes to store sufficient information on a computer to answer queries including the following:

   a Which authors have written one or more papers which discuss a particular reaction?
   b Which papers either discuss a particular reaction, or have been referred to by a paper which discusses that reaction.

By identifying the entities, attributes and relationships in the required information, derive an appropriate data structure for the conceptual schema of the research group's database.

P3.5 A medical practice has a number of doctors, with each of whom a number of patients are registered. The practice wishes to record on a computer details of drugs prescribed for its patients, and also the dates and times of consultations between the patients and particular doctors in the practice. Prescriptions, which may be for one or more drugs, are given either in consultations, or as a repeat of prescriptions or part prescriptions (i.e. prescriptions for a single drug) previously given and signed in a consultation. All repeat prescriptions, which are dated, must be signed by a doctor in the practice, not necessarily the same one who signed the original prescription. Prescriptions give not only the name of the drug, but also the amount and frequency of the dose, the total quantity to be supplied, and the date, if any, when a repeat prescription would be due.

By identifying the entities, attributes and relationships in the data which are to be stored, derive an appropriate data structure for the conceptual schema for a database to support this application.

P3.6 A travel agent wishes to use a computer database to assist him with his holiday booking service. The travel agent deals with a number of holiday firms, each of whom offer accommodation in hotels which are located in a number of resorts. The resorts are grouped into a number of distinct geographical areas, such as the French Alps. Quite often, a given hotel is booked by more than one holiday firm, across the whole range of its accommodation – bedrooms with different numbers of beds, with or without bathrooms, balconies, TVs, etc. Bedrooms are normally available to book for whole weeks, with different tariff rates applying for any given room for different weeks in the year. Obviously, once a bedroom is booked, it is not available for booking by another client!

The holiday firm also offers a complementary service in which transport may be booked from a single point in the UK to a particular resort. The itinerary may comprise several different 'legs' using different means of transport (e.g. ferry, train, coach), and each leg of the itinerary has only a certain number of places available. Some legs may be used as part of more than one itinerary. Unlike the hotel charges, the cost is independent of the season.

By identifying the entities, attributes and relationships in the data that will need to be stored, derive an appropriate data structure for each of the views, and for the conceptual schema of the travel agent's database.

P3.7 A merchant shipping company wishes to use a computer database to help with its operations. There are three distinct areas in which such assistance is desired.

First, it is required that details of the company fleet be recorded. The fleet comprises a number of types of ship: **cargo vessels** have a deadweight (cargo capacity), class of cargo carried (e.g. dry, container, grain) and number of onboard loading derricks; **oil tankers** also have a deadweight, and a class of petroleum for which they are equipped; and **passenger vessels** have a maximum passenger capacity for each of 'first' and 'tourist' classes, and a number of staterooms. All ships have a crew, which comprises a master, a number of officers and seamen. They have a length, beam, draught and displacement, and burn particular types of fuel. They also have a maximum speed and endurance. Each ship has a home port, which may or may not be the same as its port of registration.

Secondly, the officers and crew have to be paid! Their salary depends on their qualifications and current appointment – to which ship and in what capacity. There is also a 'bounty' payment made in respect of each trip made, which depends on the length of the trip and on the individual's length of service with the company. In addition, ship's officers who are sailing in less than their customary capacity (e.g. a master sailing as a first mate) receive an extra payment.

Finally, the company is required by its insurers to maintain a record of the position of each vessel; its port and date of departure, destination and estimated date of arrival; number of officers, total number on board, and total value of cargo carried, if any. Ships currently in dock for repairs must also be included in this catalogue.

By identifying the entities, attributes and relationships in the data that will need to be stored, derive appropriate data structures for the three views and the conceptual schema of the shipping company database.

4

DATA MODELLING

The next stage after data analysis, **data modelling**, consists of organizing the required data structure into a form which can be represented by appropriate software, usually a **database management system.** The end product of data analysis is a data structure diagram which represents, on paper, the structure of the data which is to be stored. The diagram could not itself be input into a computer. Rather than a graphical description (diagram) of entities, attributes and relationships, what is needed is some formal definition of the information structures which, if implemented on a computer, could be used to represent the values of the attributes and the relationships between entities.

In general terms, a set of **field** types is needed, one for each of the attributes in the data structure grouped into **record**-like structures. The actual nature, number and structure of the records will vary according to the data modelling approach which is adopted, but the fundamental concept of groups of fields being used to represent parts of the data structure is always present.

As an example, consider the college example explored in Chapter 3, and its conceptual schema as depicted in Fig. 3.7. A first step in data modelling could be to transform the data structure diagram into a figure which more closely resembles a Bachman diagram, as in Fig. 4.1. Here, the attributes of each entity type appear as fields in a record structure which has replaced the entity boxes in the diagram; however, the diagram still contains lines representing the relationship types, but with the crow's-feet replaced by arrowheads. In a classical file processing application, the data structure could then be implemented as a set of distinct files, one for each record type, with secondary indices and pointers being used to represent the relationships between the records of different files.

Such an approach, however, can hardly be said to be one of 'modelling', but rather a recipe for implementation. The logical

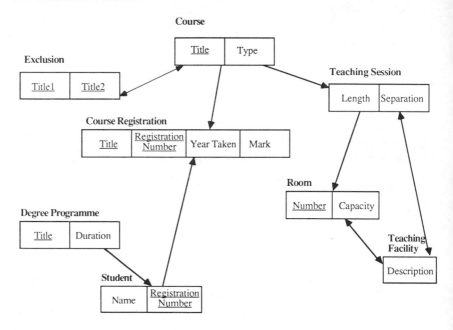

Fig. 4.1   Records diagram for college conceptual schema.

characteristics of the data structure have been lost in the detail of physical design, and operations on the logical data structure can be expressed henceforth only in terms of references to a physical file structure. By contrast, a **modelling** approach should postpone until the latest possible moment all considerations of physical implementation, and, if possible, ignore completely the **details** of such implementation. Just as, in data analysis it is the data structure rather than the instances (values) of the data which are significant, so in data modelling, it is the **shape** rather than the **content** of the data structure which matters.

A number of approaches to data modelling have emerged, some developed as an abstraction of implementation techniques, and others having a theoretical basis. Three such techniques are discussed in detail in this chapter, namely the **hierarchic**, **network** and **relational** approaches. The first relates closely to the implementation structure 'tree', and the last to the mathematical theory of relations. The network approach is based on an abstraction for plexes, and in some sense falls between the two extremes of implementation and theory. All three approaches have been used as the basis for commercial-scale database management systems, which provide facilities for manipulating the stored data in terms of the logical data structure rather than the detailed representation. From the discussion below, it will become apparent that the expressive powers of the three approaches are by no means equivalent.

4.1 DATA MODELS

Before considering these approaches to data modelling in detail, a brief reminder of what constitutes a **model** might be helpful. The essential concept is that, no matter how much care is taken, the 'real world' can never be captured in its entirety by any model. However, it is often only models which can be represented, stored and manipulated by any system, be that system the elegant language of formal mathematics, a computer, or pencil and paper. Provided that the model is well formulated, it may be used to demonstrate, despite its imperfections, all the required features of the real world which are of interest to the users of the model, or, more generally, to the users of the information contained within the model.

Thus, a model is always imperfect, but the imperfections should not interfere with the function of the model in representing the real world. In the case of data models, which are models of (part of) data structures which occur in the real world, the imperfections of the model will fall into two principal categories: an inability to **represent** some part(s) of the data structure, and an inability to **manipulate** that data structure in certain ways. Such problems will become apparent in the discussion of classical data models.

It should be noted, however, that the data structure which is being modelled is, in turn, a model of reality, and may itself suffer from either of these classes of imperfection.

4.2 THE CLASSICAL DATA MODELS

Rather than introduce the classical data models by means of formal definitions, a particular example will be considered, and three obvious representations derived for the data structure concerned which correspond to the three approaches to data modelling. The properties of the three representations will then be explored and compared in general terms.

The example to be considered is that for a number of university departments. Although it is related to the college database from Chapter 3, the data structure, which is shown in Fig. 4.2, is somewhat different. In order that the problems of representing many-to-many relationships may be illustrated, the data structure contains two such structures instead of the corresponding association entity types. In addition, the identifiers chosen for the entity types are intended to be intelligible rather than appropriate; so, for example, *name* rather than *registration number* is used as the identifier for *student*.

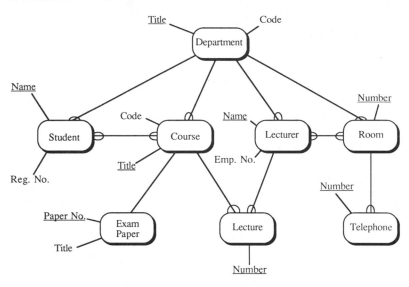

Fig. 4.2 College department example.

The process is essentially one of organizing the data structure in terms of some generic constructs (such as 'hierarchy') rather than one of wiping the slate clean, and starting all over again to deduce a 'representable' model of the data structure.

4.2.1 The hierarchic data model

Considering the university example, one could look in the data structure for an entity which is 'obviously' the root of a hierarchy. Such an entity will be involved only in relationships in which it is at the 'one' end, be they one-to-one or one-to-many. In the data structure of Fig. 4.2, an appropriate choice might be *department*, which is related to many *courses*, *lecturers*, *rooms* and *students*. An entity type such as *course*, however, would not be suitable, since, although each course is related to many *lectures* and to one *exam paper*, there is also a many-to-one relationship between *course* and *department*, and a many-to-many relationship between *course* and *student*.

Having selected an appropriate entity type as the **root**, one can imagine 'picking the structure up' by that entity type, allowing the other entity types to dangle off the first. Taking only those connected directly to the selected root, *department*, in the first instance, a tree-like or hierarchic structure is obtained, as shown in Fig. 4.3. The remaining entity types – *lecture* and *exam paper* may also be included by treating *course* as the root of a sub-tree, from which these two entities dangle, as in Fig. 4.4. Similarly, Fig. 4.5 shows the addition of the entity type *telephone*.

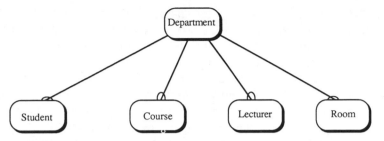

Fig. 4.3   Initial hierarchy.

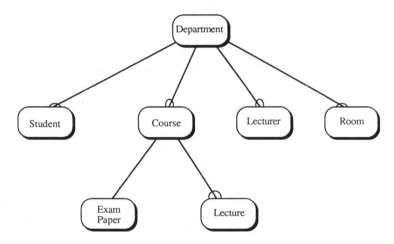

Fig. 4.4   Two-level hierarchy.

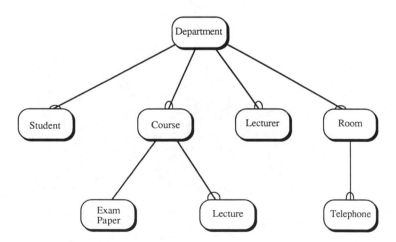

Fig. 4.5   Department hierarchy.

The **model** of the data structure then includes all the entity types, and many of the relationships. If the entity boxes are then replaced by record-like structures comprising one field for each attribute, the resulting hierarchy is a model of the data structure – albeit somewhat incomplete.

A hierarchic data model for a given data structure can be derived in this manner, and is indeed a representable model. The details of the model, and the way in which it is manipulated, are discussed further in the next section; for the moment, only the general characteristics will be considered. It should be remembered, of course, that a structure such as that in Fig. 4.5 is a structure **type** rather than an **instance**; an instance of the hierarchy would contain several, possibly many, instances of each of the pseudo-records which represent the separate entities, and might well look more like Fig. 4.6.

Like any model, a hierarchic data model is incomplete. However, the omissions of Fig. 4.5, namely, the relationships between *student* and *course*, between *lecture* and *lecturer* and between *lecturer* and *room*, are too serious to be allowed. The simple superposition of these missing relationships onto the model is not an appropriate solution, as that would destroy the hierarchic simplicity – and hence the representability – of the data model. Instead, some new structure is required. Inevitably, the imposition of such a structure will influence, and quite possibly restrict, the expressive power of the resulting model.

Considering first the relationship between *lecture* and *lecturer* – which was arbitrarily ignored in deriving the initial hierarchic model – it is readily apparent that the underlying structure is one in which the 'child'

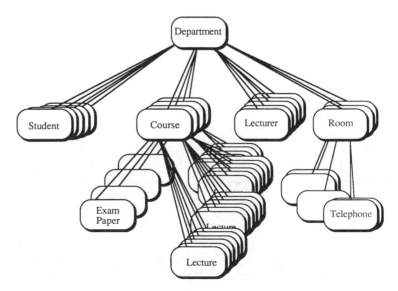

Fig. 4.6 Instance of department hierarchy.

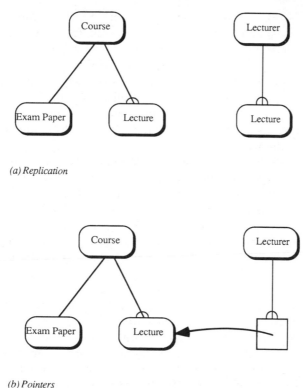

(a) Replication

(b) Pointers

Fig. 4.7   Representation of multiple parents.

node has two distinct parents. That is, each *lecture* belongs to exactly one *course*, and is also given by exactly one *lecturer*. The relationships involved being one-to-many, each *course*, for example, has many *lectures*. Since the structure is essentially symmetrical, it can be seen that the choice of which relationship to ignore initially is entirely arbitrary.

The two standard resolutions of the two-parent problem within a hierarchic organization are **replication** of each child node, so that each occurs under each of its parents, or **pointers** which allow the child node to be accessed from the parent to which it is not attached directly. These two options are illustrated in Fig. 4.7.

Since one of the prime objectives of the database approach is to minimize redundancy, the second alternative is clearly preferable, since replication which can be avoided is, by definition, redundant. However, this pointer construct, although it allows for the representation of simple networks within a hierarchic data model, does have an associated penalty. The data model is no longer a completely accurate representation of the data structure, since a symmetrical pair of relationships has been replaced by an asymmetrical arrangement of relationship and pointer. Which relationship is selected to be represented by a pointer must be chosen when the data model is constructed, and it is obvious that the choice will affect the behaviour of the model. The reader should consider the implications, for example, of the hierarchy of Fig. 4.8.

Whilst the introduction of pointers allows simple networks to be represented as part of a hierarchy, not all of the problems have been solved. There are still two relationships from the original data structure which have not been represented, but neither of these are of the same pattern as that between *lecture* and *lecturer*.

The relationship between *course* and *student* is many-to-many, so a simple pointer structure alone cannot represent it. Each student would need to be connected to a number of courses, and vice versa. The clue to an appropriate representation can be discovered by reconsidering the data analysis of that part of the data structure. As discussed in Chapter 3, the many-to-many relationship could, itself, be regarded as an association entity type, related to each of the original entity types by one-to-many relationships. Thus, the relevant portion of the data structure would become as in Fig. 4.9, and the corresponding part of the data model as in Fig. 4.10. Once again, the choice of position for the record representing the new association entity type is arbitrary.

In hierarchic terminology, the 'record' representing the association entity type is referred to as being, or rather containing, **intersection data**, in the sense that it represents the intersection between two sets of entities. Rather than corresponding to a genuine entity type, the intersection data is regarded as **decomposing** a complex network relationship between the two entity types. However, it should be borne in mind that both the terminology and the viewpoint pre-date modern data

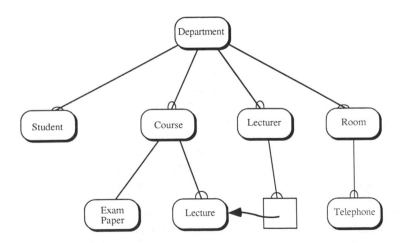

Fig. 4.8 Hierarchy with single pointer.

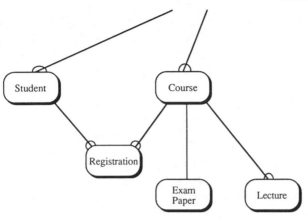

Fig. 4.9 Resolution of many-to-many relationship.

analysis in which non-concrete objects, such as associations, are considered to be entity types in their own right.

Returning to the original goal of this section, the organization of the data structure into a representable model, it is apparent that by taking a particular approach, a model has been derived based on hierarchies. The fundamental characteristic is that the model is defined in terms of hierarchies of record-like structures, with the parent–child relationships corresponding to one-to-many relationships in the original data structure. Those relationships which cannot be represented directly by such means appear as pointers between nodes in the hierarchy, associated sometimes with intersection data.

The way in which pointers and intersection data have been introduced

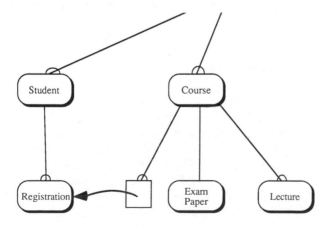

Fig. 4.10 Pointer and intersection record for many-to-many relationship.

in this discussion mirrors the historical development of the hierarchic data model. Rather than being a theoretical model which was formulated and then applied to a set of problems, the hierarchic data model has the character of a *post-hoc* justification for the fundamental implementation structure of a widely used database management system, IBM's Information Management System (IMS). IMS was developed in the early 1960s in response to a particular problem – that of finding a better way of storing data for development projects. Although it pre-dated data analysis based on abstraction, it did introduce a completely new, although somewhat pragmatic, way of looking at data. It was only really when Codd proposed his relational data model in 1970 that the hierarchic 'model' – and, for that matter, the network 'model' – were abstracted from existing implementations.

In fairness, it must be emphasized that IMS was, until recently, by far the most widely used database management system in existence. It had attained that position largely due to the fact that, when it was introduced, IMS was a considerable advance on the facilities then available, which comprised little more than the standard file structures. It should also be borne in mind that hierarchic structures are intrinsically user-oriented: organizations are arranged in hierarchies; filing cabinets are arranged hierarchically; even books are essentially hierarchic. It has long been known that cross-references are difficult to deal with – indeed, it is questionable whether many people can maintain adequate mental representations of information plexes other than hierarchies. Thus it should be no surprise that cross-reference-like structures have to be dealt with rather oddly in IMS.

In addition, in common with all other software products, the IMS concept was being continually extended and enhanced. Hence, the appearance, to the user, of modern IMS is some way removed from the hierarchic model as derived in this chapter, although the roots are still there.

4.2.2 The network data model

Given the intrinsic advantages of the hierarchic model – apparent user orientation, simple implementation structures, market dominance, and the backing of a major computer manufacturer – it may seem strange that alternative approaches should be considered. However, the asymmetric modelling of network structures in the hierarchic model is not satisfactory, and provides the justification for returning to the drawing board. Instead of trying to find a unique root for a single all-embracing structure, it is possible to construct a model based on the individual relationships.

Each relationship in the original data structure is binary, in the sense

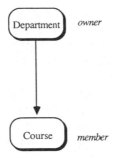

(a) A Set TYPE

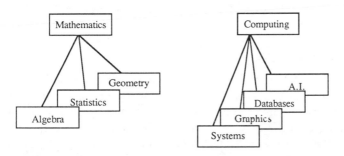

(b) Instances of the Department - Course Set

Fig. 4.11   Sets — type and instance.

that it relates instances of exactly two entity types. The degree of the relationships, and their optionality, may vary, but the data structure is composed essentially of a number of relationships between certain entity types. What makes it a data structure, rather than a set, is that collection of relationships.

The network data model uses as its fundamental building block a **set**, which comprises two entity types between which there is a one-to-many relationship. The entity type at the 'one' end of the relationship is said to **own** the set, and the other entity, at the 'many' end of the relationship, is said to be a **member** of the set. A data model is built up by identifying a set type for each relationship in the underlying data structure, and adding it to the collection of sets. Entities are permitted to belong to more than one set-type, as either owners or members, so that the complete data structure is represented by overlapping the appropriate building blocks.

One example of a set, taken from the university database, is that comprising *department*, *course*, and the one-to-many relationship between them. As Fig. 4.11(a) illustrates, the set type is **owned** by the entity type *department*, and the *course* entities are **members** of the set type. However, as with all types, it is important to remember the distinction between **type** and **instance**; Fig. 4.11(b) shows two instances of the *department–course* set type.

Since the relationship represented by a set is one-to-many, it follows that no entity may be a member of more than one set (instance), unless the multiple sets are all owned by the same entity. Given this restriction, it follows that any such duplication must be redundant, since a single instance of a relationship would be represented more than once. Further, multiple sets of the same type, and owned by the same entity, would represent a partitioning of the one-to-many relationship in a way not present in the original data structure; hence the multiplicity of sets is also undesirable. Thus, it is not unreasonable to impose the restrictions that:

a no instance of an entity type can be the **owner** of more than one set of the same type;

b no instance of an entity type can be a **member** of more than one set of the same type.

Provided that these conditions are satisfied, it is permissible for any entity type to own one or more sets (of different types), and/or to be a member of one or more sets, again of different types. (There is an additional restriction that no entity type may both own and be a member of the same set type; this will be discussed later.)

For example, Fig. 4.12 shows that the *course* entity in the example is the owner of two sets, one with *lectures* as members, and one with *exam*

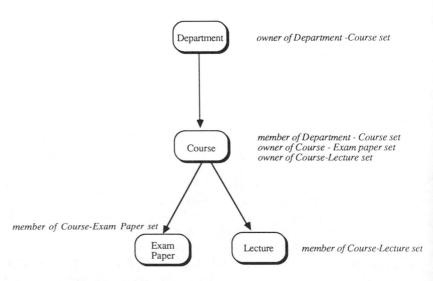

Fig. 4.12 Multiple set types.

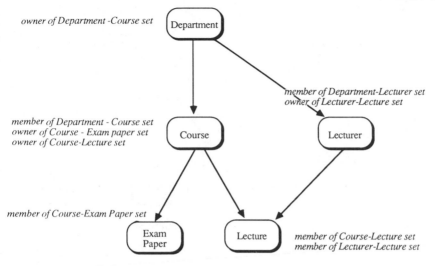

owner of Department -Course set

Department

member of Department-Lecturer set
owner of Lecturer-Lecture set

member of Department - Course set
owner of Course - Exam paper set
owner of Course-Lecture set

Course

Lecturer

member of Course-Exam Paper set

Exam
Paper

Lecture

member of Course-Lecture set
member of Lecturer-Lecture set

Fig. 4.13   Overlapping set types.

papers; it is also a member of the set owned by *department*. Since each relationship is represented by a separate set, rather than an overall hierarchic structure requiring that each entity has only one 'parent' within the data model, the *lecture* entity can also be a member of a set type owned by *lecturer*, so that each *lecture* is related both to a *course* and to a *lecturer*. This was one of the parts of the data structure which presented problems with the hierarchic model, but here it is straightforward, and requires no additional constructs, as Fig. 4.13 demonstrates.

The more complex, many-to-many relationship between *courses* and *students*, however, is still not solved. Sets can represent only one-to-many relationships, not many-to-many. Indeed, that is one of the basic requirements of the model, in order to render it implementable. It is necessary, as with the hierarchic model, to resort to intersection records to decompose the complex network into a simple one, as in Fig. 4.14. It should be noted that, unless there is some genuine intersection data, then the intersection record will contain only the identifiers of the two entities involved in the many-to-many relationship – that is, the identifier of the association entity type which might have been present in a differently analysed data structure.

Adding the intersection records to the data model, the final version is as in Fig. 4.15. Unlike the hierarchic data model, there is no requirement for a unique root, or entry point, for the network model, although it happens that, in this particular example *department* is such a root. As will be shown in the next section, rather than manipulating the data structure by traversing a tree – and having to remember to take special action at

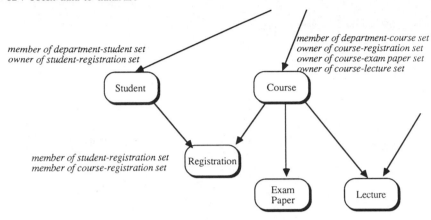

member of department-student set
owner of student-registration set

member of department-course set
owner of course-registration set
owner of course-exam paper set
owner of course-lecture set

Student

Course

member of student-registration set
member of course-registration set

Registration

Exam Paper

Lecture

Fig. 4.14   Resolution of many-to-many relationship in network model.

pointers – a network data model is amenable to more flexible processing. Since the fundamental concept, the set, involves only a single relationship, then the model is processed in a manner based on taking only one step at a time. Thus, what is important is where the current entity is in the actual structure, and what other entities are in sets of which that entity is either owner or a member.

The penalty paid for the additional expressive power of the network data model is the greater complexity involved in manipulating the structure. Whilst in a hierarchy one can only move up or down the structure, or jump via a pointer, in a network model there can be many directions in which one can move, since each entity can be involved in many sets. Nevertheless, since the objective is to represent a real-world

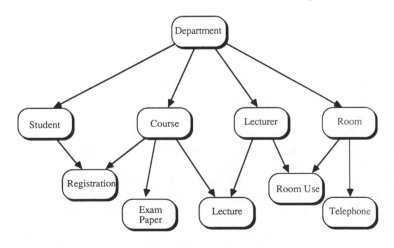

Fig. 4.15   Network data model for department example.

data structure which is itself complex, it is generally considered that the trade-off is more than worthwhile.

Indeed, the network model as derived here is essentially that proposed by the CODASYL (Conference on Data Systems Languages) Data Base Task Group (DBTG) as a standard for database systems. Although its acceptance as a standard inevitably suffered in the committee process, the model, usually referred to as the CODASYL–DBTG, CODASYL or DBTG model, has been used as the basis for several commercial database management systems.

The CODASYL–DBTG model might be said to be something of an advance on the hierarchic model, which was in turn an advance on the *ad-hoc* systems based on inverted files and the like. In essence, the advances being made were that the underlying, logical structure of the information which was to be represented is given ever greater importance as one progresses from inverted files through trees (easy to implement) to sets (more difficult, but also more flexible). As the level of abstraction increases, so does the expressive power of the model. The only restrictions on the CODASYL–DBTG model relate to various complex structures which should probably be decomposed at the data analysis stage rather than in data modelling. It should, of course, be remembered that the CODASYL–DBTG proposals pre-dated modern data analysis practice, as did the introduction of the hierarchic model, so that intersection records and similar constructs are part of the CODASYL folklore.

4.2.3 The relational data model

Although the CODASYL–DBTG model has much to offer in comparison with the hierarchic model, it is still based on the same fundamental concept: building an implementable physical structure which can be traversed in some sense. In order to advance any further, a different approach is needed, such as that popularized by E. F. Codd in 1970.

Rather than consider the data structure in terms of what could be represented, Codd considered what the data structure represented – in abstract terms. He recognized that the various relationships in a data structure could be mapped onto the mathematical theory of relations, and that it would then be possible to apply the theorems and results from that branch of mathematics to the problem of manipulating the underlying data. It happens that the data model which he proposed is stunningly simple, but that its expressive power is at least equivalent to that of the CODASYL–DBTG model.

The relational data model is based on the simplest of structures – the table. Each column of a table corresponds to an attribute, and the columns are chosen so that the combination of attribute values in each

Course

Code	Title	Credit

CMP 201	Systems Architecture	full
CMP 251	Computation Structures	half
CMP 254	Graphics	half
CMP 255	Information Management I	half
CMP 355	Information Management II	half

Fig. 4.16 A simple relation.

row of the table represents some fact(s); in fact, the table represents a **relation** over the attributes which it contains, and the tables are, therefore, referred to as **relations**.

The same simple structure is used both for entities and for relationships. No additional structures (such as the pointers introduced for the hierarchic model) are required, and even complex structures, such as many-to-many relationships, can be represented directly.

Taking as an example the *course* entity from the university example, the attributes determined by data analysis might be *course code, title* and *credit*. A relation can be constructed for this entity type merely by defining a table with columns whose names are the attributes which are to be represented, as, for example, in Fig. 4.16. Each row of the table then contains a set of values which describe a single occurrence of the entity type. For example, 'CMP355', 'Information Management II' and 'half' pertain to one instance of the *course* entity, whereas 'CMP201', 'Systems Architecture' and 'full' correspond to another.

Although a relation may look on paper exactly like a simple table, each row is an **unordered collection** of values, rather than a structured record. The order of the columns – and hence of the attributes – is completely immaterial to the meaning of a relation. The relation in Fig. 4.17 would be equally as valid as that of Fig. 4.16, since they both allow the same correspondence between attribute values to be represented. To emphasize the set-like nature of the row, rather than an apparent record-like nature, each row is called a **tuple**. A tuple which contains n attribute values is properly called an **n-tuple**, but the prefix 'n-' is normally dropped.

Similarly, the order of the tuples is immaterial. Just as an individual tuple contains a set of values, so a relation contains a set of tuples (sets of values). Not only is the order of the tuples irrelevant as far as the information stored is concerned, but it also follows that, if the relation comprises a set of tuples, then there can be no duplicate tuples. A moment's thought should show that such duplicate tuples, if they could

Course'

Credit	Code	Title
full	CMP 201	Systems Architecture
half	CMP 251	Computation Structures
half	CMP 254	Graphics
half	CMP 255	Information Management I
half	CMP 355	Information Management II

Fig. 4.17   An alternative relation.

exist, would refer to the same underlying instance of the entity type, assuming that the attribute set includes the identifier of the entity; thus, provided that the data analysis has been correct, such duplicate tuples would be completely redundant.

However, if a relation does not include all of the attributes of an entity, it may not, in fact, include the complete identifier of the entity. In such cases, different entity occurrences could correspond to identical tuples. Since duplicate tuples represent the same underlying fact, and are not permissible in true relations, such an incomplete relation would be able to represent only the relationship between the attribute values it actually contained, and not necessarily have a distinct tuple for each entity occurrence. This point will be discussed further when the manipulation of relations is considered.

Before leaving the nomenclature of the relation, three further terms should be introduced. The **degree** of a relation is, in effect, the number of attribute values which it contains, or the number of values in each tuple. The **cardinality** of the relation is the number of tuples which it contains at any instant; this is, of course, simply a count of the number of members of the set of tuples which comprise the relation. The third term refers to the attributes which appear in the relation; each column is correctly called a **domain** of the relation, rather than 'attribute' or some similar term, although in many practical cases 'attribute' will suffice. The reasoning behind the term 'domain' is roughly as follows. The relation represents, not the actual attribute values, but the correspondence **between** the values of different attributes. Thus, rather than the tuples consisting of a number of 'slots' into which arbitrary values may be written, there is a concept of an underlying **domain** of values from which each attribute value may be selected for any instance, and each tuple corresponds to a selection of one value from each domain to describe a single entity occurrence.

The mathematical significance of a particular tuple in a relation is that it represents an instance of a **mapping** between the **domains** from which the attribute values are drawn. Although there is a formal definition of a domain, for the purpose of this discussion a domain can be considered simply to be the set of all possible values for a particular attribute, or a set of attributes. For example, the *course code* domain would comprise all possible values for the *course code* attribute. Since the definition of the domain – whether formal or informal – includes not only the specification of a data type, but also the (implicit) enumeration of all the possible values, it follows that two attributes can draw their values from the same domain only if their types match and they can, in principle, take exactly the same set of values. Thus, the columns of a relation are more properly termed, not attributes, but domains, and each tuple represents an instance of a mapping between, or relation over, the domains. It is this concept which gives rise to the term **relational** to describe this particular data model.

Some simple properties of relations follow trivially from the mathematical concepts on which they are based. Firstly, since a mapping between two (or more) domains is bi-directional – even if it may not be single-value in both directions – it follows that there is no significance to the ordering of the domains, and hence that the ordering of the columns within the relation is irrelevant. Secondly, since the only concept being represented is the mapping between particular elements of the domains, duplicate rows would be nonsensical, since they would imply the co-existence of multiple mappings between the domains. Finally, since the domains are sets of values, there is no order imposed on the elements of the domains, and hence there is no order which can be ascribed to the tuples which represent the mapping. The relation is simply a set of instances of the mapping.

It is likely that, at first, the mathematical pedantry introduced at this stage will seem to be an unnecessary complication for a trivial information structure. However, it will become apparent that the manipulation of relations is based on a mathematical theory, the validity of which relies on these concepts being well understood.

Having created a relation for an entity type, exactly the same procedure can be followed for a relationship. The domains of the relation are the sets of values between which it is required that a relationship or mapping is represented. Thus, in most cases, a relationship is represented by a relation whose domains are the identifiers of the entities involved. An example is given in Fig. 4.18 for the one-to-many relationship between *department* and *course*. As with all relations, the ordering of the domains is insignificant.

The same structure can be used equally well for one-to-one and many-to-many relationships, as in Fig. 4.19. In the latter case, it is interesting to note that the domains of the relation, being the identifiers of the entities involved, comprise the identifier of the underlying conceptual entity type which might well have been deduced in the data analysis stage. It is, of

Courses

Department	Course Title
Mathematics	Algebra
Computing	Systems Architecture
Computing	Computation Structures
Mathematics	Statistics
Computing	Graphics
Mathematics	Geometry
Computing	Information Management I

Fig. 4.18   A relation representing a relationship.

Course Exams

Paper No.	Course Title
IS 201	Systems Architecture
IS 251	Computation Structures
IS 254	Graphics
IS 255	Information Management I
IS 355	Information Management II

(a) Relation for a one-to-one relationship

Registration

Student Name	Course Title
Smith	Systems Architecture
Smith	Information Managment I
Smith	Graphics
Jones	Graphics
Brown	Systems Architecture
Brown	Information Managment I
Jones	Artificial Intelligence
Jones	Systems Architecture
Brown	Artificial Intelligence

(b) Relation for a Many to Many Relationship

Fig. 4.19   Relations for (a) a one-to-one and (b) a many-to-many relationship.

course, the same information as would appear in an intersection record in either the hierarchic or CODASYL models, but the distinction is that the relation itself represents the relationship, rather than being an 'extra' record type which is introduced so that the many-to-many relationship can be represented – by pointers or set membership – by two one-to-many relationships.

It happens that relations can be constructed to represent directly higher order relationships such as the cyclic relationships of Fig. 3.18, and also recursive relationships such as the 'bill of parts' structure, in which each of a number of components is in turn composed of a number of other components, or the 'prerequisite' structure, where some courses may be taken only after the completion of other courses. Data structure diagrams and relations for these two structures are shown in Fig. 4.20.

An interesting point arises with such relations, and also with those in which a number of distinct relationships, corresponding to different roles, between a pair of entity types are represented simultaneously. It appears at first glance that the two domains in a recursive relationship are, in fact, the same; if they are, and therefore are called the same, how can the two be distinguished, bearing in mind that the ordering of the domains is immaterial? Putting the problem more plainly, how is it possible to tell which component is part of what component, or which course of the two in a tuple is the prerequisite? In the case of musicians who can be related to a particular performance as either composer, conductor or soloist, how is it possible to determine the role of a particular musician?

The answer, at least for the first case, is straightforward. Since the structure represented is a hierarchy, there must be some components which are elemental, and have no components themselves, and some others which correspond to the highest degree of sophistication in the system, and are not themselves components of a higher object. Thus, the two domains are, in fact, slightly different, and can formally be given different names, even though they have considerable overlap. The same argument can be applied to the prerequisite case, and, indeed, to any structure which is recursive in type but not in instance.

However, this largely begs the question, since the same can not be said of musicians fulfilling different roles in respect to a particular perform-ance. Here, it is quite possible, within the closed world represented by a database, that each and every musician could be composer, conductor or soloist. Although relational theory relies strictly on a domain having the same name wherever it occurs, either in a single or in multiple relations, it is necessary for some data structures to be represented by relations which contain, essentially, alias names for certain domains. The problems thus introduced are at the implementation level, ensuring that the system knows that, for example, *conductor* is the same domain as *musician*, or being able to specify that one wishes to refer to the *musician* domain that is actually called *soloist*.

Performance

Work	Orchestra	Conductor	Soloist
"A Wandering Minstrel, I"	Pro Arte	Sargent	Richard Lewis
Brahms Violin Concerto in D	Brabant	Jordans	Herman Krebbers
Grieg Piano Concerto in A minor	Philharmonia	Menges	Moura Lympany
Beethoven Violin Concerto in D	Radio Frankfurt	Krannhals	Manoug Parikian
Schumann Piano Concerto in A minor	Royal Philharmonic	Silvestri	Moura Lympany

(a) Relation for a Cyclic Data Structure ("complex fan trap")

Prerequisites

Course	Prerequisite
CMP 355	CMP 201
CMP 355	CMP 255
CMP 255	CMP 101
CMP 201	CMP 101

(b) Relation for a recursive data structure

Fig. 4.20   Relations for complex data structures.

Having demonstrated that it is possible to represent any component of a data structure in a single relation, it follows that a complete data structure may be represented as a set of relations. To a first approximation, the set of relations would comprise one for each entity type plus one for each relationship in the data structure, but it will be shown in the next chapter that it is possible to combine some of these relations without loss of expressive power.

In specifying a complete data model, a diagrammatic technique consisting of skeleton tables, whilst possibly clear, would be somewhat clumsy. Hence, a shorthand notation is used, in which a relation is represented by its name, and the names of its domains enclosed in parentheses. Thus, the complete data model for the university database might be represented as in Fig. 4.21.

It is often convenient to indicate, as in Fig. 4.21, the **key** of a relation by underlining the domain(s) which form(s) the key. The concept of key, or identifier, is slightly different from that in file processing, where the key value corresponds to a physical access path to a record, perhaps through an index or a hashing mechanism. In the context of a relation, a key is merely the combination of attribute values which are necessary to

```
Student      (Name, reg. no)
Department  (Title , Code)
Course      ( Title , Code )
Lecturer    ( Name , Emp. no.)
Room        (Number )
Exam Paper ( Paper No. , Title)
Lecture     ( Number )
Telephone   ( Number )
```

Student - Department	(Name , title)
Course-Department	(course-title , dept.-title)
Lecturer - Department	(Name , Title)
Room - Department	(Number , Title)
Student - Course	(Name , Title)
Lecturer - Room	(Name , Number)
Course - Exam Paper	(Paper No , course - title)
Course - Lecture	(Number , Title)
Lecture - Lecturer	(Number , Name)
Telephone - Room	(Telephone - number , room - number)

Fig. 4.21   Relational schema for college department.

identify a particular tuple. If the relation is representing an entity, this will simply be the identifier of the entity. If the relation corresponds to a relationship, the key will be one or possibly both of the identifier(s) of the participating entities, depending on the degree of the relationship. It is quite possible for a relation to be 'all-key', as, for example, in the case of a many-to-many relationship. Equally, it is possible for there to be multiple candidate keys. The presence or absence of a specified key is, however, immaterial to the underlying relational model, since it can always be assumed that the relation is all-key, as all tuples are distinct. Nevertheless, the specification of a key is usually convenient for the user. In particular, when the key of one relation, being the identifier of the entity which it represents, appears in a second relation to represent a relationship with that entity, it is referred to as a **foreign key**.

The relational data model, as it has been derived here, is generally thought to be the 'best' of the three classical models. However, since the fundamental structure, the relation, was selected for its logical properties rather than for its ease of implementation, it has proved to be somewhat of a problem to implement in commercial scale software. Products have been available since the late 1970s which are based on the relational model, and they are now being adopted by users. However, in the relational model, there are no physical links or pointers between entity occurrences, and hence manipulation of the entire data structure has to be based instead on value matching. Since this is a potentially expensive process, the performance of relational database management systems has proved to be a significant drawback.

The advantage of a relational system over a hierarchic, or even a CODASYL system is, of course, that no 'artificial' constructs (not present in the underlying data structure) have been introduced by the modelling process. Further, since the structure is entirely value-based, rather than structure-based, no restriction is placed on the processing which may be performed. In the case of the hierarchic model, queries addressed to such a database must be couched in terms of traversing a physical tree, and for a CODASYL database, navigating a network of overlapping sets. It is claimed that the relational model frees the user from such restrictions and, further, that the manipulation can be performed using an interface based in mathematics rather than in programming. Whilst to a large extent this is true, it is also worth commenting that few existing systems actually provide such a mathematical interface; most revert to a 'semi-procedural' programming language!

To summarize the general characteristics of the three models, the **hierarchic** model represents as much as possible of the data structure as a hierarchy, using pointers and intersection records where departures from a pure hierarchy are necessary; the **CODASYL–DBTG** (network) model uses as its basic construct a set, which represents a single one-to-many relationship, many overlapping sets being required to represent the entire data structure; and the **relational** model uses table-like structures called relations to represent both entities and relationships in a symmetrical but rather abstract manner.

4.3 DATA DEFINITION AND MANIPULATION

Having introduced the three classical data models as plausible ways of representing an arbitrary data structure, it is necessary to introduce a little formalism. For each of the three models, the basic building blocks are defined, and then the information which must be given to define the data structure and to manipulate it. Detailed syntax is not given for either of these operations, since the languages used are somewhat implement-ation dependent, rather than being features of the underlying model itself. Readers who require such detail are directed in each case to authors who have devoted more space to their treatment of the data models.

System which are based on one or other of the models are usually provided with two **data sub-languages**, one for defining the data structure, and the other for manipulating it. These two languages are given the rather unimaginative names **data definition language** and **data manipulation language**.

Manipulation of a relational data model is usually expressed, not in terms of an implemented language, but using a mathematical abstraction of the operations required. Two forms of abstraction are common, one algebraic in nature, and the other more declarative (the calculus); both are presented below. Both have been used as the basis for implemented languages, but it is instructive to consider them in their 'pure' form.

4.3.1 The hierarchic data model

In its basic form, the hierarchic model is relatively simple. However, over the years a number of enhancements have been added to IMS, mainly to overcome the restrictions imposed by hierarchic data modelling. Whilst they do make the system more usable, they also tend to obscure the underlying model, and they are not covered in detail here. It would not be fair to say that these additional features modify the underlying model, since they mainly provide mechanisms for (logically) reformatting an IMS database to be another instance of the same type of model.

The basic elements

The definition is based on the inherent structures in DL/1, the data sub-language of IBM's IMS.

A **field** is the smallest unit of data which can be referenced in the system, and would normally hold a single attribute value. It is exactly analogous to a field in a file structure.

A **segment** is an ordered group of fields, and is the 'record-like' structure which is used to hold information about a single entity. A segment corresponds to a node in the hierarchy. One field in each segment is denoted the **sequence field**, and is used to impose a logical order on segments of a given type.

Segments are related by a hierarchic structure, that is, one in which any given segment has exactly one **parent** segment (or none if it is the **root** segment), and zero or more **child** segments, possibly of more than one type. It may also have zero or many siblings, of either the same or different segment type. A given segment type may occur in only one position in the hierarchy.

A **database record** is a hierarchically structured group of segments. The distinction between type and occurrence is important: in the definition of the hierarchy, a segment type can occur in only one place, but in an occurrence of the tree, there may be many instances of a given segment type, and no two occurrences of a tree will necessarily have the same physical structure.

A **database** is a collection of database records of one or more types.

Within a database, the concept of 'primary key' is served by the **fully concatenated key** of a segment. This is merely, as the name suggests, the concatenation of all the sequence fields on the hierarchic path to the segment from and including the root segment. Within a given database, this may not be unique if some of the sequence fields are not constrained to be unique.

If a given segment needs to be linked to more than one parent

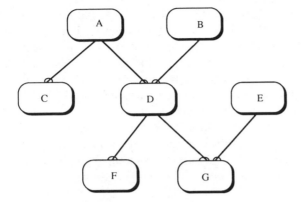

(a) Complex Data Structure

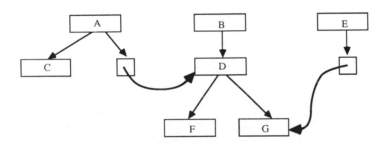

(b) Hierarchic Data Model

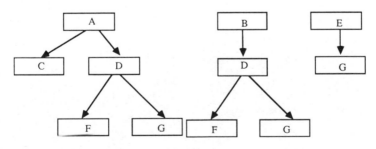

(c) Hierarchic Views

Fig. 4.22   Complex data structures in the hierarchic data model.

segment, **pointers** are included in the data structure. Although the actual scheme developed for IMS is somewhat complex, what it allows, in essence, is for multiple views of the hierarchy to co-exist in such a way that the given segment type can appear in different positions in the hierarchy in the different views. Each view is processed separately, as a hierarchy, and communication between the views is limited. For example, the data structure in Fig. 4.22(a) might be represented by a hierarchic model as in Fig. 4.22(b), which would be processed as a set of hierarchies as in Fig. 4.22(c). It must be borne in mind, of course, that the pointers are a means of overcoming a fundamental weakness of the model, and that as a result the system becomes somewhat complex.

Data definition

Each segment within a hierarchic database has to be defined to the system, as does the hierarchic structure relating them. The two are defined together in IMS, by the simple technique of declaring the segments in pre-order traversal sequence for each hierarchy. Each segment, of course, has a name and a number of fields, which in turn have names and sizes. All but the root segment have a parent segment. Pointers are included by defining 'logical parents' and 'logical child(ren)'. Fig. 4.23 contains the information required to define part of the hierarchic data model of Fig. 4.10, including the pointer link between *mark* and *course*. Although the general character of the data definition language is preserved, many details are omitted in order to keep the example as simple as possible. The restrictions on the length of both keywords and names which are imposed by IMS are, of course, not significant as far as the underlying hierarchic structure is concerned.

```
DBD       NAME=DEPTDB
SEGM      NAME=DEPT, BYTES=64
FIELD     NAME=TITLE, BYTES=56,START=1
FIELD     (NAME=CODE,SEQ), BYTES=8,START=57
SEGM      NAME=STUDENT, PARENT=DEPT,BYTES=64
FIELD     NAME=NAME,BYTES=56,START=1
          . . . . .
SEGM      NAME=MARK,POINTER=LPRNT,.....
          PARENT=((STUDENT), (COURSE, ... ),....
FIELD     NAME=.....
          . . . . .
SEGM      NAME=COURSE, PARENT=DEPT, ...
LCHILD    NAME=(MARK,DEPTDB)
FIELD     NAME=.....
          . . . . .
SEGM      NAME=EXAM PAPER,PARENT=COURSE,...
```

Fig. 4.23   IMS database definition for part of department database (many details omitted).

Data manipulation

In DL/1, data manipulation is based on two concepts: descending or traversing the hierarchy, and searching all the segments in the hierarchy for a particular value. In most cases, a search would establish an initial position from which a traversal and/or descent could commence.

There are three basic traversal operations:

a GET UNIQUE (GU). Get the first segment, in hierarchic sequence, which satisfies the specified search criteria.
b GET NEXT (GN). Get the next segment, in hierarchic sequence, of the specified type. If there are no more segments of the specified type under the current parent segment, the next segment of the 'parent' type is selected, and then the first segment of the required type beneath the new parent.
c GET NEXT WITHIN PARENT (GNP). As GET NEXT, but returning an 'end-of-file' condition if there are no more segments of the specified type under the current parent segment.

The searching criterion is specified as a **segment search argument** which is appended to a GET UNIQUE operation. The segment search argument (SSA) comprises simply a predicate based on the field values which occur in the segment.

The operation of GETting a segment implies that the values which it contains are transferred to a **user work area** (UWA), which is the means of communication between the database management software and a host language in which the data manipulation instructions are embedded. It is the host language which must provide all the control structures – such as selection and repetition – which will allow a sensible database program to be constructed using the above traversal instructions, and will also permit the data from the database to be processed as required.

Databases are, of course, essentially dynamic, and it must be possible to effect updates to the data which they contain. In IMS, using DL/1, updates (including insertion and deletion of segments) must be effected on a segment-by-segment basis. Modified versions of the traversal instructions (GET HOLD UNIQUE (GHU), GET HOLD NEXT (GHN) and GET HOLD NEXT WITHIN PARENT (GHNP)) not only select a specified segment and transfer it to the user work area, but also hold its position in the database ready for update. Update commands are available to update (i.e. re-write), delete or insert a segment at the 'held' position.

Sample queries against the hierarchy of Fig. 4.10 are expressed, informally, in Fig. 4.24.

(a) GU   DEPT   (TITLE='Computing')
         STUDENT
     while not end-of-file
         print student name etc.
         GNP STUDENT
     end while

(b) GU   DEPT   (TITLE='Computing')
         STUDENT
     while not end-of-file
         print student details
         GU REGISTRATION (TITLE='Systems')
         print details of registration (mark?) for systems course
         GNP STUDENT
     end while

(c) GU   DEPT   (TITLE='Computing')
         STUDENT
     while not end-of-file
         print student details
         GU REGISTRATION
         while not end-of-file
             Print registration details
             GNP REGISTRATION
         end while
         GNP STUDENT
     end while

Fig. 4.24   DL/1 queries against department database. (a) Generate a list of
students in the computing department; (b) for each student in
computing, print details of registration for systems; (c) for each student
in computing, print details of all registrations.

4.3.2 The network (CODASYL–DBTG) model

Unlike the hierarchic model, which has been abstracted from IMS, the
CODASYL–DBTG model is defined in terms of a standard, from which
implementations are developed. One result of this is that different
implementations are very similar in detail as well as in general concept,
and the model can be described quite adequately in terms of the standard
itself.

The CODASYL–DBTG model is somewhat complex, to say the least.
As with the hierarchic model, space permits only an outline sketch of the
model to be included here, and this inevitably can give only a partial
picture of the model. However, the salient features of the model are
presented here, and, in particular, those which distinguish the character
of the CODASYL model from the hierarchic and relational models.

The basic elements

At the lowest level, many of the building blocks from which the
CODASYL model is constructed are similar to those for the hierarchic

model. What distinguishes the two models is the way in which these components are combined to make the higher-level constructs of the model.

A **data item** is the smallest addressable unit of data, and can hold a single attribute value.

Where an attribute is multivalued, data items can be grouped together as a **vector data aggregate**, which is analogous to a single-dimensioned array in programming languages. Each element of the vector data aggregate is of the same type, and can hold exactly one value.

If the data structure requires groups of values to occur multiple times, then a **repeating group data aggregate** can be defined, which is, in effect, a sub-record. Each instance of the group comprises the same data items in the same order. Repeating group data aggregates can themselves include other data aggregates, either 'vector' or 'repeating group', with nesting to an arbitrary depth.

A **record** is an ordered collection of data items and/or data aggregates. Since repeating group data aggregates can be nested to an arbitrary depth within a record, it follows that an entire hierarchy can be represented within a single record. Thus, in some senses, a CODASYL record is similar to an IMS database record. However, whereas the definition of an IMS record specifies only which segments occur where, and not how many instances of each type of segment there may be, a CODASYL record may contain only a specified maximum number of each repeating group.

The repeating group construction is intended primarily for structures in which there are a small, fixed number of occurrences of the group, and efficiency can be improved by making the repeating group part of a particular record rather than separate records. It would be an abuse of the remainder of the CODASYL model if a hierarchic application were modelled entirely within a single CODASYL record. For example, the data structure of Fig. 4.25(a) could, in principle, be represented by either of the record structures in Fig. 4.25(b) and (c). The structure of 4.25(b) would normally be preferable, since it is more in keeping with the use of a database, which represents both data and relationships, than is the structure of Fig. 4.25(c). Nevertheless, if there were a small, fixed upper limit (of the order of, say , 7) on the number of instances of the repeating groups which could occur within any record, and it were known that the entire set of repeating groups would be required for processing whenever the main record were processed, then it might be more efficient to use the repeating group structure of Fig. 4.25(c).

A further distinction between IMS and CODASYL records lies in the way in which they are used. In that context, a CODASYL record is much more like an IMS segment, since it is the record, rather than any part of it, which is associated with a logical position within the database structure. Indeed, it may be misleading to compare CODASYL and IMS

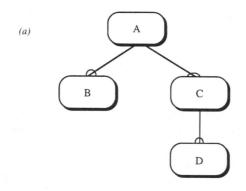

(a)

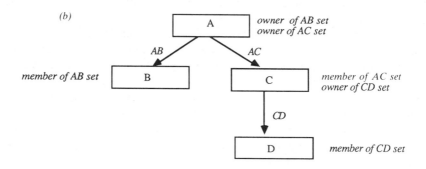

(b)

(c)

Fig. 4.25   (a) Repeating group structures in CODASYL; (b) standard CODASYL data structure; (c) CODASYL data model using repeating groups.

records, because in the majority of applications a CODASYL record is simply a group of fields which is treated as the smallest retrievable unit of data, in the same way as a segment is the smallest retrievable unit of a hierarchic database. Even that is not a complete picture, because it is only for the purpose of location within the database that a CODASYL record is indivisible. Since record retrieval in a CODASYL is a two-stage process, it is possible to retrieve, in the sense of make available to an applications program, either the entire record or only specified fields, as required. Further, the concept of a record in CODASYL is logical rather than physical, there being no requirement for the stored version of a record to look like the logical version which is manipulated by an application.

The fundamental construct within the CODASYL model which distinguishes it from other systems is the **set**. A CODASYL set, sometimes termed a **coset** to distinguish it from the mathematical notion of set, is a representation of a one-to-many relationship between a single instance of one record type and multiple instances of one or more record types. Since a diagrammatic representation of such a set resembles a fan, a CODASYL set is sometimes termed a **fanset**.

A simple set is an ordered collection of records of the same structure, termed **set members**, and a single record which is the **owner** of the set. The owner record for a particular set identifies a particular collection of set members, described as a **set occurrence**. It is possible for a set to contain two – or more – types of record as set members, in which case an occurrence of that set would comprise a collection of each of the types of member record.

The ordering of the set members can be determined either by the value of some particular data item in the record, or by the application program which creates the database. If the order is determined by a data item, then it also possible for an **index** to be defined on the ordering data item. The existence of such an index merely increases the efficiency of access to records on the basis of a corresponding data item value; there is no restriction on which data items may be used for selecting records by value.

When the network model was 'derived' earlier in this chapter, in terms of entity types rather than record types, restrictions were imposed on the membership (by entities) of different set types. These restrictions are inherent to the CODASYL model, and are reiterated here in terms of records:

a   no occurrence of a record type may be either owner or member of more than one occurrence of any set type;
b   no record type may be both owner and member of any set type.

The second of these restrictions, which was not mentioned earlier, is to prevent ambiguities which could arise in processing set types for which the owner and member records were of the same type. Provided that these restrictions are satisfied, then any record type can be a member of many (different) set types, so that any occurrence of that record type may also be a member of many occurrences of different set types. Similarly, any record type may be the owner of any number of set types, and any record type may both own set types and be a member of other set types.

Set membership for any record may be specified to be either **mandatory** or **optional**, and, independently, either **automatic** or **manual**. Mandatory membership implies that the record must belong to an instance of the set type, whereas with optional membership it can be removed (disconnected) from that set type, and still exist in the database. Automatic and manual membership refer to the way in which the record becomes a member of the set. If membership is automatic, then the record is connected by the system to whatever instance of the set type is 'current' (see below) when the record is first stored. If membership is manual, then it is up to the application program to connect the record to an instance of the set type before completing the task.

A final concept on which the CODASYL model is founded is that of a **realm**. A realm is a subset of the record occurrences in a database. Any record type may be present in more than one realm, and any realm can contain records of more than one type. When a database is processed, each realm has to be made available to the process individually, and, obviously, only records in a realm which has been made available can be processed.

Whilst an arbitrary distribution of records between realms could cause confusion, if not chaos, the concept does have some potential advantages. It is possible to make different realms available to an applications program with different access rights. For example, the program could have read-only access to one realm, and write access to another realm. Such an arrangement could protect part of the database from accidental corruption by the program. Alternatively, if one particular realm contained a subset of the database which was confidential or sensitive, then a given applications program might be denied any access to that realm.

Data definition

Two types of schema must be defined for a CODASYL database. The **schema**, which corresponds to the ANSI/SPARC conceptual schema, is defined using a free-standing Schema Data Definition Language (Schema DDL) which was specified as part of the CODASYL standard. Every application accesses the database via a **sub-schema**, (ANSI/SPARC external schema), defined using a language-specific Sub-schema Data Definition Language.

The underlying philosophy of the CODASYL model is that it should be hosted in a high-level language which can provide the iteration and recursion structures required for record-at-a-time manipulation. An applications program written in such a language would have to include a definition of the sub-schema which it was intending to use. The specification of the Sub-schema DDL was a little less rigid than for the Schema DDL, since it was assumed that those implementing the CODASYL model for a particular language would design an appropriate DDL which reflected the character of the high-level language. The original proposal included a definition of the Sub-schema DDL for

COBOL, and an outline for a FORTRAN version, but was less specific about the details for other languages.

The schema definition has to include complete definitions for both records and sets. A sub-schema definition specifies which of the record types and set types present in the schema will be available to a user of the sub-schema.

For records, the names, data types and sizes of the data items are required. For any data aggregates, the number of repetitions must also be defined. It is also possible to specify whether or not duplicate values are allowed for particular data items. In addition, the **location mode** for each record must be specified. The choices of location mode are essentially **calc**, **via a set** and **direct**.

The CODASYL model does not really support the concept of primary key, although it does permit the exclusion of duplicate values for any data item(s). The majority of the records in a CODASYL database are accessed by navigating through a logical network. However, at least one entry point is needed for the network. Entry points are provided by specifying that certain record types have a location mode of **calc**, that is, they are to be located by calculating a position in the physical database from the value of some data item (i.e. simple hashing on one field).

The majority of the remainder of the records will then be accessed via a particular set. Specifying a particular set in the location mode of a record does not imply that it can be accessed only via that set; it merely ensures that access via that set is relatively efficient. In essence, it ensures that each occurrence of that record type is located physically close to the owner of the instance of the specified set to which it belongs. Thus, once the set is identified, by accessing the owner, all the member records are clustered close by. The DDL even allows particular records to be located close to the owner record for a particular set, but displaced by a specified number of disk pages, so that clusters of records representing different set instances need not overlap. Whatever the physical location of a physical record, it can always be accessed via any set of which it is the owner or a member; however, such access may correspond to random access, which may have performance implications.

The remaining access mode, **direct**, allows efficient 'long jumps' across the database structure. Essentially, whenever a record is stored in the database, the physical address is returned, and can be stored in another record for future direct access. Although this undoubtedly permits increased efficiency, the inclusion of an explicit pointer in this manner tends to obscure the nature of the CODASYL model. However, since efficiency in real systems, as distinct from academic exercises, is extremely important, such facilities can be useful.

An example of a record definition, expressed in a rather informal version of Schema DDL, is shown in Fig. 4.26(a).

Set definition comprises the specification of a name for the set, which

```
RECORD NAME IS DEPARTMENT
    LOCATION MODE IS CALC USING CODE;

    02    TITLE    PIC X(56).
    02    CODE     PIC X(8).

RECORD NAME IS STUDENT
    LOCATION MODE IS VIA DEPARTMENT-STUDENT SET;

    02    NAME     PIC X(56).
    02    REGNO    PIC X(8).
```

(a) Sample Record Definitions for CODASYL schema

```
SET NAME IS DEPARTMENT-STUDENT;
    ORDER IS SORTED;
    OWNER IS DEPARTMENT;
    MEMBER IS STUDENT PERMANENT AUTOMATIC
        ASCENDING KEY IS NAME;
```

(b) a set definition

Fig. 4.26   CODASYL data definitions.

record type is the owner, and which record type(s) are the members. For each member record type, the insertion (automatic/manual) and retention (mandatory/optional) requirements must also be specified, whether or not duplicates are permitted, and whether any data item is used to sort (order) the record occurrences within the set. If the membership is automatic, it is also possible to specify that the system should select the appropriate set occurrence automatically, either by using the value held in the user work area for some data item in the owner of the set, or by matching some data item in the new record to the corresponding data item in the owner record. A sample set definition is shown in Fig. 4.26(b).

A sub-schema is defined in terms of the underlying schema. Essentially, the sub-schema is just a 'shopping list' of those components of the schema which are to be available to users of the sub-schema. A sub-schema definition may omit:

a data items or data aggregates from any record;
b record types or occurrences;
c sets;
d realms.

In addition, the order of data items within a given record may be changed.

Data manipulation

Most implementations of the CODASYL model provide a data manipulation language which is hosted in a high-level language, such as

COBOL, FORTRAN or PL/1. Since CODASYL data manipulation is performed record-at-a-time, such hosting is required to provide the iteration and recursion required to retrieve and process multiple records.

The fundamental concept in manipulating a CODASYL database is that of establishing **currency**. Currency is not unlike the idea of 'current record' within a conventional file processing system. The database can be regarded as a (rather large) data structure through which the user – or his applications program – 'navigates'. From any 'position' in the structure, it is possible to move to another 'position' by stepping through the various sets which comprise the database. The operator to move from one record in the data structure to another is FIND, which has many forms corresponding to the variety of ways in which the move may be specified.

After any operation, one particular record will be **current record**, and will correspond to the 'position' within the database. As well as the record itself being current, its selection, by whatever means, will also have established a **current** instance of each **set** of which it is either an owner or a member. Since a record can be a member of many set types, currency of a particular record implies the currency of possibly many set instances. Further, although only one record can be the current record, the most recently found occurrence of each record type is termed the **current of** (that) **record type.** Finally, currency may have been established for some set type(s), and not altered as a result of finding subsequent records; such current sets remain current until superseded.

Before expanding on the concept of currency, by means of an extended example, the remaining data manipulation concepts will be introduced.

Once a particular record is established as current, it is possible to GET the record, that is, transfer the values of its data items to a user work area. As indicated earlier, not all the data items of the record need to be transferred, since it is possible to specify that only certain data items should be 'got'. Since FINDing a record is often followed immediately by GETting it, a combined operator, OBTAIN, is usually provided. OBTAIN has essentially the same syntax as FIND, since it is performing the same navigation function, but it implies a GET once the record has been found.

Other operations which are obviously required, again for the current record, are MODIFY, STORE and ERASE. MODIFY copies an image of the current record from the user work area to replace that held in the database. If the new version of the record contains altered values for the data item(s) used for ordering the records within any set, the position of the modified record within those set(s) is altered accordingly.

STORE also copies a record image from the work area into the database, but creates a new occurrence of the record. The new record is connected as a member of the current instance of each of the set types of which the record is an **automatic** member. Obviously, this implies that the user has ensured that the current instances of these sets are correct. For those sets of which the record is a **manual** member, the user has to issue specific CONNECT instructions, again having ensured that the current instance of each set is the correct one. Should the record have been connected to the wrong occurrence of some set, the DISCONNECT operator may be used to remove the record from the set instance before connecting it to another. The newly stored record is established as the current record, and all the set occurrences of which it is a member are the current instances of their type.

As with the hierarchic model, the consequences of ERASing a record may be a little unexpected. A record which owns no sets can be erased with no difficulty. However, if a record owns any non-empty set occurrences, it is necessary to specify the action to be applied to those sets, since the removal of the owner effectively deletes the set occurrence. There are essentially two options:

a to erase ALL members of the owned sets;
b to erase only those members of the sets which have MANDATORY members.

The logic of the latter option is that records which have **optional** membership of the erased set can exist without reference to an instance of that set. However, if an optional member record is then a member of no sets, and owns no sets of its own, it no longer forms part of the data structure, although it could be accessed by stepping through all the occurrences of that record type within the realm. To deal with this situation, some implementations offer a third erase option, SELECTIVE, in which optional records are themselves erased if, following the removal of the set, they are no longer members of any set. Whichever option is specified, the ERASE operation is recursive, with the same option being applied at each level. It should be noted that it would, in principle, be possible to delete the entire database just by deleting a single record with the option ALL specified.

Before manipulation of the database may start, the applications program must specify which sub-schema is to be used, and which realms are to be opened. BIND establishes that the current task (**run unit**) will use a specified sub-schema. READY prepares one or more realms for processing, and may also be used to impose restrictions on the type of operations that may be performed on records in the realm – for example, a realm can be made ready for RETRIEVAL or for UPDATE.

The concept of currency, which forms the basis for most of the data manipulation operations, can be illustrated by means of an example. A small part of the schema which has been used as an example in this chapter is sufficient to show the basic ideas, and such a part is shown in Fig. 4.27. Since the *degree* and *course* records are only owners of sets, and not members, it is appropriate to assume that those records would have CALC access. It is immaterial to the discussion here via which of

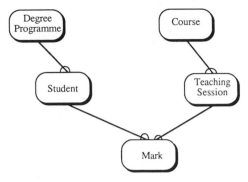

(a) Data Structure

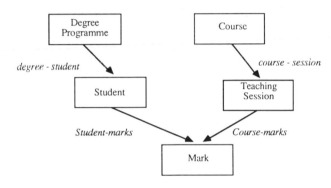

(b) CODASYL Schema

Fig. 4.27   Sample CODASYL data structure.

the two sets, *course–marks* and *student–marks*, the *marks* records are normally accessed, although one would have to be chosen in the data definition to determine around which owner record the *marks* records would be clustered.

A sample instance of the data structure is depicted in Fig. 4.28. From that diagram, it can be seen that, for example, the record for student *Smith* is a member of the *degree–student* set owned by the *computer science* record, and itself owns an instance of the *student–marks* set which has members with values α, β, and α. Those *mark* records are themselves members of three different instances of the *course–marks* set, owned respectively by records for *systems (architecture)*, *databases* and *graphics*. There is no record which links student *Smith* to the course in *A.I. (artificial intelligence)*, presumably because (s)he has not taken the course. The remainder of the diagram has similar semantics, with each record instance being indicated by a box, and each set occurrence by a set of lines from the owner record to the members.

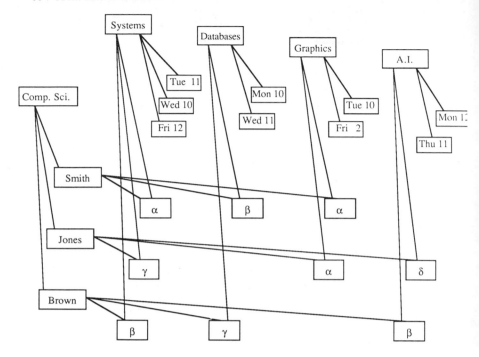

Fig. 4.28   An instance of the data structure.

The first operation required would be to establish one record as an entry point to the data structure (Fig. 4.29). For simplicity, this will be chosen to be one of those with CALC access, namely the *computer science* degree record. That record could be established by

FIND CALC *degree*

having copied the appropriate degree value to the work area. On finding this record, not only does the record become current (indicated by emboldening of the box), but it is also the current-of-run-unit (indicated by the arrowhead), and the instance of the *degree–student* set which it owns is also made current (indicated by the emboldening of the lines for the set).

Assuming that the ordering within each set is shown top-to-bottom for *degree–student*, *course–marks* and *course–session*, and left-to-right for *student–marks*, then the result of the two operations

FIND FIRST *student* WITHIN *degree–student*
FIND FIRST *mark* WITHIN *student–marks*

would be as shown in Fig. 4.30. Not only is the first mark record in the set owned by *Smith* established as the current-of-run-unit, but currency is

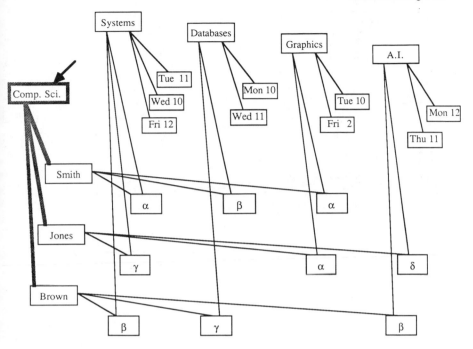

Fig. 4.29   Currency after FINDing *Comp. Sci.*

also established for the two set instances of which that record is a member. The *comp. sci.* and *Smith* records remain the current of their respective record types, as does the instance of the *degree–student* set.

From that position, it would be possible to

FIND OWNER WITHIN *course–marks*

establishing *systems* as current-of-run-unit, and then

FIND FIRST *session* WITHIN *course–session*

giving the position in Fig. 4.31. At this stage, there is a current record of each type, and also a current instance of each set type.

Thus far, the establishing of currency has been fairly straightforward. However, things get a little more complicated when a new current record of any type is subsequently established. It is probable at this stage that those who swear at the CODASYL model become separated from those who swear **by** it: its behaviour is quite predictable and easy to follow if you can hold the right sort of picture in your mind!

Consider, for example, the operation

FIND NEXT *mark* WITHIN *student–marks*

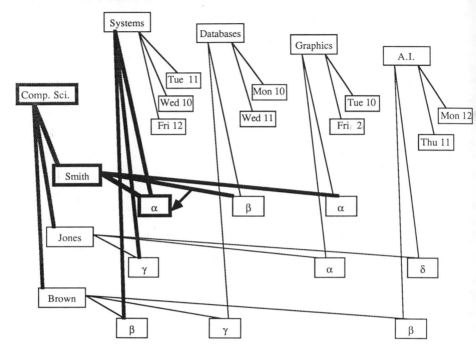

Fig. 4.30   Currency after FINDing the first *mark* for *Smith*.

which establishes the β mark obtained by *Smith* for *databases* as the current record, as shown in Fig. 4.32. However, the current *course* record is still *systems*, even though the current instance of the *course–marks* set is that owned by *databases*. Further, the current instance of the *course–session* set is that owned by *systems*. Nevertheless, this is all perfectly well defined, and causes no trouble provided that no rash assumptions are made. If, however, it is assumed that the set instances change in step with the current record automatically, no matter how far removed the sets might be, then unpredictable results might result. For example, finding the first *session* record within the *course–session* set from the position in Fig. 4.32 would yield *Tue 11*, rather than *Mon 10*, which might, unwisely, have been anticipated.

The situation could become slightly more complicated if, for example, it was decided to

FIND NEXT *student* WITHIN *degree–student*

which would result in the position of Fig. 4.33. It happens that the new current student, *Jones*, does not have a mark for *databases*, even though the current instance of the set *course–marks* is owned by the *databases* record.

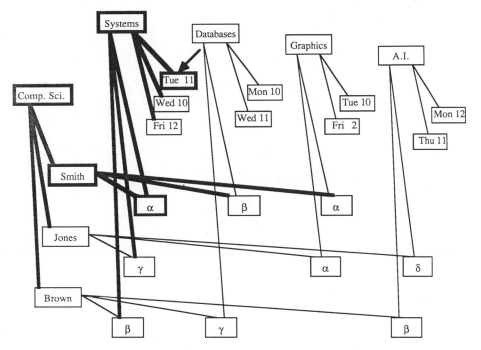

Fig. 4.31 Currency after FINDing the first *teaching session* for *systems*.

Logical positions other than first and next can be specified, such as

FIND LAST *mark* WITHIN *student–marks*

which should lead to the position of Fig. 4.34. Finally, there is no precedence between the *course–marks* and *student–marks* sets, so it would be quite possible then to

FIND NEXT *mark* WITHIN *course–marks*

leading to the position of Fig. 4.35.

The full syntax of the FIND and OBTAIN commands is summarized in Fig. 4.36. Alternatives are enclosed in curly brackets, and optional items in square brackets. Clearly, there is even more variety possible than has been illustrated here; several details having been omitted for clarity.

The above examples may suggest that manipulating a CODASYL database is exceedingly complicated. However, the examples were chosen to illustrate the complications that can arise for the unwary. It is relatively simple to construct an algorithm which could retrieve in turn the record for each student, obtaining for each student a set of course titles and marks. For example, using a suitable pseudo–code for the looping constructs

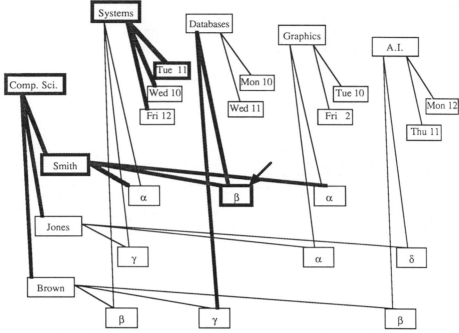

Fig. 4.32   Currency after FINDing the next *mark* within *student–marks*.

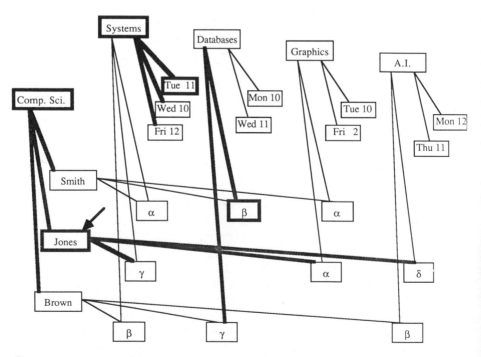

Fig. 4.33   Currency after FINDing the next *student* within *degree–student*.

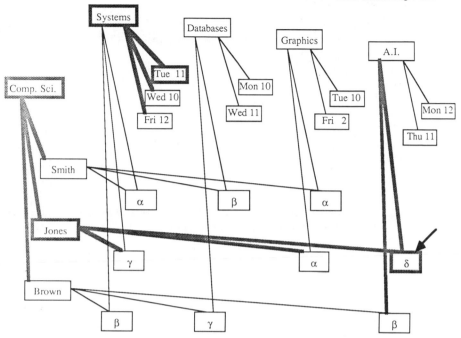

Fig. 4.34 Currency after FINDing the last *mark* within student–marks.

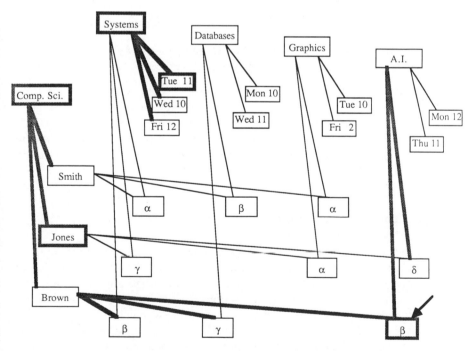

Fig. 4.35 Currency after FINDing the next *mark* within *course–marks*.

$$\left\{ {FIND \atop OBTAIN} \right\} \left\{ \begin{array}{l} \left\{ \begin{array}{l} CURRENT \\ FIRST \\ LAST \\ NEXT \\ PRIOR \\ n \end{array} \right\} \; [\,recordname\,] \quad [\,WITHIN \; \left\{ {realm\ name \atop set\ name} \right\} \;] \\ \\ OWNER\ WITHIN\ set\ name \\ \\ \left\{ {ANY \atop CALC} \right\} \quad recordname\ USING\ variable\ name \end{array} \right\}$$

Fig. 4.36   Simplified syntax for FIND and OBTAIN. Items in square brackets are optional; alternatives are bracketed together.

FIND CALC *degree*
FIND FIRST *student* WITHIN *degree–student*
While not end-of-file (*degree–student*)
  GET
  PRINT …
  FIND FIRST *mark* WITHIN *student–marks*
  While not end-of-file (*student–marks*)
    OBTAIN OWNER WITHIN *course–marks*
    Print …..
    OBTAIN NEXT *mark* WITHIN *student–marks*
  FIND NEXT *student* WITHIN *degree–student*

Other applications could clearly be constructed with similar ease. All that is required is a clear picture of how the currency changes at each stage. It is not surprising that some implementations, for example DEC's VAX–DBMS, provide an interactive query prototyping facility in which a 'picture' can be drawn on the screen of the current position in the database.

4.3.3   The relational model

Unlike the hierarchic and CODASYL models, the relational model is not based on an established implementation. Indeed, several years elapsed between the publication of Codd's proposals in 1970 and the emergence of any commercial systems based on the relational model. In addition, the two interfaces proposed by Codd – relational algebra and relational calculus – were intended more as ideal abstractions rather than as end-user interfaces. Thus, although both are described here, very few systems offer an interface which adheres rigorously to either.

Since there is no established system from which the relational model was deduced, and as the building blocks are relatively simple, there is little that could usefully be said here about data definition; hence, there is no data definition section for the relational model.

However, owing to the importance of the relational model, and, in particular, of the interfaces to relational models, there are sections for each of the relational algebra and relational calculus.

The basic elements

For the relational data model, the basic elements are simply **relations**. A relation is a **named set** of n-ary mappings between n **domains**. Each instance of the mapping is represented by one value or **attribute** drawn from each domain. The set of attributes representing a single instance of the mapping is termed an n-**tuple** or simply **tuple**. Just as the ordering of tuples within a relation is irrelevant, so also is the ordering of the attributes within a tuple.

A domain is simply a homogeneous collection of the possible values for an attribute. It might, for example, be the set of all valid dates, or it might be more specific, such as the dates of all Mondays in 1987. The parallel with data types in languages such as Pascal should be obvious.

A relation in which each tuple has n attributes is said to be of **degree** n. If the relation contains m tuples, each representing an instance of the n-ary mapping, it is said to have **cardinality** m. Since a relation is a set, not only is there no ordering of the tuples within the relation, but every tuple must be unique. Thus, a relation cannot contain duplicate tuples. Further, although the ordering of the attributes within each tuple is irrelevant, every tuple within a relation must have attributes drawn from all of the domains of the relation.

Within a relation, there must be some combination of attributes which together identify every tuple of the relation. Since every tuple must be unique, it follows that the entire tuple must always be able to act as an identifier, but in many cases a shorter identifier will exist. The identifier is termed the **key** of the relation, by comparison with file processing concepts.

Relations are conventionally represented as **tables**, in which the columns represent the attributes, and the rows the instances (tuples) of the relation. Each column has a name. Strictly, the name should be that of the underlying domain from which the attribute values are drawn; however, most implementations based on the relational model do not enforce this requirement. In any case, such a requirement can cause problems if two or more attributes are drawn from the same domain, representing distinct roles. For example, a relation which represents trips between towns must contain two town names, one for the start and the other for the finish. The domains for the two towns are the same, but the roles are different. Since the ordering of the attributes within a relation is not significant, the two roles can be distinguished only if the attributes have different names. Thus, it follows that they cannot both bear the name of the underlying domain.

A representation of the structure of a relation is simply the relation name and a list of attribute (domain) names enclosed in brackets. Those attributes which together comprise the key of the relation are normally underlined. Thus, for example,

student (*regno*, *surname*, *forename*)

would represent a relation in which each tuple contained three attributes. One, drawn from the domain of possible registration numbers, would be the identifier of each tuple. The other two attributes would be drawn respectively from the domains of possible surnames and possible forenames.

Relational algebra

Since a relation is a set, it follows that the standard set operators can be applied to relations. The results of such operations will also be relations, and further operators may be applied to those result relations. A data manipulation language for relations can be founded on the set operators, in which manipulation of the relations is performed on the complete set of tuples. Some operators are required in addition to the standard set operators, to provide for the selection of tuples from a relation, the selection of attributes from a relation, and the joining together of two relations to generate a third.

The relational algebra is an idealized language in which each operator is set-based. The standard set operators – UNION, DIFFERENCE, INTERSECTION, cartesian PRODUCT and DIVISION – are all supported, together with the specific relational operators, SELECT, PROJECT and JOIN. All of the operators produce a relation as their result, so that operations can be nested to an arbitrary depth.

Since relational algebra is a design target for an interface to relational databases, rather than an actual implementation, the syntax of the operators is less well defined than it might be. The style adopted here is intended to be illustrative of the characteristics of the language, rather than to be a candidate for implementation.

As with CODASYL DML, it is probably helpful to illustrate the operation of the algebra by means of an example. Fig. 4.37 shows an instance of a relational schema which contains the same information as the CODASYL structure of Fig. 4.28. The justification for the choice of the three relations

student (*student*, *degree*)
marks (*student*, *course*, *mark*)
courses (*course*, *session*)

should become apparent on reading the next chapter. For the moment, the reader will have to accept that the selected structure is a valid representation of the data structure. It should be noted, however, that, in order to make the examples more obvious, the identifiers are referred to as *student*, *course* and *session*, rather than *name*, *title* and *time* respectively.

In order for the UNION operator to be applied to two relations, they must be **union-compatible**. Obviously, they must be of the same degree. In addition, both relations must have the same attributes, ranging over the same domains. Strictly, the order of the attributes in the two relations is immaterial, but the discussion here will assume, for simplicity, that the ordering remains the same.

In pure relational algebra, new data must be added to the database by means of the UNION operator. For example Fig. 4.38 indicates three sets of additions to the database of Fig. 4.37. The additions are presented as three small relations – *new student*, *new marks* and *new course* which are union-compatible with the original *student*, *marks* and *course* relations. The result of the UNION operation is shown for each case.

For the first two additions, the UNION results simply in the tuples for the new data being added to the database. The new information about the *databases* course is, however, an addition to the times of the teaching

Student

Student	Degree
Smith	Comp.Sci.
Jones	Comp.Sci.
Brown	Comp.Sci.

Marks

Student	Course	Mark
Smith	Systems	α
Smith	Database	β
Smith	Graphics	α
Jones	Graphics	α
Brown	Systems	β
Brown	Database	γ
Jones	A.I.	δ
Jones	Systems	γ
Brown	A.I.	β

Course

Course	Session
Systems	Tue 11
Systems	Wed 10
Systems	Fri 12
Database	Mon 10
Graphics	Fri 2
Graphics	Tue 10
A.I.	Mon 11
Database	Wed 11
A.I.	Thu 11

Fig. 4.37   Instance of relational schema.

Student

Student	Degree
Smith	Comp.Sci.
Jones	Comp.Sci.
Brown	Comp.Sci.

Marks

Student	Course	Mark
Smith	Systems	α
Smith	Database	β
Smith	Graphics	α
Jones	Graphics	α
Brown	Systems	β
Brown	Database	γ
Jones	A.I.	δ
Jones	Systems	γ
Brown	A.I.	β

Course

Course	Session
Systems	Tue 11
Systems	Wed 10
Systems	Fri 12
Database	Mon 10
Graphics	Fri 2
Graphics	Tue 10
A.I.	Mon 11
Database	Wed 11
A.I.	Thu 11

New Student

Student	Degree
White	Data Proc.

New Marks

Student	Course	Mark
White	Systems	δ
White	Database	β
White	Graphics	γ

New Course

Course	Session
Database	Mon 10
Database	Wed 11
Database	Fri 9

Student ∪ New Student

Student	Degree
Smith	Comp.Sci.
Jones	Comp.Sci.
Brown	Comp.Sci.
White	Data Proc.

Marks ∪ New Marks

Student	Course	Mark
Smith	Systems	α
Smith	Database	β
Smith	Graphics	α
Jones	Graphics	α
Brown	Systems	β
Brown	Database	γ
Jones	A.I.	δ
Jones	Systems	γ
Brown	A.I.	β
White	Systems	δ
White	Database	β
White	Graphics	γ

Course ∪ New Course

Course	Session
Systems	Tue 11
Systems	Wed 10
Systems	Fri 12
Database	Mon 10
Graphics	Fri 2
Graphics	Tue 10
A.I.	Mon 11
Database	Wed 11
A.I.	Thu 11
Database	Fri 9

Fig. 4.38 UNION of relations.

sessions. Two of the sessions are already recorded in the *courses* relation. Thus, although these two sessions are also present in the *new courses* relation, the result of the UNION is to add just one tuple to the *course* relation, corresponding to the new session. The tuples which occur in the result relation for UNION are those which occur in either **or both** of the operand relations.

Figure 4.39 shows the results of two further set operators, DIFFERENCE and INTERSECT. The former is usually referred to as MINUS. For both operators, the operand relations must be union-compatible. The result of MINUS is a relation which contains only those tuples of the first operand which are **not** present in the second. Thus, the relation *course* MINUS *new course* does not contain tuples for either of the *database* sessions – *Mon 10* and *Wed 11* – which are present in both relations. The existence of the third tuple in *new course* has no effect on the result relation.

For INTERSECT, the result relation contains only those tuples which are present **in both** operand relations. In this case, it contains only the two tuples which were removed by the MINUS operator.

As with standard set theory, it is the case that the UNION of the two result relations, *course* MINUS *new course* and *course* INTERSECT *new course* is identical to the original relation, *course*. That is, in general,

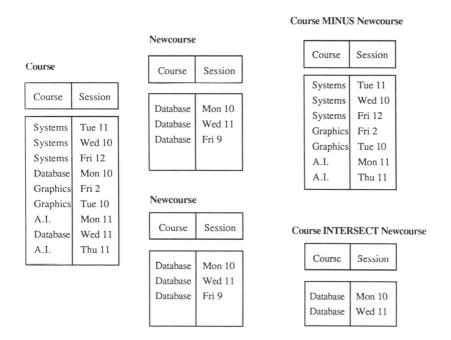

Fig. 4.39   DIFFERENCE (MINUS) and INTERSECT.

$(a$ MINUS $b)$ UNION $(a$ INTERSECT $b) = a$

Although this result is not profound in itself, it is an example of the set operators being applied to the results of earlier operations. The operands for the UNION operator are both themselves algebraic expressions enclosed in parentheses. The fact that the result is as would be expected confirms that such nesting of operations is valid.

The cartesian PRODUCT operator, TIMES, or '×', forms a relation

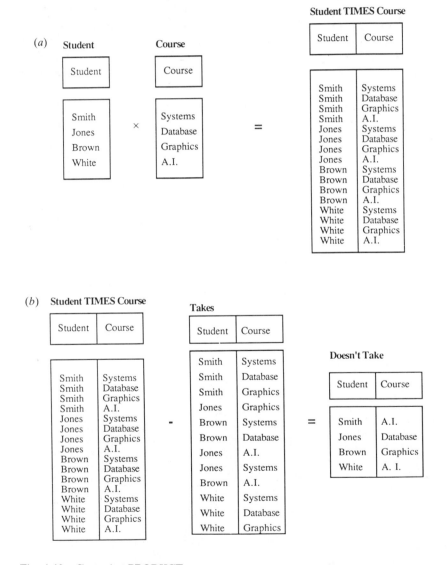

Fig. 4.40   Cartesian PRODUCT.

whose attributes are the concatenation of the attributes of the two operand relations, and which contains one tuple for every possible combination of the tuples of the operand relations. Figure 4.40(a) depicts the result of such a product. Although the ordering of the tuples in each relation is immaterial, the result relation is shown with the ordering preserved, to clarify the pattern of tuples in the result.

As before, it is possible to use the result of the PRODUCT operation as an operand for another operation. The cartesian PRODUCT of all

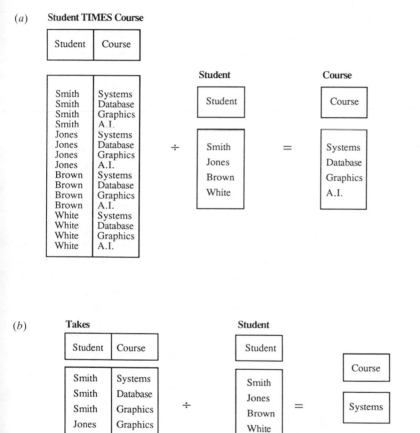

(a)   Student TIMES Course

(b)   Takes

Fig. 4.41   DIVISION.

courses with all *students* gives all the possible *student–course* combinations. Hence, taking the difference between that product and the list of courses actually taken by the students gives a list of which courses are **not** taken by each student, as shown in Fig. 4.40(b).

DIVISION is a set operation which is defined simply to be the inverse of TIMES. If the dividend is a 'complete' product of the divisor, as in Fig. 4.41(a), where the dividend is the product from Fig. 4.40, then the quotient is simple to deduce. The general case, however, is slightly more complex.

A tuple appears in the quotient if, in the dividend, it appears concatenated with **all** of the tuples from the divisor. Whilst this is trivially true for the simple case of Fig. 4.41(a), the two examples of Fig. 4.41(b) are probably more interesting. In these examples, the dividend is the set of actual course registrations. The first divisor is a relation containing all four students. The only course for which all four students are registered, or which appears concatenated with each of the student names in *takes* is *systems*; thus that is the only course to appear in the quotient relation. Similarly, for the second divisor, the only students who are taking both *systems* and *databases* courses are *Smith*, *Brown* and *White*, the three students who appear in the quotient.

DIVIDE is not a primitive operator, in the sense that it can be defined in terms of the other set operators together with PROJECT and SELECT; however, the definition is so clumsy that DIVIDE is normally regarded as one of the relational algebra operators. Unfortunately, not all the implementations based on relational algebra which exist include DIVIDE as an operator, with the result that it is difficult in such systems to perform 'set matching' operations such as in Fig. 4.41(b).

SELECT applies a predicate, or condition, to a single relation (which may be the result of another operation) to select a subset of the tuples. In essence, SELECT forms a 'horizontal subset' of the relation. Each tuple in the result contains all the attributes present in the operand relation, but only those tuples which satisfy the condition. Figure 4.42 shows two such selections from the *marks* relation.

It happens that the word SELECT is redundant, in the sense that the presence of a condition implies that the operation is selection. Thus, rather than

SELECT *marks* WHERE *course* = *database*

it would be acceptable to write

marks WHERE *course* = *databases*

This shorter form is usually employed in complex algebraic expressions in which either the selection is being applied to some result relation, or the result of the selection is an operand for a further relation.

PROJECT specifies a subset of the attributes of a relation for inclusion

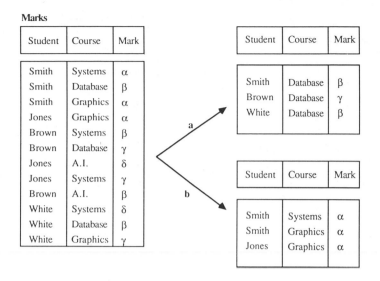

(a) - SELECT marks WHERE course = 'database'

(b) - SELECT marks WHERE mark = 'α'

Fig. 4.42   SELECT.

in the result relation. By comparison with the SELECT operator, PROJECT can be regarded as an operator which generates a 'vertical subset' of a relation. As with SELECT, the actual word, PROJECT, is redundant, since a list of attributes over which projection is to be performed implies that the operation is projection. Hence, the usual notation for PROJECT is simply a list of attributes for the result relation, enclosed in square brackets, following the relation name.

Since a relation contains no duplicates, the result of a PROJECT must also contain no duplicates. If the projection omits one or more attributes which form part of the key of the operand relation, then the projection will result in a relation not only of lower degree, but also of reduced cardinality, since duplication will be eliminated. For example, Fig. 4.43 depicts the results of three projections of *marks*. The first, *marks [student, course]* contains the same number of tuples as does *marks*, since both key attributes have been included in the projection. This projection is, in fact, the *takes* relation which was used in the discussion of some of the other set operators.

Projecting *marks* over the single field *student* does not preserve the full key of *marks*. Taking just the *student* attribute of *marks* yields a set of values in which each name occurs three times. Since duplication is not permitted in a relation, the result of the operation is a relation containing

Marks

Student	Course	Mark
Smith	Systems	α
Smith	Database	β
Smith	Graphics	α
Jones	Graphics	α
Brown	Systems	β
Brown	Database	γ
Jones	A.I.	δ
Jones	Systems	γ
Brown	A.I.	β
White	Systems	δ
White	Database	β
White	Graphics	γ

Marks [Student, Course]

Student	Course
Smith	Systems
Smith	Database
Smith	Graphics
Jones	Graphics
Brown	Systems
Brown	Database
Jones	A.I.
Jones	Systems
Brown	A.I.
White	Systems
White	Database
White	Graphics

Marks [Student]

Student
Smith
Jones
Brown
White

(Marks [Student , Course]) [Course]

Course
Systems
Database
Graphics
A. I.

Fig. 4.43 PROJECT.

just four tuples, one for each distinct name. A similar argument applies to the projection of *takes* (itself a projection of *marks*) over the single attribute *course*. Again, the result relation comprises just four tuples.

The final operator which is included in the relational algebra is, like DIVIDE, not a primitive operator, in the sense that it can be expressed as a combination of the other operators. However, the operation which it performs is so common that it is normally regarded as being indispensable. JOIN can be defined in a number of ways. The most common is termed the **NATURAL EQUI-JOIN**; it is this version which is described here.

JOIN is used to combine two relations on the basis of the value of a shared attribute. The result relation contains all the attributes from each operand relation, but with the shared attribute occurring only once. The tuples in the result relation are formed by concatenating tuples from the two operands whenever the value of the shared attribute is equal in the two operands.

Marks

Student	Course	Mark
Smith	Systems	α
Smith	Database	β
Smith	Graphics	α
Jones	Graphics	α
Brown	Systems	β
Brown	Database	γ
Jones	A.I.	δ
Jones	Systems	γ
Brown	A.I.	β
White	Systems	δ
White	Database	β
White	Graphics	γ

Student

Student	Degree
Smith	Comp.Sci.
Jones	Comp.Sci.
Brown	Comp.Sci.
White	Data Proc.

Marks JOIN Student

Student	Course	Mark	Degree
Smith	Systems	α	Comp. Sci.
Smith	Database	β	Comp. Sci.
Smith	Graphics	α	Comp. Sci.
Jones	Graphics	α	Comp. Sci.
Brown	Systems	β	Comp. Sci.
Brown	Database	γ	Comp. Sci.
Jones	A.I.	δ	Comp. Sci.
Jones	Systems	γ	Comp. Sci.
Brown	A.I.	β	Comp. Sci.
White	Systems	δ	Data Proc.
White	Database	β	Data Proc.
White	Graphics	γ	Data Proc.

Fig. 4.44 JOIN.

For example, Fig. 4.44 shows the natural equi-join of the *marks* and *student* relations. The arrows in the diagram indicate the mapping between the two relations which is implied by the values of the shared attribute *student*. Each tuple in the *student* relation matches three tuples from the *marks* relation. The resultant relation comprises tuples with four attributes, namely all the attributes from the two operand relations, but with the shared attribute *student* occurring once only.

Other forms of JOIN can be defined in which the comparison is not equality, but, for example, 'greater than'. For such joins, it would be normal to retain both versions of the shared attribute, since the two values for any tuple would differ. Alternatively, a JOIN operation can be performed by comparing attributes from the two operands which are not common to both, but which are based on the same domain. For example, a relation of the form

employee (employee#, name, manager#)

could be joined with itself to form tuples containing not only the name of the employee, but also the name of his manager, assuming that *manager#* and *employee#* are drawn on the same domain. For this type of join, where the attributes in the two operands have to be specified, the syntax of the operation is less well defined, and tends to vary between implementations. One possible version might be,

employee JOIN [manager# = employee#] employee

implying that the value of *manager#* in the first operand must be equal to the value of *employee#* in the second. However, the syntax is not entirely satisfactory, and it also ignores the question of what the attributes of the result relation will be called. Even if the equality condition implies that one of the attributes used in the comparison can be omitted, that still leaves two attributes called *name* and *manager#* in the result. In this case, the normal solution, of **qualifying** each attribute name in the result relation by preceding it with the name of the relation from which it is copied, fails to distinguish the attributes. It may be necessary to prohibit the join of a relation with itself, and to require instead that if such an operation is required, then one of the operands must be an ALIAS for the operand relation, so that the two operands effectively have different names.

It will be apparent that the JOIN operator is simply the cartesian PRODUCT followed by a SELECTION and, in the case where the duplicate attribute is removed, a PROJECTION. It is in this sense that JOIN is not primitive. However, it is such a common operation that it is useful to have an explicit shorthand.

Complex queries can be built up by nesting the operators of the relational algebra, as for example in Fig. 4.45, in which a timetable is deduced for student *Jones*.

Some additional operators may be provided in an implemented system which is based on relational algebra. Typical operators would be INSERT, MODIFY and DELETE. However, whilst such operators do simplify the corresponding tasks, they fly somewhat counter to the philosophy of the algebra, since they are operations to be performed on single tuples rather than set-based operations performed on the relation as a whole. Nevertheless, although it is possible to express these operations in terms of the algebra operators, it is not particularly convenient, so that any usable system would probably include INSERT, MODIFY and DELETE.

Marks

Student	Course	Mark
Smith	Systems	α
Smith	Database	β
Smith	Graphics	α
Jones	Graphics	α
Brown	Systems	β
Brown	Database	γ
Jones	A.I.	δ
Jones	Systems	γ
Brown	A.I.	β
White	Systems	δ
White	Database	β
White	Graphics	γ

Courses

Course	Session
Systems	Tue 11
Systems	Wed 10
Systems	Fri 12
Database	Mon 10
Graphics	Fri 2
Graphics	Tue 10
A.I.	Mon 11
Database	Wed 11
A.I.	Thu 11
Database	Fri 9

Course	Session
Systems	Tue 11
Systems	Wed 10
Systems	Fri 12
Graphics	Tue 10
Graphics	Fri 2
A. I.	Mon 12
A. I.	Thu 11

((Marks WHERE student = 'Jones') JOIN courses) [course, session]

Fig. 4.45   Complex query.

Other operations which might be defined in a practical system might include such as SORT. Since relations are unordered sets, sorting is clearly meaningless in pure relational terms. However, at the level where real users are using a relational system to manipulate real data, it must be recognized that sorting is often a genuine requirement. Thus, although operations such as SORT are not part of relational algebra, they would normally be provided.

Relational calculus

The relational algebra is essentially a set-based language, which is procedural to the extent that a sequence of relational operations are specified. By contrast, relational calculus is an application of **predicate calculus** which is **non-procedural**. Various forms of the calculus exist, the most common of which is **tuple calculus**. Codd's original proposal for a calculus-based language. Data Sub Language Alpha (DSL-alpha) was essentially tuple calculus. In common with the algebra, any relational calculus is an idealized manipulation language, and various implementations capture the essence of the calculus with differing success.

Tuple calculus is based on the notions of **tuple variables** and **well formed formulae**. Tuple variables are simply variables which can take the value of a complete tuple drawn from a single relation. Each tuple variable is defined to range over a certain relation, and its value must be an element of that relation. Thus, one can use a standard set denotation for a tuple variable, such as

$cx \in course$

which can be read as

the tuple variable cx takes a value which is an element of the relation *course*

or, alternatively,

cx ranges over *course*

A tuple calculus expression will involve one or more tuple variables, each of which must be defined in this manner. Depending on the particular query, it may be necessary to define two or more tuple variables ranging over a single relation.

The second element of tuple calculus, well formed formulae, are essentially just **conditions**. However, there are certain restrictions on how the conditions may be constructed. The 'well formed' qualification just means that these restrictions have been observed.

A relational calculus expression has a value which is a relation, just as the result of an algebraic expression is a relation. In its simplest form, the expression consists of a list of attributes drawn from one or more tuple variables. Figure 4.46(a) shows two such expressions, and the relations which are the values of those expressions. Each attribute in the list is denoted by the attribute name qualified by the tuple variable name. It can be seen that, in this simple form the calculus expressions are equivalent to the algebraic PROJECT operator.

In most cases, a tuple calculus expression includes a condition or **predicate**. The predicate is introduced by the word 'where', and contains an arbitrary boolean combination of elementary conditions on individual attributes. Figure 4.46(b) shows two expressions with conditions, and the resulting relations.

If the expression involves more than one tuple variable, the form can be just the same as for a single variable expression, provided that all the

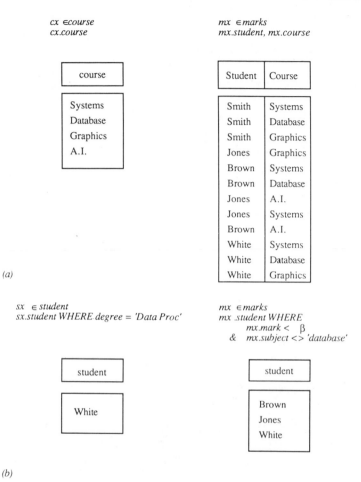

(a)

(b)

Fig. 4.46   Simple calculus expressions.

variables involved appear in the list of attributes of the result relation. Such an example is shown in Fig. 4.47(a), which lists students registered for the *computing science* degree who have obtained at least one mark worse than β. Inspection of this example might suggest that it would be immaterial which of *sx.student* and *mx.student* appeared in the list of attributes for the result relation. However, if the latter were to be specified instead of the former, then the meaning of the two conditions involving attributes of *sx* would be unclear. What would be meant would be that there would have to be some tuple in the relation over which *sx* ranged which could satisfy the condition. This is expressed by introducing the **existential quantifier**, ∃, as in Fig. 4.47(b).

$mx \in marks$
$sx \in marks$

$sx.student, mx.course \ WHERE$
    $mx.mark < \quad \beta$
    $\& \ sx.degree = 'Comp. \ Sci'$
    $\& \ mx.student = sx.student$

(a) Calculus Expression involving two tuple variables

student	course
Brown	Database
Jones	A.I.
Jones	Systems

$mx \in marks$
$sx \in student$

$mx.student, mx.course \ WHERE \quad \exists \ sx \ ($
    $sx.degree = 'Comp \ Sci'$
    $\& \ sx.student = mx.student$
    $\& \ mx.mark < \beta \ )$

(b) Alternative expression with Existential Quantifier and bound variable

Fig. 4.47   Calculus expressions over two relations.

The existential quantifier is required whenever a particular tuple variable does not feature in the list of attributes in the result. One common situation in which this arises is where a tuple from one relation is used to link two others, without being part of the result. The example in Fig. 4.48 is typical of such queries. The tuple variable mx must be quantified since none of its attributes appear in the result. The expression generates a list of *degrees* and *sessions*, where for each pair there is at least one student who is taking the course for which the session is scheduled, and who is registered for the degree. Thus, the result relation contains a 'timetable' for each degree programme.

A tuple variable which is quantified by the existential quantifier is local to the expression, and plays no part in the result of the expression. The quantified variable is said to be **bound**, as opposed to the other variables which are not quantified, and are termed **free**.

Occasionally, a different form of quantification is required. One such case corresponds to the algebraic DIVIDE operator. The problem of determining which courses are taken by all students could be expressed as

$sx \in student$
$mx \in marks$

sx ∈ *student*
mx ∈ *marks*
cx ∈ *course*

sx.degree, cx.session WHERE ∃ *mx (*
    sx.student = mx.student
& *mx.course = cx.course)*

degree	session
Comp Sci	Tue 11
Comp Sci	Wed 10
Comp Sci	Fri 12
Comp Sci	Mon 10
Comp Sci	Fri 2
Comp Sci	Tue 10
Comp Sci	Mon 11
Comp Sci	Wed 11
Comp Sci	Thu 11
Data Proc	Fri 9
Data Proc	Tue 11
Data Proc	Wed 10
Data Proc	Fri 12
Data Proc	Mon 10
Data Proc	Fri 2
Data Proc	Tue 10
Data Proc	Wed 11
Data Proc	Fri 9

Fig. 4.48   Calculus expression with bound variable.

my ∈ *marks*
mx. course WHERE ¬∃*sx* (¬∃*my* (
    my.course = mx.course
&   *my.student = sx.student*))

which generates a set of courses from *marks* where there exists no tuple in *student* for which there is no matching tuple in *marks* which is for that course. A moment's thought may be needed to convince oneself of the validity of this expression.

Part of the problem lies in the double negation of the quantification. The expression may be more intelligible if it is rewritten using the **universal quantifier**, ∀, read as, 'for all':

sx ∈ *student*
mx ∈ *marks*
my ∈ *marks*

mx. course WHERE ∀*sx* (∃*my* (
    my.course = mx.course
&   *my.student = sx.student*))

This expression is slightly more intelligible. A particular course is included provided that for all students there exists a tuple (*my*) linking the student to the course. The universal quantifier is not necessary, in the sense that it is precisely equivalent to '¬∃¬'. However, the universal quantifier can be less confusing than double negation.

The more complex queries involving more than one quantifier have been shown in **prenex normal form**, with all the quantifiers collected together at the start of the predicate. The rules for performing this transformation are well established in logic, and will not be considered in detail here. Nevertheless, one or two points are worth making concerning the order of the quantifiers. If the only quantifiers are existential, with no negation, then the order of the quantifiers is immaterial; that is, the quantifiers **commute**. This property is lost, however, if any quantifier, or the expression which it quantifies, is negated. Since the universal quantifier is equivalent to a negated existential quantifier plus a negation, it follows that existential and universal quantifiers do not commute. Provided that a little thought is given to the meaning of the various quantifiers, it should be relatively straightforward to ensure that the quantifiers are in the correct order. Although the question of the order of the quantifiers should be borne in mind, it should not be a problem in most cases.

Although the mathematical nature of relational calculus expressions does not lend itself to implementation as a user interface, a number of relational database systems have data manipulation languages based on relational calculus. One such system, which also exploits the non-procedural nature of the calculus, is INGRES, for which the DML is QUEL.

The relational calculus is one of a number of alternative styles of data manipulation language for a relational database. It is said to be **relationally complete**, meaning that its expressive power is at least as great as that of the relational algebra, without requiring any specific iteration or recursion constructs. A number of other interfaces which have been implemented for relational database systems either are, or come close to being, relationally complete, but some are based on iteration over the set of tuples in each relation. Although iterative languages may have the same effective expressive power as the algebra, they are not strictly set-at-a-time languages, and fall short of relational completeness on that criterion.

4.4 EXPRESSIVE POWER

The three classical data models have been introduced as methods of organizing a data structure into a form suitable for implementation. In essence, the data structure is implemented by modelling it using primitives of a certain type – tree, set or relation. If these three primitives offered the same expressive power, there would be nothing to choose between the three models excepting performance and, perhaps, comprehensibility.

However, in the case of the hierarchic approach, and to a lesser extent for the network approach, the modelling process is imperfect, and imposes some restrictions both on the data structure which can be represented and on the manner in which it can be processed. Although there are ardent advocates of each of the three model types, it is largely the differences in expressive power of the approaches which influence their suitability for particular applications.

Clearly, the hierarchic approach imposes the most severe constraints on the data model. Not only is the structure forced into a hierarchic form, but the data manipulation language is entirely hierarchic also. Thus, even though cross-links in the hierarchy can be represented internally, using pointers, there is no provision in the DML to traverse the structure using those links rather than the basic tree structure.

In fact, in IMS it is possible to define distinct views of the data structure, termed **logical databases**, in which the relationship(s) represented by pointers appear to be part of the hierarchy, and other relationships – which happen to be represented directly in the underlying data model – are omitted. Such logical databases are allowed to co-exist with the 'real' database, but although they may be processed in parallel with the physical hierarchy, all communication with the host program must be independent. In effect, any program which needs to use both the physical structure and the logical pointers must comprise a number of interleaved processes, each of which processes exactly one physical or logical database, and which communicate by passing **values** in program variables.

When the underlying data structure is purely hierarchic – as can occasionally happen – there is no real difference in the expressive power of the hierarchic and network approaches. Both can represent the structure directly, and both rely on physical navigation of a stored data structure. However, the network approach does not require the use of logical pointers to represent relationships which are not purely hierarchic, since a record can be a member of an arbitrary number of set types. Since the entire structure is represented in a homogeneous manner, a CODASYL data model of arbitrary complexity can always be manipulated by a single process. Nevertheless, the CODASYL approach still shares one restriction with the hierarchic model, in that processing is based on navigation of a physical structure, using only those links (relationships) which have been included explicitly in the data model.

The principal difference between the relational model and the other two would appear to be be in its manner of manipulation. Rather than manipulation of the model involving the selection of a sequence of records or segments within a physical data structure, involving navigation along pre-defined routes (i.e. those which are actually represented), a relational model can be manipulated either in a non-procedural manner, or using set-at-a-time operators. In essence, of course, this process still involves navigation – from one relation to another – but, in this case, navigation **by value** rather than in a physical sense. Further, the 'route' which can be taken is not restricted by access paths which were built in to the model, since relational DMLs place virtually no restrictions on the type of query which can be processed.

It is worth noting that the only real difference between a relational model and a CODASYL model of the same structure is the distinction between physical and logical navigation. In terms of the data structures which can be modelled, the expressive powers of the two modelling techiniques are the same. The only 'problem' structure for a network model is a complex network, such as a 'many-to-many' relationship. In a CODASYL model, this relationship is represented by an intersection record which belongs to sets owned by each of the records involved in the many-to-many relationship. The contents of the intersection record, however, are identical with those of the relation which would be used to represent directly the same many-to-many relationship. Hence, it can be seen that the expressive powers of the two data modelling techniques are essentially equivalent.

SUMMARY
Chapter 4

Data modelling, as defined in this text, is the process of organizing a data structure into a form which can readily be implemented on a computer. The three classical data models – hierarchic, network and relational – can be derived by approaching the data structure in different ways.

The hierarchic model organizes the data structure as a set of hierarchies. The roots of the hierarchies correspond to entity types which are involved only at the 'one' end of one-to-many relationships. Each node in the hierarchy is represented by a **segment**, and a hierarchic collection of segments is termed a **database record**. Where the 'real' data structure is not a pure hierarchy, **pointers** are used to provide cross-links in the structure. However, the resulting plex is still manipulated as a set of hierarchies. Data manipulation is performed by **navigation** of the hierarchic structure to select the required segments, and transfer them to a user work area. Iteration and other control structures must be provided by a host language.

The network, or CODASYL–DBTG, data model uses a **set** as its fundamental component. A set represents a one-to-many relationship between two record types, one of which is the **owner** of the set, and the other the **member**. Each relationship in the data structure is thus modelled independently of the others, and any record may be involved in any number of set types. As with the hierarchic model, the data is manipulated by navigating through the data model, selecting records and transferring the required data to a user work area. Again, the data manipulation language must be hosted in a high-level language which can provide the necessary iteration and other control structures. Record selection is based on the notion of **currency**, both for records and sets, and on the logical position of records within sets.

The relational model employs a tabular structure or **relation** to model the data. Each row of the table is called a **tuple**, and represents an n-ary mapping between the n **domains** over which the relation exists. The relational model can represent directly virtually all of the data structure components encountered during data analysis. Data manipulation is effected in terms either of **relational algebra** or **relational calculus**. The former is a high-level set-at-a-time language, comprising the standard set operators and three additional operators – PROJECT, SELECT and JOIN – specific for relations. The latter is a non-procedural language based on predicate calculus. Since the relational model is based on the mathematical theory of relations, various assertions can be made about the expressive power both of the model and the languages, and, in particular, whether a language is **relationally complete** in the sense that it has at least the expressive power of the algebra.

When choosing between the three data models, the expressive powers of the CODASYL and relational models are essentially equivalent, and that of the hierarchic model is less than for either. The principal distinction between the record-based models (hierarchic and CODASYL) and the set-based relational model is the way in which the data are manipulated.

PROBLEMS
Chapter 4

P4.1 A university library has various pieces of information concerning books, borrowers, reservations, books kept for binding and the like. A book is described by a unique reference number allocated to the particular volume, a title, authors and classification category. Each borrower must have recorded not only his name but his department, a borrower number and an indicator to show status, i.e. staff, postgraduate, undergraduate, etc.

Books may be on the shelves, out to a particular borrower or being bound or rebound and thus not available. They may also be reserved by borrowers. Borrowers may have varying numbers of books depending on their status, and all borrowers may make reservations for books which are currently out.

The types of queries which the library expects to generate include:

i   What books does a particular borrower have?

ii   Is a particular book in, out, reserved, etc.?

iii Given a particular book reference number, or possibly author and title, where is the book? If it is out, which borrower has the book?

iv   List all books or borrower's books in particular categories, etc. It is anticipated that these lists will be required infrequently compared to the other queries mentioned above.

   a Prepare and discuss a hierarchic (DL/1) schema for the library database. Consider the DML instructions required to effect the queries suggested above.

   b Repeat the exercise with a CODASYL-like schema and the corresponding CODASYL DML.

P4.2 Typical queries to be addressed to the vehicle fleet database derived for P3.3 of Chapter 3 might include:

i   find details of the vehicles allocated to a particular department;

ii   for a given employee, find a list of vehicles which he is authorized to drive;

iii find which employees have been in accidents involving company vehicles;

iv find the current replacement value of all vehicles in a particular class;

v find the service history of a particular vehicle.

a Prepare a hierarchic (DL/1) schema for the company database, and consider the DML instructions required to effect the queries suggested above.

b Prepare an alternative schema based on the CODASYL model, and show how the suggested queries could be effected using CODASYL DML.

c For both the hierarchic and CODASYL schemata, consider how much of the schema would have to be available to each group of users to satisfy their requirements.

P4.3 Construct skeleton relational data models for the following data structures. Consider merging relations where appropriate.

a

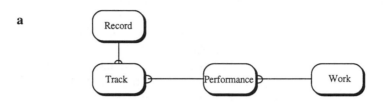

b

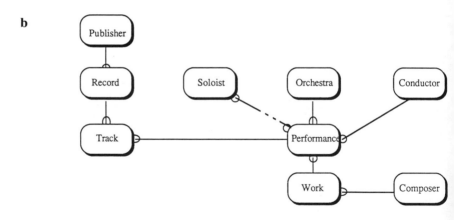

c

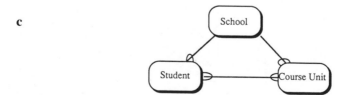

P4.4 Write relational calculus expressions for the following queries on the sample relations shown:

    a Find the names of all students registered for CMP356.

    b Find the initials of all the advisers.

    c Identify the course codes for which students advised by 'PJM' are registered.

    d For each student advised by 'PAD', find the titles of the courses for which (s)he is registered.

P4.5 Translate the queries of P4.4 into relational algebra expressions.

P4.6 Express the following relational algebra operators in terms of the other relational and set operators:

    a JOIN

    b DIVIDEBY

What is a MINIMAL set of relational algebra operators?

Sample relations for questions 4.4 and 4.5

Studcourse

Srmum,	Cucode
81001	CMP301
81001	CMP353
81001	CMP355
81001	CMP356
81002	CMP301
81002	CMP353
81002	CMP355
81002	CMP357
81003	CMP301
81003	CMP353
81003	CMP355
81003	CMP356
81004	CMP301
81004	CMP353
81004	CMP356
81004	CMP357
81005	CMP301
81005	CMP353
81005	CMP355
81005	CMP357

Student

Srnum,	Name,	Adviser
81001	Brown	PJM
81002	Green	PAD
81003	Jones	PJM
81004	Smith	PAD
81005	White	RDD

Course

Cucode,	Title,	Length
CMP301	Project	1
CMP353	Prog.Sys.II.	1/2
CMP355	Inf.Man.II.	1/2
CMP356	Sys.Anal.II.	1/2
CMP357	Op.Res.II.	1/2

P4.7 Consider the expression of **each** of the relational algebra operations in terms of relational calculus.

Is the translation any easier in the other direction?

Compare the expressive power of the two relational languages.

P4.8 'The relational data model can represent certain types of data structure more readily than the network (CODASYL) model, which in turn can represent certain data structures more readily than the hierarchic model.'

Discuss the extent to which this assertion is valid.

P4.9 It is sometimes asserted that the hierarchic data model is peculiarly suited to representing hierarchic structures, whereas the network (CODASYL) and relational models are more general, and logically equivalent to each other.

In the context of this assertion, discuss the representation of the relationships between *objects* and *components*, where *objects* are real-world entities which are composed of a number of *components*.

How does the discussion alter if:

a *components* may themselves be composed of other *components*;

b *components* may be part of more than one object type;

c both **a** and **b**?

P4.10 The hierarchic and network (CODASYL) data models are said to be navigational, whereas the relational model is said to be non-navigational. To what extent is this a valid distinction?

Discuss, in detail, the advantages of navigational and non-navigational approaches in the context of *ad-hoc* query formulation.

5

NORMALIZATION AND SYNTHESIS

5.1 REDUNDANCY

One of the principal justifications for adopting the database approach for a particular set of applications is that it can allow data to be **shared** between a number of distinct applications. The obvious corollary of this is that the data need not be duplicated. Only one copy of the data needs to exist, and all modifications to the data can be made to that single copy. If this were not the case, then there could be many copies of any given data item, each of which would have to be updated in synchrony with the others: if a change were to be made to the value of one such data item, it would have to be applied also to all the other copies before the 'database' could be considered to be consistent. Clearly, if many data items were duplicated, then the scope for inconsistencies between the different versions of data would, to say the least, be considerable.

However, merely using a database approach does not guarantee that the resulting data model will be free of unnecessary duplication, and therefore automatically consistent. Whichever modelling approach is adopted, it is quite possible, and sometimes easy, to generate a data model which either requires duplication of some data, or which implies certain undesirable dependencies between different data items. Whilst this problem is most apparent in the case of the relational model, which assumes no underlying physical structure for the data model as a whole, the CODASYL model and the hierarchic model are also vulnerable.

The objectives of this chapter are to identify the problems which can occur, deduce their consequences, and determine how they might best be overcome. In keeping with the historical development of the underlying theory, the concepts are presented primarily in terms of relational structures. However, once understood, the ideas may be applied also to other types of data model.

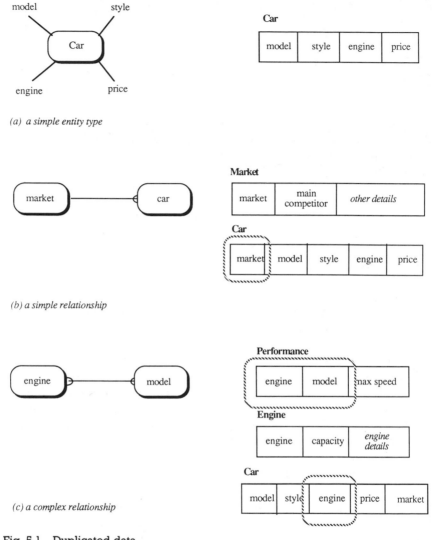

(a) a simple entity type

(b) a simple relationship

(c) a complex relationship

Fig. 5.1   Duplicated data.

5.1.1   Redundancy versus duplication

It is first necessary to recognize when duplication of data is undesirable. Data whose presence in the database is undesirable, in the sense that it can cause problems in maintaining consistency, is termed **redundant** data.

It is not true that all duplicated data are redundant, although redundant data are nearly always duplicated. In general, in order for it to be possible for data to be redundant, then those data must occur elsewhere in the database. The exception to this is where the data in question could be deduced in some manner from other data, without needing to exist in their own right. Clearly, if the data in question are neither present explicitly nor deducible, then some information must be lost if they are removed from the database; hence, such data would not be redundant. For example, if a particular value were to occur as two separate instances in a database, representing the same fact, then it is quite possible that one of those occurrences might be redundant. Alternatively, if that value were a count of how many instances of a particular entity type were currently represented in the database, then the value could be deduced by counting those instances, and, again, the specific representation of the value might be redundant.

However, it does not follow that **all** duplicated or derived values are redundant. Duplicated attribute values are fairly common, and are by no means redundant. For example, the fact that a particular make of car is a saloon is information about a particular instance of the entity type *car*. It is not redundant merely because it is the same as the value of the 'style' attribute for another car make which also happens to be a saloon. The two values, *saloon*, represent two distinct facts, and neither can be deduced from the other. The removal of either value would detract from the information in the database.

Style may be just one of the attributes of *car* whose value may be repeated. Figure 5.1(a) depicts a possible entity type, *car*, with four possible attributes. The associated record structure, comprising one field for each attribute, could equally well be a record in a simple file system, a segment in a hierarchic database, a record type in a CODASYL database, or a relation. It can be assumed, for simplicity, that each instance of the structure is intended to represent a possible configuration for the entity type *car*, rather than a record of a physical car which actually exists.

Whatever the modelling approach, however, a given value could occur in many instances of the structure. There is no reason why a particular model of car (e.g. *popular* or *1500*) should be restricted to exactly one style (e.g. *saloon*, *hatchback*, *coupé* etc.). Similarly, any model may be available with several sizes – and types – of engine. Thus, in principle, any value for any of the attributes could be duplicated any number of times, but on each occasion a separate fact would be represented. It is not possible to deduce, for example, the style of a particular *car* merely because some of the other *cars* are *hatchbacks*.

Further, it may be no coincidence that two competing cars have the same price, but if that is determined by the marketing policy of the two manufacturers rather than by rules available to the database, then the one may not be deducible from the other. Thus, as far as the database is concerned, both values, although the same, are required, and neither is redundant.

There is clearly a distinction between two entities happening by coincidence to have the same value for some attribute, and two entities always having the same value for some attribute because they are both related to some other entity which determines the value of the attribute.

Figure 5.2 shows some possible instances of the *car* entity type. Note that each row of the table, whether it corresponds to a record, segment or tuple, represents a different mapping between attribute values drawn from the four domains – *model*, *style*, *engine* and *price*. Each mapping happens to be distinct, and therefore none is redundant. Despite the obvious repetition of many of the individual attribute values, none of the *combinations* of attribute values can be deduced from any other.

Considering first just the values for the *model* and *style* attributes, it might appear that it would be possible to deduce from the second row of the table (*macho coupé 2900s £11,340*) that the third row should also start with *macho coupé*. That is, since the attribute values *macho* and *coupé* occur together in the second row, it might be suggested that no information is conveyed by their occurring together again in the third row. However, closer inspection reveals that the *engine* attribute must be considered as well.

Although there is a *macho coupé* with a *2400s* engine, there is no *macho convertible* available with the same engine. Thus, the table does not represent pairings of *model* and *style*, each of which can occur with any one of a set of *engines*. Rather, it represents a three-way mapping between the three attribute values. Even though the mapping appears to be exhaustive in the case of the *fiasco* model, where both *saloon* and *estate* styles can occur with each of the engines possible, that is an exception rather than the rule. In general, it cannot be deduced that a particular combination of *model*, *style* and *engine* will occur merely because, for example, that particular *model* is available in that particular

model	style	engine	price
macho	convertible	2900s	£12,900
macho	coupe	2900s	£11,340
macho	coupe	2400s	£ 9,990
fiasco	saloon	2400s	£10,950
fiasco	estate	2400s	£11,470
fiasco	saloon	2400t	£ 9,990
fiasco	estate	2400t	£10,370
commando	saloon	2400t	£ 8,400
commando	estate	2400t	£ 8,700
commando	saloon	1900	£ 7,100
domino	saloon	1900	£ 4,990
domino	estate	1900	£ 5,350
domino	saloon	1400	£ 4,450
domino	hatchback	1400	£ 4,100

Fig. 5.2   Instances of *car* entity type.

style, and there is some **other** *style* of that *model* which has the *engine* in question. Thus, although many of the attribute values are **duplicated**, none, in this case, are **redundant**.

As an aside, it is worth noting that it might be possible to draw a different conclusion if only a subset of the data were considered. It has been commented already that the mapping between *engines* and *model–style* pairings appears to be complete for the *fiasco* model. Thus, if only data for the *fiasco* were available, it might be deduced that the table contained duplicated data which was also redundant, and steps might be taken to remove such unnecessary duplication. If the full data were subsequently to become available, it might be a bit difficult to load it into the 'improved' data structure. Such problems are quite likely to arise if judgements about the possible relationships between data items are deduced from a **subset** of the instances of that data, rather than from the complete set of all **possible** values, or, more realistically, an appropriate data model.

Similar arguments apply to relationships between two or more entity types. If, for example, there is a one-to-many relationship between the entity types *market* and *car*, where the former entity represents the principal market in which any given car (type) is sold, then it follows that several *car* instances will be related to a single instance of *market*. A possible record-like structure which might be used to represent this fact is shown in Fig. 5.1(b).

Although the 'record' structure is obviously relational rather than, say, CODASYL, it should be borne in mind that the connection between the two record types may be represented in many ways. Whilst in a relational model, the connection is represented by the presence of *market* as a foreign key in the *car* relation, the same fact would be represented by common set membership in a CODASYL model. The foreign key and the common set membership represent exactly the same information. Although it is obvious in the relational case that a given value of *market* will be duplicated for each car aimed at that market, the shared set membership of the CODASYL model is, in fact, duplicating exactly the same information. However, instead of the actual attribute value being duplicated, it is a physical pointer or other physical location information which is duplicated.

In either case, information is duplicated, but it can hardly be said to be redundant. Considering Fig. 5.3(a), which shows some possible instances of the relationship, there is clearly no way of deducing, for example, that a *fiasco saloon* is aimed at the *executive* market, merely because a *macho coupé* is also aimed at that market. However, the figure implies that the market at which a particular car is aimed is determined only by the *model* and *style*, and that the *engine* fitted is of no relevance. This **determinacy** will be noted later when the process of normalization is considered.

Clearly, it would be possible to extend the table of Fig. 5.2 to include,

model	style	market

model	style	market
macho	convertible	sports
macho	coupe	executive
fiasco	saloon	executive
fiasco	estate	commuter
commando	saloon	commuter
commando	estate	commuter
domino	saloon	domestic
domino	estate	domestic
domino	hatchback	domestic

market	main competitor

market	main competitor
sports	expresso
executive	gyro
commuter	trio
domestic	poncho

(a) tables representing relationships only

model	style	engine	price	market	main competitor

model	style	engine	price	market	main competitor
macho	convertible	2900s	£12,900	sports	expresso
macho	coupe	2900s	£11,340	executive	gyro
macho	coupe	2400s	£ 9,990	executive	gyro
fiasco	saloon	2400s	£10,950	executive	gyro
fiasco	estate	2400s	£11,470	commuter	trio
fiasco	saloon	2400t	£ 9,990	executive	gyro
fiasco	estate	2400t	£10,370	commuter	trio
commando	saloon	2400t	£ 8,400	commuter	trio
commando	estate	2400t	£ 8,700	commuter	trio
commando	saloon	1900	£ 7,100	commuter	trio
domino	saloon	1900	£ 4,990	domestic	poncho
domino	estate	1900	£ 5,350	domestic	poncho
domino	saloon	1400	£ 4,450	domestic	poncho
domino	hatchback	1400	£ 4,100	domestic	poncho

(b) relationships incorporated into larger table

Fig. 5.3   Instances of simple relationship type.

for each car, the market at which it is aimed, and the principal competitor it will face in that market. Such a table is shown in Fig. 5.3(b). In this table, it is apparent that there is more duplication than in either Fig. 5.2 or Fig. 5.3(a). It happens that some of the duplicated values are also redundant. For example, the fact that the main competitor for a *macho coupé 2400s* is a *gyro* can be deduced from the fact that the *gyro* is the main competitor for a *macho coupé 2900s*, or indeed for a *fiasco saloon 2400s*, since all three are aimed at the same market.

Thus, returning to Fig. 5.1(b), the *market* attribute of the *car* record can be said to be **duplicated**, but not **redundant**. However, some duplicated fields in the table of Fig. 5.3(b) are redundant.

Figure 5.1(c) depicts a complex, many-to-many relationship between *engine* and *model*. Astute readers will notice that this is one of the many-to-many relationships which forms part of the complex fan trap between *model*, *engine* and *style*, which is resolved by the three-way mapping of Fig. 5.2. However, it is quite possible that particular information can be attached to the single many-to-many association, for example, maximum speed, as shown in the *performance* record type.

Instances of these record types are shown in Fig. 5.4(a), where it is again obvious that the foreign key fields, *engine* and *model* in the *performance* and *car* records contain duplicated data. As with the simple relationship between *market* and *car*, however, the duplication is not redundant, but each duplicate value represents a different instance of the relationship.

However, if the three tables are combined, as in Fig. 5.4(b), more duplication is introduced, and that additional duplication, in the *max speed* and *capacity* columns, is redundant.

If the performance data were more realistic, such as that shown in Fig. 5.5, in which the maximum speed depends on the body style as well as on the engine and the model, then the *max speed* column in the combined table would not contain redundant data. However, the dependence of the maximum speed on the body style will be ignored for the purposes of this discussion.

Combining the attribute values for each of the three parts of the car example gives the table of Fig. 5.6. The discussion of the remainder of this section will be based on these data.

It has been demonstrated that the 'complete' table contains duplicated data, some of which are redundant. In Fig. 5.7(a), all **duplicated** attribute values are shaded, whereas in Fig. 5.7(b), only those values which are **redundant** are shaded. A moment's consideration of the values shaded in Fig. 5.7(b) should show why those values are redundant, or rather, how else they could be deduced. (Although the order of the tuples in a relation is insignificant, it happens that the table in Fig. 5.7(b) is ordered so that the redundant data occur immediately below another tuple from which they can be deduced.)

It should be noted that all the redundant values in the table are also duplicated. However, there are a large number of duplicated attribute values which are **not** redundant, as shown in Fig. 5.7(c). Hence, the assertion earlier in this section that (nearly) all redundant data are duplicated, but not all duplicated data are redundant.

It is worth noting that some attempt might be made to reduce the amount of both duplicated and redundant data by departing from the rectangular nature of the table. Essentially, for each *model* of car, there are a number of *engines* which can be fitted, and for each *model/engine* combination, there are a number of body *styles* available. This information can be represented by a structure which includes **repeating groups**. Figure 5.8 shows those attribute values which would still appear

model	style	engine	price	market
macho	convertible	2900s	£12,900	sports
macho	coupe	2900s	£11,340	executive
macho	coupe	2400s	£ 9,990	executive
fiasco	saloon	2400s	£10,950	executive
fiasco	estate	2400s	£11,470	commuter
fiasco	saloon	2400t	£ 9,990	executive
fiasco	estate	2400t	£10,370	commuter
commando	saloon	2400t	£ 8,400	commuter
commando	estate	2400t	£ 8,700	commuter
commando	saloon	1900	£ 7,100	commuter
domino	saloon	1900	£ 4,990	domestic
domino	estate	1900	£ 5,350	domestic
domino	saloon	1400	£ 4,450	domestic
domino	hatchback	1400	£ 4,100	domestic

engine	model	max speed
2900s	macho	155
2400s	macho	131
2400s	fiasco	117
2400t	fiasco	101
2400t	commando	105
1900	commando	83
1900	domino	91
1400	domino	79

engine	capacity
2900s	2847
2400s	2395
2400t	2395
1900	1898
1400	1365

(a) Tables for complex relationships

model	style	engine	capacity	max speed	price	market
macho	convertible	2900s	2847	155	£12,900	sports
macho	coupe	2900s	2847	155	£11,340	executive
macho	coupe	2400s	2395	131	£ 9,990	executive
fiasco	saloon	2400s	2395	117	£10,950	executive
fiasco	estate	2400s	2395	117	£11,470	commuter
fiasco	saloon	2400t	2395	101	£ 9,990	executive
fiasco	estate	2400t	2395	101	£10,370	commuter
commando	saloon	2400t	2395	105	£ 8,400	commuter
commando	estate	2400t	2395	105	£ 8,700	commuter
commando	saloon	1900	1898	83	£ 7,100	commuter
domino	saloon	1900	1898	91	£ 4,990	domestic
domino	estate	1900	1898	91	£ 5,350	domestic
domino	saloon	1400	1365	79	£ 4,450	domestic
domino	hatchback	1400	1365	79	£ 4,100	domestic

(b) table incorporating complex relationships

Fig. 5.4 Instances of complex relationship type.

in the new structure, and it can be seen that some duplicated values, both redundant and non-redundant, have disappeared. The structure is more clearly visible in Fig. 5.9. The first representation merely shows the fields reordered, so that it is clear which group of fields is repeating at any stage. In the second representation, the nesting of the repeating groups within the new, variable length records is emphasized. It should be noted that, not only are the records of varying length, but so also are the repeating groups themselves.

model	style	engine	max speed
macho	convertible	2900s	153
macho	coupe	2900s	155
macho	coupe	2400s	131
fiasco	saloon	2400s	117
fiasco	estate	2400s	108
fiasco	saloon	2400t	101
fiasco	estate	2400t	93
commando	saloon	2400t	105
commando	estate	2400t	98
commando	saloon	1900	83
domino	saloon	1900	91
domino	estate	1900	85
domino	saloon	1400	77
domino	hatchback	1400	79

Fig. 5.5 Alternative speed data.

model	style	engine	capacity	max speed	price	market	main competitor
macho	convertible	2900s	2847	155	£12,900	sports	expresso
macho	coupe	2900s	2847	155	£11,340	executive	gyro
macho	coupe	2400s	2395	131	£ 9,990	executive	gyro
fiasco	saloon	2400s	2395	117	£10,950	executive	gyro
fiasco	estate	2400s	2395	117	£11,470	commuter	trio
fiasco	saloon	2400t	2395	101	£ 9,990	executive	gyro
fiasco	estate	2400t	2395	101	£10,370	commuter	trio
commando	saloon	2400t	2395	105	£ 8,400	commuter	trio
commando	estate	2400t	2395	105	£ 8,700	commuter	trio
commando	saloon	1900	1898	83	£ 7,100	commuter	trio
domino	saloon	1900	1898	91	£ 4,990	domestic	poncho
domino	estate	1900	1898	91	£ 5,350	domestic	poncho
domino	saloon	1400	1365	79	£ 4,450	domestic	poncho
domino	hatchback	1400	1365	79	£ 4,100	domestic	poncho

Fig. 5.6 Complete car data.

Of course, since the mapping between *model*, *style* and *engine* is three-way, the order in which the attributes have been paired for this exercise is arbitrary. It happens that other pairings produce different savings in duplication and redundancy. However, the general principles are the same.

5.1.2 Consequences

One obvious consequence of using a structure which includes redundant data is that space must be wasted in storing those data. Not only does this

model	style	engine	capacity	max speed	price	market	main competitor
macho	convertible	2900s	2847	155	£12,900	sports	expresso
macho	coupe	2900s	2847	155	£11,340	executive	gyro
macho	coupe	2400s	2395	131	£ 9,990	executive	gyro
fiasco	saloon	2400s	2395	117	£10,950	executive	gyro
fiasco	estate	2400s	2395	117	£11,470	commuter	trio
fiasco	saloon	2400t	2395	101	£ 9,990	executive	gyro
fiasco	estate	2400t	2395	101	£10,370	commuter	trio
commando	saloon	2400t	2395	105	£ 8,400	commuter	trio
commando	estate	2400t	2395	105	£ 8,700	commuter	trio
commando	saloon	1900	1898	83	£ 7,100	commuter	trio
domino	saloon	1900	1898	91	£ 4,990	domestic	poncho
domino	estate	1900	1898	91	£ 5,350	domestic	poncho
domino	saloon	1400	1365	79	£ 4,450	domestic	poncho
domino	hatchback	1400	1365	79	£ 4,100	domestic	poncho

(a) duplicated data

model	style	engine	capacity	max speed	price	market	main competitor
macho	convertible	2900s	2847	155	£12,900	sports	expresso
macho	coupe	2900s	2847	155	£11,340	executive	gyro
macho	coupe	2400s	2395	131	£ 9,990	executive	gyro
fiasco	saloon	2400s	2395	117	£10,950	executive	gyro
fiasco	estate	2400s	2395	117	£11,470	commuter	trio
fiasco	saloon	2400t	2395	101	£ 9,990	executive	gyro
fiasco	estate	2400t	2395	101	£10,370	commuter	trio
commando	saloon	2400t	2395	105	£ 8,400	commuter	trio
commando	estate	2400t	2395	105	£ 8,700	commuter	trio
commando	saloon	1900	1898	83	£ 7,100	commuter	trio
domino	saloon	1900	1898	91	£ 4,990	domestic	poncho
domino	estate	1900	1898	91	£ 5,350	domestic	poncho
domino	saloon	1400	1365	79	£ 4,450	domestic	poncho
domino	hatchback	1400	1365	79	£ 4,100	domestic	poncho

(b) redundant data

imply a cost penalty, in that more space is needed to store the data, and space costs money, but there can also be a performance cost. The performance of most database systems is governed, not by the speed of the computer, but by the speed at which data can be transferred into the computer from secondary storage. Clearly, if more data have to be transferred, more time will be required. Thus, if the data structure contains redundant data, extra time will be required to transfer those data into the computer for processing, and hence performance can be downgraded.

However, this argument is not complete, and the consequences of excessive zeal in eliminating redundant data can also affect performance

model	style	engine	capacity	max speed	price	market	main competitor
macho	convertible	2900s	2847	155	£12,900	sports	expresso
macho	coupe	2900s	2847	155	£11,340	executive	gyro
macho	coupe	2400s	2395	131	£ 9,990	executive	gyro
fiasco	saloon	2400s	2395	117	£10,950	executive	gyro
fiasco	estate	2400s	2395	117	£11,470	commuter	trio
fiasco	saloon	2400t	2395	101	£ 9,990	executive	gyro
fiasco	estate	2400t	2395	101	£10,370	commuter	trio
commando	saloon	2400t	2395	105	£ 8,400	commuter	trio
commando	estate	2400t	2395	105	£ 8,700	commuter	trio
commando	saloon	1900	1898	83	£ 7,100	commuter	trio
domino	saloon	1900	1898	91	£ 4,990	domestic	poncho
domino	estate	1900	1898	91	£ 5,350	domestic	poncho
domino	saloon	1400	1365	79	£ 4,450	domestic	poncho
domino	hatchback	1400	1365	79	£ 4,100	domestic	poncho

(c) non-redundant duplicated data

Fig. 5.7 (a) Duplicated; (b) redundant; and (c) non-redundant duplicated data.

model	style	engine	capacity	max speed	price	market	main competitor
macho	convertible	2900s	2847	155	£12,900	sports	expresso
	coupe				£11,340	executive	gyro
	coupe	2400s	2395	131	£ 9,990	executive	gyro
fiasco	saloon	2400s	2395	117	£10,950	executive	gyro
	estate				£11,470	commuter	trio
	saloon	2400t	2395	101	£ 9,990	executive	gyro
	estate				£10,370	commuter	trio
commando	saloon	2400t	2395	105	£ 8,400	commuter	trio
	estate				£ 8,700	commuter	trio
	saloon	1900	1898	83	£ 7,100	commuter	trio
domino	saloon	1900	1898	91	£ 4,990	domestic	poncho
	estate				£ 5,350	domestic	poncho
	saloon	1400	1365	79	£ 4,450	domestic	poncho
	hatchback				£ 4,100	domestic	poncho

Fig. 5.8 Repeating groups.

adversely. This point is discussed further in the last section of this chapter.

More subtle problems arise when data which are redundant are subject to update. There are two broad categories of problem. The first relates to maintaining consistency between duplicated values, and the second to the fact that structures which include redundancy tend to represent sets of facts rather than atomic facts.

If several copies exist of a particular attribute value, and that attribute value itself represents a single fact, then it follows that, if the **fact** changes, then so must **all** of the duplicate values. Consider, for example,

(a)

model	engine	capacity	max speed	style	price	market	main competitor
				style	price	market	main competitor
	engine	capacity	max speed	style	price	market	main competitor
model	engine	capacity	max speed	style	price	market	main competitor
				style	price	market	main competitor
	engine	capacity	max speed	style	price	market	main competitor
				style	price	market	main competitor
model	engine	capacity	max speed	style	price	market	main competitor

(b)

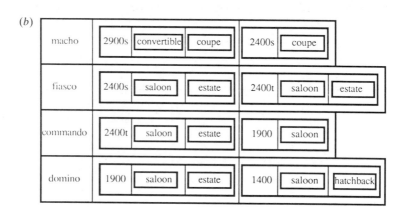

Fig. 5.9   Repeating group structures.

the table in Fig. 5.10(a). If the *main competitor* in the *domestic* market changes – perhaps because a new car comes onto the market – then it is necessary to replace not one, but **all** of the values *poncho* in the table, as shown. Similarly, if, following a refinement to the production process, the *capacity* of the 2400t engine is henceforth to be *2391* rather than *2395*, then the *capacity* attribute must be altered for each car which can have that engine fitted.

The duplication of both of these attributes is, in fact, redundant, since the multiple values in each case represent only a single fact – that the main competitor in the *domestic* market is (was) the *poncho*, and that the capacity of the *2400t* engine is *2395*. Thus, a desire to avoid such update

model	style	engine	capacity	max speed	price	market	main competitor
macho	convertible	2900s	2847	155	£12,900	sports	expresso
macho	coupe	2900s	2847	155	£11,340	executive	gyro
macho	coupe	2400s	2395	131	£ 9,990	executive	gyro
fiasco	saloon	2400s	2395	117	£10,950	executive	gyro
fiasco	estate	2400s	2395	117	£11,470	commuter	trio
fiasco	saloon	2400t	2395	101	£ 9,990	executive	gyro
fiasco	estate	2400t	2395	101	£10,370	commuter	trio
commando	saloon	2400t	2395	105	£ 8,400	commuter	trio
commando	estate	2400t	2395	105	£ 8,700	commuter	trio
commando	saloon	1900	1898	83	£ 7,100	commuter	trio
domino	saloon	1900	1898	91	£ 4,990	domestic	poncho
domino	estate	1900	1898	91	£ 5,350	domestic	poncho
domino	saloon	1400	1365	79	£ 4,450	domestic	poncho
domino	hatchback	1400	1365	79	£ 4,100	domestic	poncho

(a) examples of data which must be updated consistently

model	style	engine	capacity	max speed	price	market	main competitor
macho		2900s	2847	155	£12,900	sports	expresso
macho		2900s	2847	155	£11,340	executive	gyro
macho		2400s	2395	131	£ 9,990	executive	gyro
fiasco	saloon	2400s	2395	117	£10,950	executive	gyro
fiasco	estate	2400s	2395	117	£11,470	commuter	gyro
fiasco	saloon	2400t	2395	101	£ 9,990	executive	gyro
fiasco	estate	2400t	2395	101	£10,370	commuter	gyro
commando	saloon	2400t	2395	105	£ 8,400	commuter	trio
commando	estate	2400t	2395	105	£ 8,700	commuter	trio
commando	saloon	1900	1898	83	£ 7,100	commuter	poncho
domino	saloon	1900	1898	91	£ 4,990	domestic	poncho
domino	estate	1900	1898	91	£ 5,350	domestic	poncho
domino	saloon	1400	1365	79	£ 4,450	domestic	poncho
domino	hatchback	1400	1365	79	£ 4,100	domestic	poncho

(b) examples of data which can be lost on deletion of other data

3500x	3468

runabout	solo

(c) information which cannot be inserted in isolation

Fig. 5.10   Update, deletion and insertion problems.

problems is further justification for the elimination of redundancy.

However, it should be noted that problems can occur if it is necessary to update any attribute whose value is duplicated, even if no redundancy is involved. For example, if, following a marketing survey, it were decided to replace the term *saloon* by, say, *carriage*, then it would be necessary to replace each of the duplicated values in Fig. 5.10(a). The same problem of maintaining consistency, and ensuring that **all** the relevant values are updated, arises as for redundant data, even though no redundancy is involved in this case.

The composite table of Fig. 5.6 represents, in each record, not one but several facts. Unless 'missing' or 'unknown' values are to be permitted, it follows that a record cannot exist unless there is a 'value' for each of these facts. Thus, problems can arise both when deleting facts which already exist, or introducing new facts in isolation.

Figure 5.10(b) shows that, if the model *macho* were to be withdrawn, then the whole of the first three rows of the table would have to be deleted. Not only would this eradicate information specific to the *macho*, but it would also remove information concerning the *2900s* engine, and the *sports* market. Neither of the facts so removed occur elsewhere in the table. However, there is no reason to suppose that either the engine or the market cease to exist merely because one particular model of car is no longer produced.

Similarly, if the *2400t* engine were to be withdrawn, the deletion of the corresponding rows of the table would lose the information that the *commando* is available as an *estate*. Again, it does not follow that the removal of an engine implies the removal of a particular style for any model.

Not only do difficulties arise when deleting information; problems can also occur with the converse operation, inserting new information. For example, no information can be inserted about a new engine, the *3500x*, until there is some car in which it is fitted. Similarly, the recognition of a new market, *runabout*, in which the main competitor is the *solo*, can not be recorded until there is some car aimed at that market.

Both the deletion and insertion problems result from the non-atomicity of the information represented in a single row of the table. It is not just that each row represents more than one fact – i.e. that it contains more than one attribute value – but that some of the facts represented in a single row are independent. The existence of a particular engine is independent of the existence of some market, or of some model. Whether some style of body is made for a particular model does not depend on the existence of any specific engine. However, the table structure of Fig. 5.6 does not allow these facts to be represented independently, but only in combination.

5.2 NORMALIZATION

The discussion of the previous section has shown that the presence of redundancy in a database can lead to problems when the database needs to be updated. Not only can the consistency of the database be threatened, single individual facts may be represented more than once, but it may not be possible to insert or delete information if it does not correspond precisely to the organization of the storage structure.

It follows that there may be some benefit in ensuring that any given database schema does not include redundancy. The process of identifying and removing redundant features from a schema is termed **normalization**. As with the discussion of redundancy, the concepts are developed here in terms of relational schemata. Although the mechanism may not be the same, many of the concepts are equally relevant for CODASYL and hierarchic schemata.

5.2.1 Objectives

The principal objectives of normalization are, quite simply, to **identify** and to **remove** redundancy from a schema. The process must be executed in terms of the **structure** of the schema, rather than on the basis of particular instances of data, although consideration of such instances can often help.

As has been shown, there is an important distinction between redundancy and duplication. The process of normalization may apparently **increase** the level of duplication, particularly in a relational schema, since a normalized schema usually comprises many more relations than one which is un-normalized (i.e. contains redundancy). The mappings between the separate relations are represented by the presence of foreign keys. Whenever the mapping is one-to-many or many-to-many, the field representing the foreign key is bound to contain duplicate values. However, it will become apparent that it is only the values of the foreign keys themselves which are duplicated, and not those of data which are dependent on the foreign key. Further, although the duplication of some foreign keys may, in fact, increase, the increase is only marginal, and, overall, there can be a considerable reduction in duplication even of foreign key values.

It should be stressed at this point that the reasons for seeking to eliminate redundancy relate to questions of consistency and accuracy rather than to any concept of efficiency. As will be discussed in a later section, the actual processing of a normalized schema may be very much less efficient than for an un-normalized schema.

In addition, it should be borne in mind that the normalization is effected in terms of the **conceptual** schema only. The problems which normalization is addressing are relevant only if it is possible for users to perform operations such as UPDATE for some records (tuples) but not for others which share some duplicated values. If, however, any user of the database can see only a normalized schema which contains no redundancy, it is of absolutely no consequence if there is a **transparent** mapping between that conceptual schema and one, or more, internal schemata which are not normalized to the same extent. Although the internal schema(ta) will contain redundant data, updates to any values which happen to be duplicated in an internal schema should be applied automatically to all instances of those data. Since the mapping from conceptual schema to internal schema is performed automatically by the database management system, there **should** be no possibility of the updates being applied only partially.

Thus, the objective of the normalization process can be restated as the **minimization** of redundancy in a **conceptual** schema.

5.2.2 Functional dependencies

The normalization process is based on the concept of functional dependency, or **determinacy**, between two or more attribute values. Functional dependency between any pair of attribute values means that the value of one of the attributes **implies**, in a mathematical sense, the value of the second. The concept is related closely to those of primary key in file processing, and identifier in data analysis. However, the attribute whose value determines the value of the second need not necessarily be the primary key of the relation in which it occurs. Also, as with primary keys and identifiers, the determining attribute may, in fact, be a combination of attributes.

Considering the 'complete' car data represented in Fig. 5.6, which has been shown to contain considerable redundancy, the key for the rows of the table is the combination of attribute values *model*, *style*, *engine*. None on their own uniquely determines a single record, but in this instance it is this combination which is the smallest suitable key for the table.

Price on its own is almost sufficient, but is excluded by the duplicate value £9,990. Taking *price* together with *max speed*, the data of Fig. 5.6 suggest that the two attributes together could be a candidate key, but there are two important points to be borne in mind. Firstly, there is no particular reason why the combination should be unique. Both *price* and *max speed* are attributes which represent qualities of the car in question. Neither on its own is unique, and it is only by looking at the data which are present **at the moment** that it might be deduced that the combination is unique. However, there is no real evidence for this, and to make such an assumption would be rash. Secondly, the table as a whole represents configurations of *car* which correspond to different instances of a three-way relationship between the entity types *model*, *style* and *engine*. Thus, it would make most sense to select as primary key for the table a combination of attributes which reflects that mapping, rather than attributes of the mapping.

It happens that, if the combination *model*, *style*, *engine* is chosen as primary key, then the only attribute whose value is determined directly by that combination is, in fact, *price*. As the problem was developed, it was stated, for example, that the *max speed* was determined by the combination of *model* and *engine* – only part of the primary key for the table. Similarly, the principal *market* is determined by the combination of *model* and *style*, again only part of the primary key. Finally, the *capacity* of an engine is determined by the type of engine, not the car in which it is mounted, and the *main competitor* in a market is a feature of the market itself, and not of the cars aimed at that market.

Each of these determinacies can be expressed as a **functional dependency** of one attribute on the value of another. The dependencies can be depicted graphically as in Fig. 5.11, in which the ringed attributes are those which determine the value of the attribute at the arrowhead. Conversely, the value of the attribute at an arrowhead is functionally dependent on the values of the attribute(s) enclosed in the corresponding ring(s). That is, whenever a particular value, or combination of values, occurs for the ringed attribute(s), then the **same** value occurs for the functionally dependent attribute. This can be verified by inspection of Fig. 5.6. For example, both versions of the *fiasco saloon* are aimed at the

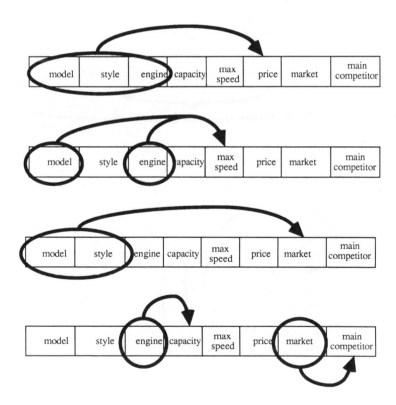

Fig. 5.11 Functional dependencies in the *cars* data.

executive market, whereas both versions of the *fiasco estate* are aimed at the *commuter* market. Similarly, in all four cars fitted with a *2400t* engine, the *capacity* is *2395*.

It is often helpful to show all the functional dependencies for a particular table on a single diagram, as in Fig. 5.12(a). (The different styles of line are merely for clarity, rather than to indicate some convention.) The figure shows also the two nested repeating groups which were identified in Fig. 5.9, although the order of nesting has been reversed. Since normalization removes the nested groups, the distinction is immaterial at this stage, although the reader may care to re-work the next section assuming that the repeating groups had been nested in the sense shown in Fig. 5.9.

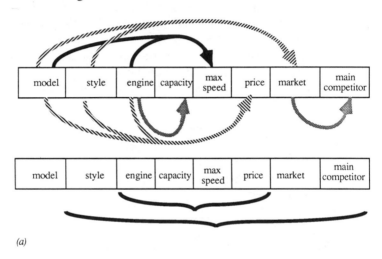

(a)

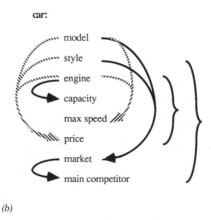

(b)

Fig. 5.12 Functional dependencies and repeating groups.

Figure 5.12(b) presents the same information as Fig. 5.12(a), but in a slightly more concise manner. It is this layout which will be used in the description of the normalization process.

5.2.3 Zeroth normal form

Putting a relation into zeroth normal form is nothing more than transforming it from a structure such as that of Fig. 5.9 to a rectangular format such as in Fig. 5.6. More formally, it ensures that each domain is **atomic**, containing only simple values rather than repeating groups. It also makes the relation simpler to handle, since each tuple is the same 'shape'.

Often, the process will be unnecessary, since the 'original' table will already be in zeroth normal form. Indeed, there is some discussion about whether zeroth normal form really exists in its own right. However, since it is the usual starting point for the normalization process, it seems sensible at least to describe it. Nevertheless, an un-normalized relation can be normalized directly into first normal form without going through the intermediate stage of zeroth normal form.

Should it be necessary to re-arrange an existing table, perhaps with the structure of Fig. 5.9(b), into zeroth normal form, the process is quite simple. The first stage is simply to arrange the repeating groups one under the other, as in Fig. 5.9(a), and then to recognize that this is merely a rectangular table with a number of blanks, as in Fig. 5.8. It is then a trivial matter to insert the appropriate values into the table to produce a table such as Fig. 5.6.

5.2.4 First normal form

The intention of putting a relation into first normal form is to **remove** any repeating groups which might be present. By splitting the original relation into a number of smaller ones, two targets are achieved. Firstly, the redundancy which is introduced by transforming an un-normalized relation which contains repeating groups into zeroth normal form is eliminated. Secondly, since the resulting relations contain no repeating groups, they must be rectangular.

The process is illustrated in Fig. 5.13. The original relation for the *cars* example contains two repeating groups, which happen to be nested. The basic step at each stage is to consider each relation in turn, and to split into two any which contains a repeating group. Only one repeating group is separated out at each stage. The two relations thus produced contain:

a the key of the original relation, plus any attributes functionally dependent on the key;

b the key of the original relation **plus** whatever attributes are effectively the key of the repeating group, together with the remaining attributes from the repeating group.

Thus, in Fig. 5.13, the first stage produces two relations, one containing *model* and any attributes (in this case none) which are uniquely determined by the value of *model*, and a second which comprises the remaining attributes. The key of the second relation is the concatenation of *model* and *style*, the latter being the effective key of the repeating group. In this reduced relation, the only data which are duplicated for

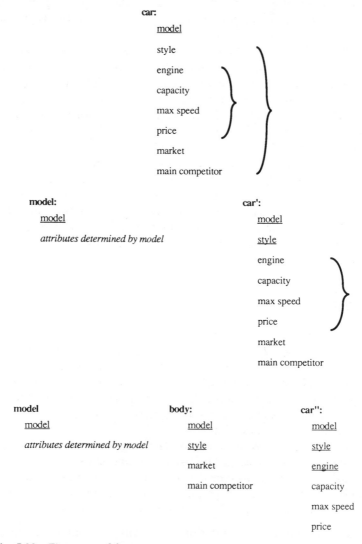

Fig. 5.13   First normal form.

each instance of the repeating group is, in fact, the key of the original relation, *model*, which is now a **foreign key**.

The process must be repeated for the resulting relations, since there is still one repeating group – with effective key *engine*. Again, the attributes which are functionally dependent on the key of the relation, namely *market* and *main competitor* remain, and the attributes from the repeating group are used to form a new relation, this time with key *model–style–engine*.

Whilst first normal form relations can be generated equally well from either un-normalized or zeroth normal form relations, it happens that it is easier if the repeating group structure is obvious. Thus, zeroth normal form may, in fact, be unhelpful, since the un-normalized relation has been artificially constrained into a rectangular format which masks that structure. Nevertheless, in many cases, the original relation is presented in zeroth normal form, and it is necessary to proceed from that point.

5.2.5 Second normal form

Although first normal form eliminates redundancy caused by repeating group structures, there can still be problems with redundancy. For example, within the first normal form relations of Fig. 5.13, the value of *capacity* occurs for each car in which a given engine is installed. Clearly, the fact that a given engine has a certain capacity is a single fact, and should be represented only once. It is duplicated, in fact, with redundancy, because the attribute value is not functionally dependent on the whole of the key of the relation.

Figure 5.14 shows the functional dependencies in the first normal form relations. Considering the *car'* relation, it is clear that, not only is *capacity* functionally dependent on *engine* rather than on the entire key of the relation, but *max speed* is, in fact, dependent on only two of the three attributes which form the key, namely, *model* and *engine*. This phenomenon is termed **partial dependency**.

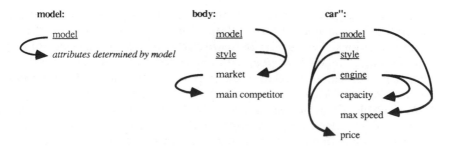

Fig. 5.14 Functional dependencies in first normal form relations.

car":

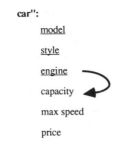

model
style
engine
capacity
max speed
price

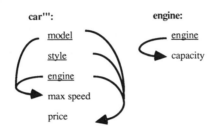

car'":

model
style
engine
max speed
price

engine:

engine
capacity

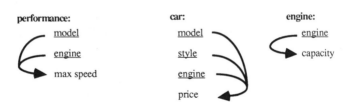

performance:

model
engine
max speed

car:

model
style
engine
price

engine:

engine
capacity

Fig. 5.15 Second normal form.

As with the generation of first normal form relations, the process of generating second normal form relations involves the formation of new, smaller relations. Taking first the *capacity* attribute, this can be split off into a separate relation, *engine*, with key *engine*, as shown in Fig. 5.15. A similar process can be applied to the *max speed* attribute, only in this case the key is *model–engine*.

As a result of this process, the drastically reduced *car* relation contains no redundant data. Each tuple represents a single fact – or, strictly, two: that the combination of a particular *model*, *style* and *engine* can exist, and that that combination has a certain price. Information such as the maximum speed for a particular combination of engine and model, or the capacity of a particular engine, are represented once only, in separate relations. Although there is some duplication, it is restricted to foreign key attributes – *engine*, *model* and *style*. In all, the total amount of duplication is reduced.

5.2.6 Third normal form

The *body* relation of Fig. 5.14 appears to be in second normal form, since there is no attribute which is partially dependent on the key of the relation. However, there is clearly considerable duplication of the attribute *main competitor*, which is repeated for every car which is targeted at a particular market.

This time, the dependency of *main competitor* on the key of the relation is not partial, but **transitive**. The value of *main competitor* is determined, not by the key of the relation, but by *market*, which is itself functionally dependent on the key. Thus, any given value of the key – that is, *model–style* – does determine the value of *main competitor*, but only indirectly.

As with partial dependency, the solution to transitive dependency is to split the relation into two. The attribute which is the intermediate in the dependency chain – in this case, *market* – becomes the key of one relation, and also remains in the original. The attribute which was transitively dependent on the key of the original relation is now functionally dependent on the key of the new relation, and so is placed there, and removed from the original relation. This process is illustrated in Fig. 5.16.

The complete set of third normal form relations generated by the successive processes of normalization are shown in Fig. 5.17. The relations contain no repeating groups, no partial dependencies, and no

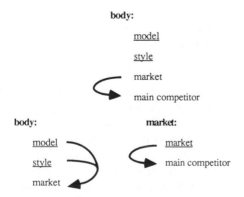

Fig. 5.16   Third normal form.

model:	engine:	market:
model	engine	market
attributes determined by model	capacity	main competitor

performance:	body:	car:
model	model	model
engine	style	style
max speed	market	engine
		price

Fig. 5.17 Complete set of third normal form relations.

transitive dependencies. As near as is possible, each relation represents single facts, or sets of related facts. None of the relations contain redundancy.

The instances of the third normal form relations, as derived from Fig. 5.6, are shown in Fig. 5.18. Clearly, although the relations are free from redundancy, there is still considerable duplication. In fact, the five relations of Fig. 5.18 contain 111 attribute values, whereas the table of Fig. 5.6 contained 112. Thus, although Fig. 5.6 contained considerable redundancy, the third normal form relations, from which that redundancy is supposed to have been eliminated, contain only one fewer attribute values.

However, the structure of the normalized relations does overcome the insertion and deletion problems illustrated by Fig. 5.10. If the *macho* were to be withdrawn, although it would imply changes to each of the *car, performance* and *body* relations, the information about the *2900s* engine and the *sports* market would be preserved. If the *2400t* engine were to be withdrawn, information about the *commando* would remain. Similarly, it would be quite possible to insert information about the *3500x* engine before it was available in a car, or to record the existence of the *runabout* market.

Although the third normal form relations do seem to embody rather excessive duplication of attribute values which happen to be foreign keys, there are two points which must be stressed in mitigation.

Firstly, as is the case with most textbook examples, the cardinalities of the sample relations are relatively low. Therefore, any saving due to the elimination of redundant duplication is often masked by the overhead of setting up a new relation. The *engine* and *market* relations, for example, grow only as the numbers of engines and markets, respectively, increase. Each new engine or market requires two attribute values in the

engine

engine	capacity
2900s	2847
2400s	2395
2400t	2395
1900	1898
1400	1365

market

market	main competitor
sports	expresso
executive	gyro
commuter	trio
domestic	poncho

performance

engine	model	max speed
2900s	macho	155
2400s	macho	131
2400s	fiasco	117
2400t	fiasco	101
2400t	commando	105
1900	commando	83
1900	domino	91
1400	domino	79

body

model	style	market
macho	convertible	sports
macho	coupe	executive
fiasco	saloon	executive
fiasco	estate	commuter
commando	saloon	commuter
commando	estate	commuter
domino	saloon	domestic
domino	estate	domestic
domino	hatchback	domestic

car

model	style	engine	price
macho	convertible	2900s	£12,900
macho	coupe	2900s	£11,340
macho	coupe	2400s	£ 9,990
fiasco	saloon	2400s	£10,950
fiasco	estate	2400s	£11,470
fiasco	saloon	2400t	£ 9,990
fiasco	estate	2400t	£10,370
commando	saloon	2400t	£ 8,400
commando	estate	2400t	£ 8,700
commando	saloon	1900	£ 7,100
domino	saloon	1900	£ 4,990
domino	estate	1900	£ 5,350
domino	saloon	1400	£ 4,450
domino	hatchback	1400	£ 4,100

Fig. 5.18   Instances of third normal form relations.

appropriate relation. Thus, a saving in number of attribute values will result only if the attribute values would otherwise have been duplicated – redundantly – more than twice. This is unlikely in examples which are small enough to present in a textbook, but less so in real-world examples.

Secondly, the example has been developed to illustrate a variety of problems without involving too many different entity types. It is perhaps more complex, given the number of data items, than one might normally expect. Indeed, in a real-world example which had the same structure, it would be likely that there would be several additional attributes. For example, an engine might develop a certain horsepower, and have one of a set of possible configurations; the main competitor in a market would, presumably have a price and manufacturer; and performance would be measured not only by maximum speed but also by fuel consumption and acceleration. If that were the case, then the un-normalized relation would comprise some 196 attribute values, whereas the third normal form relations would comprise only 145.

5.2.7 Boyce-Codd normal form

Third normal form is the usual end-point for normalization. Redundancy is largely eliminated, with each relation representing either single facts, or related sets of facts. Further, none of the redundancies which are eliminated by transforming a schema into third normal form are particularly obscure. Indeed, repeating groups, partial dependencies and transitive dependencies might even have been removed from a well-designed file processing system, designed without recourse to the database approach.

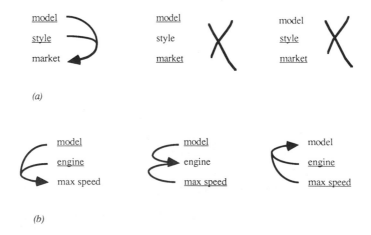

Fig. 5.19   Candidate keys.

However, the derivation of third normal form relations from a second normal form schema can obscure some hidden dependencies by making assumptions about which fields comprise the keys of the resulting relations.

There is no reason why any given relation should have just one combination of fields which can be used as a primary key. Indeed, unless the relation is all-key, so that all the attributes are required as part of the primary key, it is quite likely that there will be more than one candidate key. It is a fairly simple task to consider all possible combinations of the attributes to ascertain which are candidate keys. Any combination whose values do not completely determine all of the remaining attribute values, or which is **longer** than some other candidate key, can be discarded immediately.

Thus, for the *body* relation, the possible candidate keys are shown in Fig. 5.19(a). Although the combination *model–style* does determine the value of *market*, inspection of the instance of the relation in Fig. 5.18 shows that neither of the other combinations determines the value of the remaining attribute. Hence, the only candidate key for the *body* relation is that deduced during the normalization process, *model–style*.

For the *performance* relation, it appears that any pair of values determines the third, so that it appears that the relation has three acceptable candidate keys, as shown in Fig. 5.19(b). However, care should be taken that the determinacies deduced from an instance of the relation are general, and not just a fortuitous coincidence. Whilst it is possible that the combination *model–max speed* would determine a unique *engine*, it is slightly less credible that *engine–max speed* would determine a unique *model*. It is worth noting further that, from Fig. 5.18, it would appear that *max speed* could itself be a candidate key for this relation. As far as the instance of the relation is concerned, *max speed* is indeed unique. However, there would seem to be no sound, real-world justification for this uniqueness, and so it would be somewhat foolhardy to consider *max speed* as a candidate key for the relation.

Occasionally, when deducing the candidate keys for a particular relation, some additional dependencies can come to light which demonstrate that the relation may not, in fact, be in third normal form. The relation in Fig. 5.20(a) represents the delivery policy of the car manufacturer. Deliveries are organized by month with only one model being delivered during any month, and any dealer receives deliveries of a particular model during only one of the months during which that model is delivered. Thus, the combination *model–dealer* determines uniquely the month in which the delivery will be made. Since *delivery* is fully dependent on the combination of *dealer* and *model*, it appears that the relation is in third normal form.

However, an alternative candidate key is the combination *dealer–delivery*, since deliveries during a single month are all for the same model. Indeed, the value of *model* is not only determined by this second candidate key, but it is also dependent on the value of *delivery* itself. That dependency is a partial dependency, and so the relation would **not** be in third normal form if the combination *dealer–delivery* were taken to be primary key rather than *dealer–model*. The degree to which the relation fails to meet third normal form is illustrated in Fig. 5.20(b) by the shading

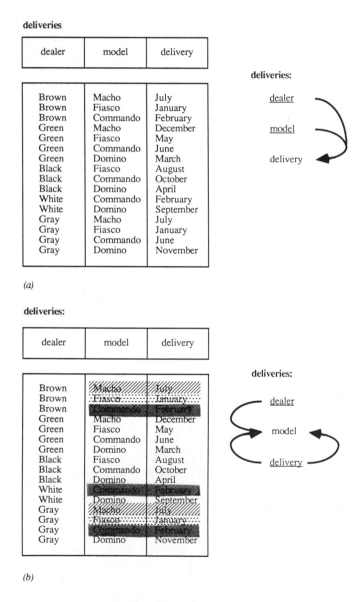

Fig. 5.20   Hidden dependencies in third normal form relations.

dealer	delivery

model	delivery

dealer	delivery
Brown	July
Brown	January
Brown	February
Green	December
Green	May
Green	June
Green	March
Black	August
Black	October
Black	April
White	February
White	September
Gray	July
Gray	January
Gray	June
Gray	November

model	delivery
Macho	July
Fiasco	January
Commando	February
Macho	December
Fiasco	May
Commando	June
Domino	March
Fiasco	August
Commando	October
Domino	April
Domino	September
Domino	November

Fig. 5.21   Boyce–Codd third normal form relations.

which shows sets of duplicated data; clearly, only one instance of each set of values is required.

Anomalies such as this can be avoided by restating the condition for a relation to be in third normal form. Instead of requiring that, 'all attributes are fully dependent on the primary key', a relation can be said to be in third normal form if, 'all attribute values are fully dependent on **each candidate key**'. This can be re-expressed as a requirement that each (combination of) attribute(s) which determines the value of another attribute must be a candidate key for the relation.

In the case of Fig. 5.20(b), the normalization is completed by splitting the data into two relations, as shown in Fig. 5.21. These relations are said to be in **Boyce–Codd normal form (BCNF)**.

It follows from the definition of Boyce–Codd normal form that any BCNF relation is also in third normal form, as defined in the previous section. However, since the classification of a relation as being in third normal form is based on the relationships between the attribute values and the chosen **primary** key, rather than with **all** candidate keys, it cannot be assumed that a relation in third normal form is also in Boyce–Codd normal form.

Since the two normal forms are so similar, it is becoming common to assume that specifying third normal form means, in fact, Boyce–Codd normal form. Thus, BCNF is subsuming third normal form as the usual end-point for the normalization process.

5.2.8 Fourth normal form

Although the normalization process usually stops at (Boyce–Codd) third normal form, it is still possible for considerable redundancy to be present. The problems here can arise if an error is made when eliminating repeating groups to generate first normal form relations.

Such problems arise most often if the un-normalized relation contains two repeating groups which are, in fact, independent of each other. The procedure for eliminating a repeating group is, of course, to split the relation into two, one containing the non-repeating attributes, and the other the repeating attributes together with the 'key' of the un-normalized relation. If there are **two** repeating groups to be eliminated, it is not immediately obvious whether each must be separated off into its own relation, or if a single relation can be made to contain both repeating groups. It is when faced with this dilemma that errors can be made which result in redundancy in the BCNF relations.

Figure 5.22 shows two un-normalized relations, each containing two repeating groups, and each with a possible instance which includes the

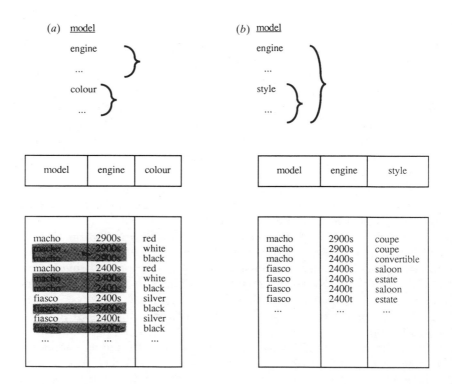

Fig. 5.22   Multiple repeating groups.

two repeating groups. In the first case, the two repeating groups, identified by *engine* and *colour*, are **independent**. Clearly, there is considerable redundancy – indicated by the shading – even though the relation satisfies the conditions to be in BCNF. (The only candidate key is the concatenation of all three attributes, each instance of which represents a single fact; hence the relation must be BCNF.)

In the case of the second example, in which the two repeating groups are nested, the resulting relation over the three key values contains no redundancy. Whereas in the case of *model, engine* and *colour*, it is possible to deduce that there will be a white *macho 2400s* from the fact that there is a white *macho 2900s*, a similar deduction is not possible in the case of *model, engine* and *style*.

Since the *colour* and *engine* repeating groups in the first relation are independent, every occurrence of one group will be associated with each occurrence of the second. That is, for each *engine* which can be installed in a particular *model*, there will be a tuple for every *colour* which is available for that model. Thus, there will be a tuple for every possible combination of *engine* and *colour*. In essence, there is one set of tuples which shows which *engines* can be installed in a particular *model*, in which the *colour* value is just a 'filler', and there is a second set of tuples showing the *colours* which are available for each model; in the case of the latter, it is the *engine* attribute which is superfluous. Strictly, the two sets do overlap, but the basis of the argument is unaffected.

In the case of *engine* and *style*, however, which *styles* are possible depends on the *engine* which is installed, or vice versa. (Note that a simple re-ordering of attributes can reverse the sense of the nesting of the repeating groups.) For example, a *macho 2900s* is available only as a *coupé*, whereas a *macho 2400s* is available only as a *convertible*. It follows that every tuple in the relation shown in Fig. 5.22(b) represents a (non-redundant) fact.

Whilst representing two **nested** repeating groups in a single relation introduces no redundancy, the same is not true for **independent** repeating

model	engine
macho	2900s
macho	2400s
fiasco	2400s
fiasco	2400t
...	...

model	colour
macho	red
macho	white
macho	black
fiasco	silver
fiasco	black
...	

Fig. 5.23   Fourth normal form relations.

groups. The strategy in such a case is to generate a separate relation for each independent repeating group which is eliminated, so that the instance of Fig. 5.22 would be replaced by two relations, such as those in Fig. 5.23.

The relationships between *model* and *engine* and between *model* and *colour* are examples of **multivalued dependencies**. A given value of the *model* attribute determines a **set** of values for the *engine* attribute, and an independent set of values for the *colour* attribute. There is, in fact, a many-to-many relationship between *model* and *engine*, and also between *model* and *colour*. However, each *model* is associated with a defined subset of the possible engines, and also with a subset of the possible colours. The attribute *model* can be said to **multiply determine** the values of *colour* and *engine*. If any attribute of a relation multidetermines more than one other attribute value, then redundancy such as that in Fig. 5.22 will result. The solution to this problem is to place each repeating group in a separate relation, as in Fig. 5.23. Although this may increase the number of attributes drawn on the domain of the multidetermining attribute, it is unlikely that this split will actually increase rather than reduce the actual duplication of any attribute value.

The relations of Fig. 5.23, in which the multivalued dependencies have been 'factored' out into separate relations are said to be in **fourth normal form**. Since the factoring process can introduce neither partial nor transitive dependencies, it follows that fourth normal form relations are also in BCNF and second normal form.

Unfortunately, problems can arise with multivalued dependencies even if a relation contains only one. If the relation contains **any** attribute which is not part of the multideterminacy then there will be some redundancy and the relation will not be in fourth normal form. Figure 5.24 shows such a case, where the multi valued dependency *model→›colour* co-exists with a functional dependency, *model→designer*. As before, there is clearly some redundancy, indicated by the shading. The redundancy can be eliminated only by splitting the relation into two binary relations.

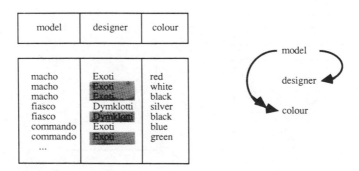

Fig. 5.24 Multivalued dependency (shown by double arrowhead).

Thus, a relational schema can be said to be normalized to fourth normal form if it is in BCNF **and** no relation contains a multivalued dependency simultaneously with any other independent functional dependency.

Since a multideterminant, by definition, determines multiple values for some attribute, it follows that a multideterminant cannot be a candidate key for a relation. Hence, there is no trivial generalization possible for the definition of BCNF which would ensure that a relation was also in fourth normal form. However, taking the definition of fourth normal form given above, it can be seen that this can be rewritten as

'a relation is in fourth normal form (4NF) if every determinant is a candidate key for the relation, **unless** it is a multideterminant, in which case the only other attributes which may be present is that which is multiply determined and any others functionally dependent on the **combination** of the first two.'

Although this is a little more clumsy than the definition of BCNF, it does not require specific checks that the relations also satisfy first and second normal forms.

Fourth normal form relations need not always be binary. Nothing in the definition of fourth normal form precludes either the multi-determinant or its dependent attribute from being a concatenation of attributes. For example, the *model–engine–style* relation of Fig. 5.22 satisfies the requirement, because the multideterminant is the concatenation of *model* and *engine*, and the only other attribute in the relation, *style*, is multivalued dependent on these two attributes. It happens that there is also a multivalued dependency between *model* and *engine*, but as it is the combination of these two attributes which is the multideterminant for *style*, the relation is still in fourth normal form. It happens that the ordering of the nesting of the multivalued dependencies is immaterial; whichever order is assumed, the relation is still in fourth normal form.

Applying the same test to the *model–engine–colour* relation of Fig. 5.22 shows it not to be in fourth normal form, since *colour* is not functionally dependent on *model–engine*, and nor is *engine* on *model–colour*. Similarly, *designer* in Fig. 5.24 is not functionally dependent on *model–colour*, and so that relation also is not in fourth normal form.

In most cases, it is not necessary to normalize a schema into fourth normal form. The possibility of relations satisfying third normal form but not fourth normal form can, to a large extent, be regarded as the result of an incorrect normalization into **first** normal form. Thus, the test for fourth normal form is little more than a check that the earlier stage was effected correctly. Although there is some theoretical significance to fourth normal form, it is not of the same degree of importance as first, second and third (Boyce–Codd) normal forms.

5.2.9 CODASYL and hierarchic models

The discussion of normalization has been developed in terms of the relational model; this is, indeed, almost universally the case. However, just as redundancy can exist in hierarchic and network data models, so also can such models be normalized.

It was noted whilst developing the concept of redundancy that the 'record-like' structures used in the discussion could be tuples, records or segments. Regardless of the underlying data model, the problems associated with redundancy are the same, and it is still an appropriate aim to eliminate redundancy. All that differs is the way in which the normalized structures are represented and inter-related.

Figure 5.25 shows a record structure which could form part of a CODASYL schema. It is, of course, identical to a tuple from the table of Fig. 5.6, and it suffers from all of the inherent redundancy of that table.

The normal method for resolving structural problems in the CODASYL model is to introduce **intersection records** which are members of two set types simultaneously. Although the CODASYL model does allow for repeating groups within records, such constructs are usually regarded as a means of tuning the performance of a database, rather than

model	style	engine	capacity	max speed	price	market	main competitor

(a) an un-normalised record

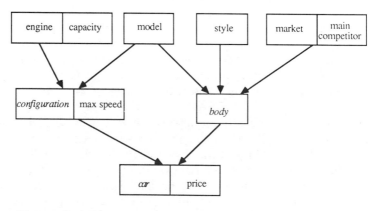

(b) a normalised schema

Fig. 5.25 Normalizing a CODASYL schema.

of reflecting the logical design. Therefore, CODASYL repeating groups will be ignored in this discussion.

Whilst the process of deducing the intersection records which are required is very similar to the derivation of first, second and third normal form relations, the resulting records are somewhat different from the normalized relations. The fundamental difference is that foreign keys are represented, not by the inclusion of the foreign key as a field, but by the record being a member of sets **owned** by the record(s) corresponding to the foreign key(s). Thus, a 'normalized' version of the original record structure might be as in Fig. 5.25(b).

Some of the records in the normalized structure correspond exactly with third normal form relations. Taking the record names to be the same as their first fields, for convenience, the *engine* and *market* record types have precise counterparts in the normalized relational schema of Fig. 5.18. The *configuration*, *body* and *car* record types also map onto third normal form relations, but with the foreign keys replaced by set membership pointers. Thus, each *configuration* record is a member of a set owned by an *engine* record, and another owned by a *model* record. The only data actually contained in the *configuration* record is, in fact, the *max speed* attainable by a given engine in a particular model. The corresponding relation, of course, comprised *engine*, *model* and *max speed* attributes.

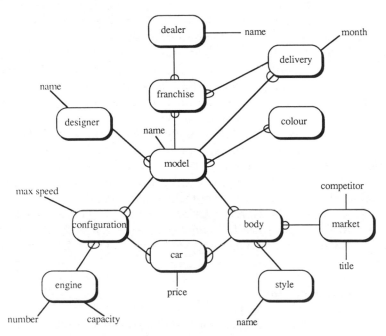

Fig. 5.26 Data structure for *cars* database.

A similar mapping can be made between the *body* record type and the normalized *body* relation. However, in this case, there are no fields actually specified for the *body* record type, since it is composed entirely of the foreign keys, now represented by set membership, *model*, *style* and *market*. Finally, the *car* record type may be mapped onto the normalized relation of the same name. The key fields of the owner record types for the sets of which *car* is a member are, respectively, *engine–model* and *model–style*. Thus, by virtue of the set membership, each *car* record is associated with foreign key values of *model*, *engine* and *style*, in exact equivalence to the presence of these attributes in the normalized relation.

It follows that the argument may be extended trivially to data models expressed in terms of the hierarchic data model; this is left as an exercise for the reader.

5.3 THE SYNTHETIC APPROACH

Normalization is usually presented as the classical design technique for deriving a relational schema free from excessive redundancy. However, the usual starting point for normalization is an un-normalized 'relation' comprising all the data items of interest to the enterprise.

Such a starting point may well arise if an existing file processing system is being upgraded into a database, because there will be existing file structures which may be used as starting points. However, data analysis techniques tend to produce a more detailed description of the data to be represented, and, in particular, the entity types and relationship types between them. In the case of the techniques discussed in this text, the end-product of data analysis is a data structure diagram, but other analysis techniques can produce equally valid descriptions of equal detail.

It would seem appropriate, therefore, to develop a technique for schema design which does not discard the structural information contained within, for example, a data structure diagram. Rather than reducing the structure to a homogeneous single record type, with functional dependencies represented separately, the aim might be to deduce the structure for a fully normalized (i.e. BCNF) schema directly from the data structure diagram. Such a technique is **relational synthesis**.

5.3.1 Requirements

The basic requirement for relational synthesis is that it should lead to the derivation of a set of relations which are all in at least third normal form, and which, together, could be used as a representation of the conceptual schema corresponding to the data structure diagram.

Such a technique must clearly capture, not only the number of entities, and their attributes, but also the degree and optionality of all of the relationship types. Assuming that the data analysis which generated the data structure diagram has been performed correctly, the correctness criterion for the resultant schema is that it should be capable of representing any instance of the data structure.

5.3.2 Skeleton data models

When discussing the relational data model, it was suggested that an initial stab at an appropriate schema could be to define one relation for each entity type, and one further relation for each relationship type. Sub-types would be represented by distinct relations, so that they would, in effect, be additional entity types. Relations sharing a primary key could then be merged, provided that the mapping such a shared key implied was complete.

Relational data models generated in this way would, indeed, be a good starting point. However, the initial 'skeleton' data model, before any relations are merged, would be likely to contain many more relations than would actually be required. Also, the process of working out which relations could, in fact, be merged could be somewhat tedious in the absence of a formal procedure for performing that merging.

It happens that, in many real-world data structures, the relations which would be invented to represent the relationships between entity types can very often be merged with the relation for one or other of the participating entity types. Since the number of relationship types is often comparable with, or greater than, the number of entity types, such merging can halve the size of the conceptual schema.

Taking the data structure diagram of Fig. 5.26 as the starting point for the analysis, and noting that the data structure includes the *dealer–franchise–delivery* and *colour* information introduced to illustrate parts of the normalization process, the initial skeleton data model would comprise 25 relations, since there are 12 entity types and 13 relationship types. The relational synthesis technique uses these initial relations as building blocks from which the final relations are synthesized. Since the starting point for the derivation of a data model is a data structure **diagram**, it is not inappropriate for the synthesis technique to be largely graphical, although each process has a theoretical basis.

5.3.3 Posting relationships

The relations for the conceptual schema are synthesized from those which comprise the initial data model. Essentially, for each relationship type in the data structure, consideration is given to merging the relation which represents the relationship type with one or other of the relations representing the corresponding entity types.

Figure 5.27 shows one such relationship in isolation. The attribute # *doors* has been introduced to ensure that the *body* entity type is not 'special', in the sense that it is all-key. In fact, the presence of this additional attribute has no effect on the result of the discussion. The three tables in the figure depict possible instances of the three relations which would be deduced for that part of the initial relational model.

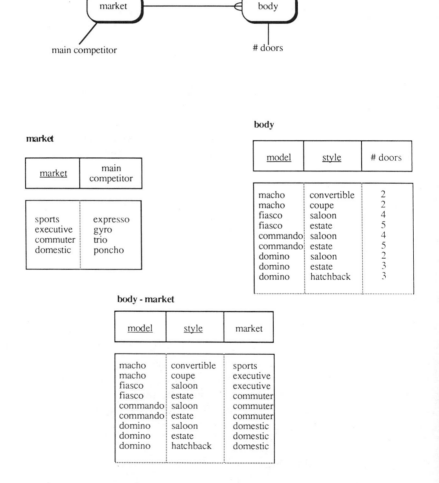

Fig. 5.27 Relations for a one-to-many relationship.

Although all of the relations are in Boyce–Codd normal form, the three relations include significant redundant duplication. Specifically, for each tuple in the *body* relation, there is a corresponding tuple in the *body–market* relation. The key of both relations is the combination of *model* and *style*. However, each permitted combination of *body* and *style* must be represented twice – once in each relation. In each case, there is one additional attribute value which is functionally dependent on the combination of *body* and *style*.

It is not merely a coincidence that every tuple in the *body* relation can be matched by a corresponding tuple in *body–market*. The relationship between the entity types *body* and *market* is fully mandatory. That is, each *market* must be associated with at least one *body*, and every *body* is associated with **exactly one** *market*.

Clearly, at least in this case, some redundancy could be eliminated by replacing the *body* and *body–market* relations by a single, **synthesized** relation, *body*, as in Fig. 5.28. The *market* relation remains unchanged. The merging of the relations can be achieved because, not only are the keys of the two relations identical, but there is also a complete mapping between the tuples of the two relations. It would not be possible to merge the relations if, for example, there were some *bodies* which were not associated with some *market*. In that case, of course, the data structure diagram would be incorrect.

The relationship between *body* and *market* is one-to-many. Rather than needing to consider every one-to-many relationship in detail, it is possible to derive a general rule for the representation of one-to-many relationships.

In the general case, which is depicted in Fig. 5.29, each relation may be considered to have exactly two attributes: the **key** attribute, and a **non-key** attribute. Either or both of these attributes may, in fact, be a combination of atomic attributes, but the discussion is pursued only in

market

market	main competitor
sports	expresso
executive	gyro
commuter	trio
domestic	poncho

body

model	style	# doors	market
macho	convertible	2	sports
macho	coupe	2	executive
fiasco	saloon	4	executive
fiasco	estate	5	commuter
commando	saloon	4	commuter
commando	estate	5	commuter
domino	saloon	2	domestic
domino	estate	3	domestic
domino	hatchback	3	domestic

Fig. 5.28 Synthesized relations for one-to-many relationship.

terms of the key and non-key part of the relation. Each is treated as a single whole, rather than as a collection of components.

The initial relations derived for the simple binary relation of Fig. 5.29 are A, B and AB, as indicated in the figure. However, not only are the keys of AB and B the same, but there is one tuple in AB for each tuple in B, because the relationship between the two entity types is fully mandatory. Thus, there is always an AB tuple for every B tuple, and the two relations can be merged, as shown in Fig. 5.29(a)

A convenient graphical notation to indicate that the two relations can be merged is to draw a curled arrow from the relationship to the entity with which it is to be combined logically. The term **posting** is sometimes used for this operation, the derivation being that the identifier of the entity at one end of the relationship is posted into the relation representing the other entity. In this case, it is, effectively, the relationship which is being posted.

It follows from the discussion that the relationship can be posted only

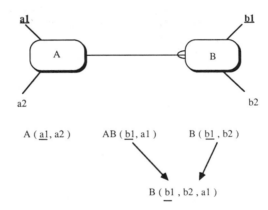

(a) Synthesising Relations

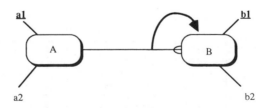

(b) 'Posting' the relationship

Fig. 5.29   One-to-many relationship — the general case.

into the relation for B and not that for A. By inspection, it is obvious that each tuple of A can be associated with an arbitrary number of B tuples. Also, of course, the two relations A and AB do **not** share a common key.

The general rule, therefore, might be that the representation of a one-to-many relationship can be posted into the relation representing the entity at the 'many' end of the relationship. That entity type is, of course, the **determinant** for the relationship type, since a particular instance of the entity type determines which instance of the second entity type will be involved in the corresponding instance of the relationship.

However, the relationship types of Figs 5.27 and 5.29 are fully

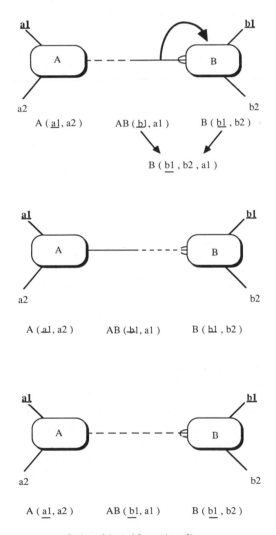

Fig. 5.30 One-to-many relationship with optionality.

mandatory. It is necessary to consider other possible configurations which include optionality.

Figure 5.30 shows the three possible configurations of a one-to-many relationship which includes optionality. Given that the relations for AB and B can be merged only if the mapping between the two is complete, it follows that the relationship can be 'posted' into the entity only if the entity instance determines the value of the second entity. From this, it follows that the relations can **not** be merged if the determining entity type (i.e. the one at the 'many' end of the relationship) has optional participation in the relationship. Thus, the only possibility for merging relations occurs if the entity type at the 'many' end of the relationship has mandatory participation in the relation. In the other two cases, shown

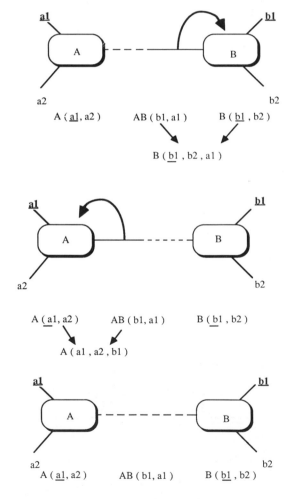

Fig. 5.31   One-to-one relationship with optionality.

also in Fig. 5.30, three separate relations are needed to represent the data structure, even though there appear to be relations with common keys.

The argument can be developed for the case of two entity types participating in a one-to-one relationship. The three possible configurations with optionality are shown in Fig. 5.31. In this case, the relationship may be posted into one of the entity types provided that at least one end of the relationship is mandatory. When the relationship is posted, it is into the entity which has mandatory participation in the relationship. In the case of a fully mandatory relationship, this implies that the relationship can be represented in the relation for **either** of the two entity types.

A more general rule for posting relationships is, therefore, that (the

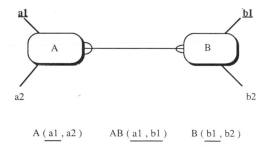

A (a1 , a2)   AB (a1 , b1)   B (b1 , b2)

(a) A Many to Many Relationship

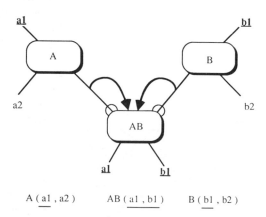

A (a1 , a2)   AB (a1 , b1)   B (b1 , b2)

(b) A Decomposed Many-to-Many Relationship

Fig. 5.32   (a) Many-to-many relationship; (b) decomposed many-to-many relationship.

representation of) a relationship may be posted if it is a **determinacy**. A determinacy is characterized by the relationship being mandatory at one end, and of degree one at the other. The relationship is posted into the entity at the **opposite** end from the degree of one.

The remaining category of relationship is, of course, the many-to-many relationship. This type of relationship represents no determinacy (apart perhaps from a multideterminacy, which is of no help when synthesizing

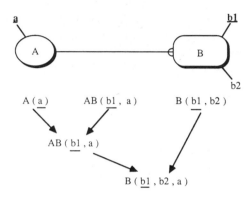

(a) Synthesised Relations

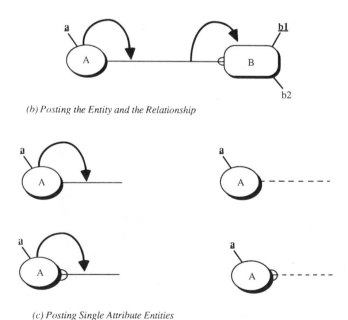

(b) Posting the Entity and the Relationship

(c) Posting Single Attribute Entities

Fig. 5.33   Single-attribute entities.

relations). Therefore, three relations are required to represent a many-to-many structure, as shown in Fig. 5.32(a). However, it is interesting to note that if the many-to-many relationship is decomposed into two one-to-many relationships, as in Fig. 5.32(b), and the rule for posting relationships is then applied, then the resulting synthesized relations are identical to the original relations in Fig. 5.32(a). Whatever the optionality of the many-to-many relationship, the intersection entity always has mandatory participation in both of the relationships.

5.3.4 Single-attribute entities

If an entity type has no attributes other than its identifier, it can be termed **single attribute**. In order to assist with the discussion of relational synthesis, a modified symbol can be used to represent single-attribute entities in a data structure diagram, namely an elliptical entity box, as in Fig. 5.33. As before, the actual criterion is that the entity type should have no non-key attributes, rather than that it should have only one atomic attribute. All key entities for which the key is compound can also be treated as single-attribute entity types.

If an entity type is key-only, then the only instances which need to be stored are the different possible values of the identifiers of the entity type. However, it is the identifier of the entity type which is used to represent a relationship between that entity and any other. If the entity participates in a relationship, therefore, the identifiers of the entity instances will appear in the relation which represents the relationship. If the participation in the relationship is mandatory, it follows that every entity instance must participate in at least one instance of the relationship, and hence that the identifier of the instance will be present in at least one tuple in the relation representing the relationship. Provided that there is no other requirement for a separate list of the entity instances, the single attribute entity can be 'posted' into the relationship, in much the same way as determinacy relationships can be posted into the appropriate entity types.

Figure 5.33(a) illustrates the general case, where A is the single-attribute entity type, participating in a one-to-many relationship with entity type B. Since A has mandatory participation in the relationship, the relation for A can be merged with that for the relationship AB. As the relationship is a determinacy, the relation AB may be merged, in turn, with the relation B. Thus, the whole structure may be represented, in fully normalized form, in a single relation.

The arrow notation used for showing how relationships are posted into identifiers may be used to show also where single-attribute entities are posted into relationships. Figure 5.33(b) depicts the same synthesis of a single relation for the complete structure as does Fig. 5.33(a).

By extending the argument above, it becomes apparent that a single-attribute entity may be posted into any relationship type in which it has mandatory participation, regardless of the degree of that relationship. However, if the single-attribute entity has only optional participation in the relationship, then posting the entity type into the relationship, and discarding the relation representing the entity itself, could lose information. In such a case, any instance of the entity type which did not participate in the relationship would not appear as a foreign key in the relation representing the relationship. Hence, such an instance would not be recorded unless either the entity had also been posted into another relationship, with which it had mandatory membership, or the basic relation for the entity type itself were preserved. This is summarized in Fig. 5.33(c).

Since posting the entity into the relationship introduces no new attributes for the relation, it follows that the posting is simply a recognition that it is unnecessary to represent the entity separately. Further, posting an entity type more than once is pointless, since once it has been 'posted' it no longer needs to be considered.

There is one minor problem that can arise if the relationship into which the entity type is posted qualifies as a determinacy. If the entity into which the relationship would have been posted is the single attribute entity which has just been posted into the relationship, there is no longer

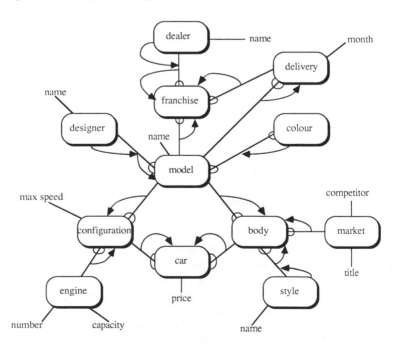

Fig. 5.34 Synthesis of conceptual schema.

anywhere to post the relationship. Either the relationship cannot be posted, or the relationship must be posted before the single-attribute entity is considered. In the latter case, the single-attribute entity would contain the foreign key corresponding to the relationship, and would no longer be single-attribute. Either way, one relation is needed to represent the relationship and the single-attribute entity, whichever one has been posted into the other!

Having derived the relational synthesis approach, it is appropriate to apply the technique to the data structure diagram of Fig. 5.26. Figure 5.34 includes the arrows showing what is posted where, and Fig. 5.35 shows the result of that process. First, the posted relationships and identifiers are effectively replaced by appropriate attributes, as shown in

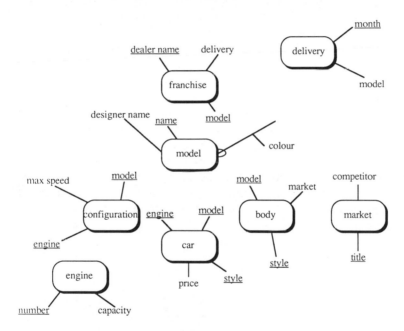

DELIVERY (month , model)
FRANCHISE (dealer, month , model)
MODEL (model , designer)
MODEL - COLOUR (model , colour)
CONFIGURATION (model, engine , max speed)
BODY (model, style, market)
MARKET (market, competitor)
ENGINE (engine, capacity)
CAR (model, style, engine, price)

Fig. 5.35   Normalized conceptual schema.

the figure. Then a relation is defined for each remaining entity type and relationship type, including the posted attributes.

It will be seen that the resulting relations are the same as those derived by normalization, with the exception of the *franchise* relation, which is in third normal form but not Boyce−Codd normal form. This anomaly is discussed later.

5.3.5 Entity sub-types

When normalizing a schema, the correct representation for entity sub-types is deduced automatically from the functional dependencies. However, a moment's thought is required to consider the correct treatment of sub-types within the synthesis approach.

Figure 5.36 shows a generalized entity type with two sub-types. Since there are three entity boxes in the diagram, three relations would be defined in the initial data model, as shown. The only point of contention is how the (non-binary) relationship between the entity and its sub-types should be represented.

Considering for the moment the three relations A, $A1$ and $A2$, it is apparent that they all share a common key A. Thus, implicitly, each tuple in, say, $A1$ is already related to the appropriate tuple in A. Similarly, $A2$ is related to A, but there is no mapping at all between $A1$ and $A2$, as sub-types are non-overlapping. The hierarchy − for that is what it is, rather than a straightforward relationship − is therefore implicit in the relations for the entity type and its sub-types, and no additional relations are required.

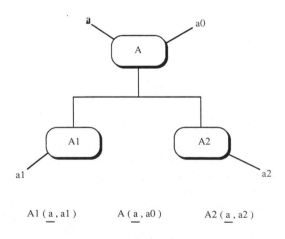

Fig. 5.36 Entity sub-types.

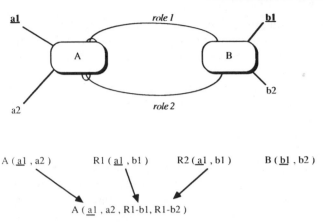

Fig. 5.37   Representation of roles.

5.3.6   Roles

The problem of multiple relationships between a pair of entity types, corresponding to different roles, is also trivial in the synthesis approach. An initial relation would be deduced for each of the relationships, and they would then be treated separately. Whether or not the relations would be merged would depend on the optionality of the relationships. However, distinct roles would be represented by different attributes in the relation, although they would be drawn on the same domain.

Figure 5.37 illustrates two entities, with two relationships between them corresponding to different roles. The synthesized version of the relation for *A* contains two attributes drawn on the domain of *B*, the identifier of the second entity type. If there were a third relationship between *A* and *B*, in which *A*'s participation was optional, then that third relationship would need to be represented by its own relation. There is no need for the posting of different roles to be 'all-or-nothing'. Each role is a separate, independent relationship, and is treated as such.

5.4   MINIMAL NORMALIZED SCHEMA

The two approaches of normalization and synthesis start at opposite extremes. Normalization starts from a single, un-normalized relation, generating additional relations to eliminate redundancy. The starting point for synthesis is an initial data model containing a large number of relations, which are merged as far as possible without introducing redundancy.

Whilst the minimum number of relations required for a schema is clearly one, in zeroth normal form, such a relation would hardly be viable as a schema. At the other extreme, a schema comprising one relation for each entity and for each relationship would seem to be unnecessarily complex. An appropriate compromise might be a schema containing the minimum number of relations which contain no redundancy. Following the arguments of this chapter, such a schema would, of course, be in fourth normal form.

Given the complexity of 'real', rather than 'textbook', schemata, it is sometimes of use to have some form of confirmation that the final version of the schema is optimal. A simple check can be based on the number of relations in such a schema. Obviously, checking that the schema contains the correct number of relations cannot ensure that the relations are the right ones. However, if there is a large discrepancy between the number of relations predicted and the number actually present, it is a fair assumption that the schema is not properly normalized,

The calculation of the number of relations in a fully normalized schema is based on the process of synthesis. It involves counting the number of entity types and relationship types in the data structure diagram for the schema, and deciding how many relationships are determinacies, and how many entity types are single-attribute. Denoting these four counts by E, R, D and S, respectively, the argument proceeds as follows.

The initial data model comprises one relation per entity type plus one per relationship type. That is, there are $E + R$ relations in that model. Relations are then merged together where possible. If a relationship is a determinacy, then the relation which represents it can be merged with that for the appropriate entity type. This reduces the number of relations required to $E + R - D$. Finally, single-attribute entity types which have mandatory participation in at least one relationship may, in effect, be posted into those relationships. Hence, the number of relations required is reduced further to $E + R - D - S$, provided that the number of single-attribute entities, S, includes only those which have mandatory participation in relationships.

Thus, a fully normalized, or **minimal** schema, should contain $E + R - D - S$ relations. If it contains more, then there are some relations which could be merged with others. If it contains fewer, then there must be some redundancy somewhere.

One *caveat* must be emphasized. It has been seen that the counting of single-attribute entities depends on which relationships are posted into which entities. It may well be that some single-attribute entity is no longer single-attribute after this posting has occurred. Clearly, this must be taken into account when counting the number of single-attribute entities which could potentially be posted.

Further, the number of entities, E, must include all sub-types, and the number of relationships, R, must **exclude** the hierarchical relationships between entity types and their sub-types.

Finally, it must be emphasized that the expression derived above for the number of relations in a minimal schema is only a crude check on the final schema. A simple scalar such as this can contain no information on **which** relations should be present in the schema, only on **how many**. Nevertheless, such a test can not only indicate the presence of gross failures in the normalization or synthesis process, but it can also alert the analyst's mind to which relations should be merged with others. The mere fact that the entities, relationships, determinacies and single-attribute entities have to be counted systematically can often help the analyst to ensure that all facets of the data structure are considered.

5.5 SYNTHESIS VERSUS NORMALIZATION

The previous section assumes implicitly that the end results of normalization and synthesis are identical. Although such an assumption might appear to be reasonable, it is worth giving some further attention to the matter. At the very least, it would be worth considering the way in which repeating groups, partial and transitive dependencies would be treated during synthesis.

Each of these three features is illustrated in Fig. 5.38, which also shows the underlying data structures. The un-normalized relation is taken, in each case, to contain all of the attributes which occur in the data structure. A moment's consideration should satisfy the reader that the three un-normalized relations display, respectively, repeating groups, partial dependency and transitive dependency.

Taking each of these abstracted cases in turn, and applying the process of synthesis to generate minimal schemata, it can be seen that the synthesized schema is in each case identical to that which would be generated by normalization.

Since the examples are both abstracted and generalized, it follows that, if the synthesized schemata are equivalent to normalized schemata in these cases, then the same will be true in any 'real' case. Thus, it can be asserted that relational synthesis generates fully normalized schemata.

However, again there is a *caveat*. It can only be guaranteed that a normalized schema will be generated from a non-redundant data structure diagram. If the data structure itself contains redundant relationship types, it is quite possible that there will be relations in the synthesized schema which are in third normal form, but not BCNF. For example, Fig. 5.39 shows part of the data structure diagram for the *cars* database, together with the relations which would be deduced for that part of the data structure. One of the resulting relations, *franchise*, is the same as that shown in Fig. 5.20, where it was shown **not** to be in BCNF.

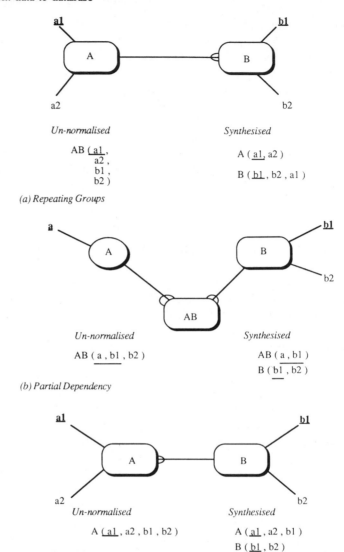

Fig. 5.38 Synthesis versus normalization.

It would appear that the synthesis technique has failed.

The reason for the apparent failure is that the data structure diagram itself contains redundancy.

The three relationships represent determinacies of the form:

franchise → delivery
delivery → model
and *franchise → model*

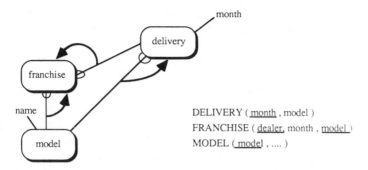

DELIVERY (<u>month</u> , model)
FRANCHISE (<u>dealer,</u> month , <u>model</u>)
MODEL (<u>model</u> , ...)

Fig. 5.39   Redundant relationship.

However,

franchise → *delivery* **and** *delivery* → *model* ⇒ *franchise* → *model*

that is, the third determinacy is implied by the first two. Hence, that determinacy, or rather, the specific relationship, is redundant.

Unfortunately, such redundancy in the data structure diagram is not detected during synthesis. Relational synthesis merges relations together as far as it can without **introducing** redundancy; if it is present already, it will remain. Hence, the prudent user of such a technique would check first for the presence of such redundant relationships, and eliminate them from the data structure diagram.

5.6   CONSEQUENCES OF NORMALIZATION

Normalization, or the alternative process of synthesizing a fully normalized schema, has been presented as an essential part of data modelling. However, it does not follow that normalization as far as third or fourth normal form is always appropriate. In particular, it may not be appropriate to implement a fully normalized **internal** schema, even if the conceptual schema is designed in fourth normal form.

5.6.1   Performance considerations

It is likely that only a very small proportion of database queries would be addressed to a single relation within a fully normalized schema. On the contrary, it is probable that most queries will address two or more relations which must be JOINed together.

Given the third normal form schema of Figs 5.17 and 5.18, for example, it is possible that most queries addressed to such a database would request all the information for a given car, or perhaps even a particular model, rather than one of the individual facts represented in the separate relations. That is, the query would probably wish to address a **view** of the database which looked more like Fig. 5.6 than Fig. 5.18. Even queries concerned only with, say, marketing might require information from two or three relations – *body*, *market* and, perhaps, *car*.

Each time relations need to be JOINed, whether explicitly in response to an algebraic query, or implicitly given a calculus query, the operation involved can be expensive. Since relations are unordered sets, in a pure relational system, the operation would comprise something akin to a **sort–merge**, which is always of order at least $N\log N$. The number of such operations required would increase as the level of normalization increased, since the number of relations in the schema would increase. What is worse is that the number of JOINs required would probably increase faster than the number of relations – perhaps even as fast as N^2 – since it might be possible for any relation to be joined separately to every other one.

Clearly, given this argument, it makes sense to minimize the number of relations in the schema, and, hence, the number of JOIN operations required for typical queries. Hence, the synthesis of the basic relations in an initial schema, to form a minimal normalized schema, makes obvious sense. There is, of course, an additional advantage, in that merging of relations leads to a **reduction** in the storage requirement, since it cuts down on the duplication of key values. If the amount of data to be stored is reduced, then so also is the amount to be transferred from secondary to primary memory. This gives an additional performance advantage.

The latter argument does not extend readily to suggest that relations of lower normal form would have a smaller storage requirement. It has been demonstrated that relations of lower normal forms include considerable redundancy, and the extra storage required to store redundant data will often exceed that saved by the reduction in duplication of key values. Thus, the storage space required for an un-normalized schema would, in nearly all cases, be greater than that for a normalized schema.

5.6.2 Trade-offs

The main conclusion to be drawn from a consideration of performance arguments must be that performance will always be improved if the number of relations in the schema is reduced. Thus, the question must be asked, why should a schema be normalized at all? The advantages to be gained, of course, are **elimination of redundancy** and **reduction in storage space**.

Normalization as far as third or fourth normal forms usually reduces the physical size of the data to be stored. Beyond that point, additional duplication is introduced, so that the storage requirement increases. However, the storage requirement argument is comparatively weak, compared with the additional processing required to join relations at execution time. That cost heavily favours less normalization rather than more.

The principal advantage of normalization lies in the elimination of redundancy. A database which includes redundant data is vulnerable to inconsistencies being introduced whenever data is updated. If a particular data item occurs ten times in the database, then every update to that value must be applied to all ten instances. If the ten occurrences are not kept in step, then different users, seeking the same value in different ways, could obtain different answers. If that value were something significant, as far as the user of the database was concerned, then such inconsistencies could be important. Ten different values for the number of seats still available on a particular air flight could cause chaos in an airline booking system. Alternatively, ten different balances co-existing for a single bank account could lead to a little confusion in the banking world.

The **disadvantages** of redundant data are, then, an increase in storage requirement, and the risk of inconsistency. The first point may or may not be significant, but it is not often overriding. However, the second point deserves greater consideration. It is the elimination of this risk which must be set against the increased processing requirements for normalized schemata.

Although any un-normalized schema may be prone to inconsistencies, such inconsistencies can only be introduced by updates applied to the database. (Corruption of the database by external means will be ignored for the purpose of this discussion.) The two options available are either to ensure that every update maintains consistency meticulously, or to eliminate the possibility of inconsistency.

Unfortunately, updates are initiated by users, and users are notoriously bad at keeping anything tidy and consistent. The temptation to update one instance of a duplicated value, and come back to do the others 'later' (=never?) can be overwhelming. Even if the user's only acccss to the database is via a tried and trusted applications program, that program must have been written by somebody in the first place. Although it might purport to ensure that all duplicate instances of updated values will be updated, it is a foolish person who has complete trust in any program. Programmers, after all, are no less human than users.

It follows that it would be naive to trust every single update to preserve consistency. If the consistency of the data is important, it follows that the objective must be to eliminate the possibility of inconsistency. Again, there are two options: to retain redundant data, but to make the system

enforce some kind of consistency checks, commonly referred to as **integrity constraints**, or to normalize the schema. The costs of normalization have been explored already, and would suggest that integrity constraints might be preferable. However, the same users who would be tempted to 'defer' updating duplicate values, would find themselves exceedingly frustrated if every time they tried to perform a 'quick' update, the update was disallowed by the database management system. In addition, the cost of enforcing the constraint would not be trivial, since all the values which **might** be duplicates would have to be considered, and, in addition, there would have to be some mechanism to control which values would have to be kept in step, and which just happened to have the same value through coincidence.

In all, the cost and complexity of a foolproof integrity checking system for an un-normalized schema is often too great. The usual option is to choose a normalized schema, and to live with the consequences.

There is an obvious trade-off, since the greater the degree of normalization, the greater the processing costs, but the smaller the risk of inconsistency. The relative frequency of updates, which could introduce inconsistency, and of complex queries, which would involve several relations in a normalized schema, will influence the degree of normaliz-ation which is appropriate in any given case.

5.6.3 Conceptual versus internal schemata

The foregoing discussion has made the implicit assumption that there is a direct mapping from conceptual schema to internal schema. However, the conceptual schema is merely the overall data structure which is visible to the user community as a whole. It need bear little resemblance to the storage schema, provided that the database management system can perform the appropriate mappings reliably.

A number of modifications can be made to the schema whilst mapping it into an appropriate storage structure, and many of these can be used to ameliorate the performance problems of fully normalized schemata.

The JOIN operation can be made simpler and more efficient, for example, if every foreign key is associated either with an index or with a physical pointer to the corresponding tuple for which it is a key. These, and other, constructs may be introduced in the storage schema whilst remaining invisible to the user. Hence, the database will appear to be purely relational, but will not suffer from the performance degradation associated with normalization.

Alternatively, there is no reason why the internal and conceptual schemata should be normalized to the same degree. Provided that the user can only **possibly** see a schema in fourth normal form, there is no reason why the internal schema should not be in, say, first normal form. It would then be possible for an intelligent query processor to optimize the query in terms, not of the conceptual schema, but of the internal schema. Provided that the system alone is responsible for maintaining consistency, the user need never know that the conceptual schema was, in effect, a logical abstraction of what was actually stored. Obviously, there may still be a worry about the reliability of the database software which performs the mapping, but it is likely to be more reliable than most users' programs.

5.6.4 Incomplete data

One of the objectives of normalization is to avoid the 'insertion anomaly', in which information concerning part of a tuple may not be inserted until values are available for all of the attributes of the relation. It would, of course, be possible to insert a partial tuple, with the 'missing' values replaced by some appropriate **null**, but the presence of null values can add significant complications to the manipulation of the database. In any case, the rules of the relational model require that the primary key attributes of a relation must never be null.

There are two broad categories of absent data. It may be that a particular attribute represents an optional relationship, in which the entity corresponding to the entity happens not to participate. Alternatively, it may be that the value is not known yet, but it is anticipated that it will (should?) become known at some (indeterminate) time in the future. In the former case, the absence of data does not violate in any way the system description or the data model. In the latter case, the absence of the data can be regarded as a temporary aberration which will eventually be rectified.

Whilst no degree of normalization can equip a schema to deal with data which are temporarily missing, the level of normalization can certainly influence the ease with which optionality can be represented.

If it is likely that there will be some **missing** data, it may be tempting to use the same 'null' mechanism when data are absent due to optionality. Such a scheme is likely to cause problems, since a single mechanism – null values – is being used to represent two distinct phenomena. In any case, the **semantics** of null values within a database has aroused considerable discussion in recent years.

SUMMARY
Chapter 5

Duplication of data within a database is often **redundant**, in the sense that such data could be deduced from other data in the database. The presence of redundant data can cause problems for **update**, **deletion** and **insertion**.

Normalization is the process of eliminating redundancy. Although usually described in terms of the relational model, normalization can apply also to other data models. Relations in **first normal form** are free from **repeating groups**. Relations in **second normal form** are also free from **partial dependencies**. Relations in **third normal form** are also free from **transitive dependencies**. An alternative, and stricter, definition of third normal form, **Boyce–Codd normal form (BCNF)** requires that every determinant is a candidate key. Relations in **fourth normal form** are in third normal form (or BCNF), and are free from **multivalued dependencies**.

Relational synthesis is a technique which is the converse of normalization. The starting point for relational synthesis is the **data structure diagram** for the conceptual schema. An **initial data model** is constructed having one relation for each entity type or sub-type, and one relation for each relationship type. Relationships which are determinacies may be **posted** into the determining entity type. Entity types which are all-key ('single-attribute entities') and which have mandatory participation in at least one relationship type, may be posted into that relationship. A fully normalized schema is generated by forming one relation for each entity type or sub-type, and one for each relationship type, remaining **after** the posting operations above. The minimum number of relations in a fully normalized schema is given by $E + R - D - S$, where E is the number of entities, R the number of relationships, D the number of determinacies, and S the number of single-attribute entities. A schema generated by relational synthesis will be in **fourth normal form**, provided that the data structure diagram itself is free from redundancy.

Due to the additional processing costs associated with fully normalized schemata, it is not always appropriate to normalize the **internal schema** to fourth normal form. However, a normalized conceptual schema should still be prepared in most cases.

PROBLEMS
Chapter 5

P5.1 Starting from the un-normalized *student* relation given below, derive an equivalent set of third normal form relations, showing also the first and second normal form relations derived en route.

Student   *Student registration number (SRnum)*
       Name
       School
       Adviser name
       Adviser school
       Course code
       Course title ⎫ repeating group
       Lecturer name ⎫ repeating group ⎬
       Lecturer school ⎭ ⎭

Repeat the exercise starting from the following data structure diagram and applying the synthesis technique.

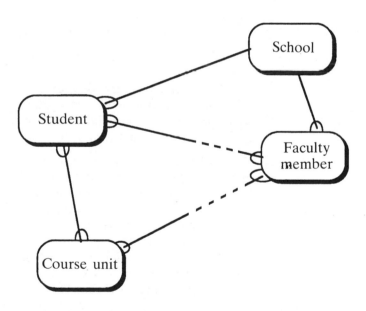

Compare the two results.

P5.2 Apply normalization techniques to these alternative un-normalized relations for P3.1 of Chapter 3. Verify that the relational schemata comprise the minimum number of relations.

Record Record #
     Publisher name
     Record speed
     Track #
     Performance date
     Performance location
     Soloist
     Orchestra
     Conductor
     Work title
     Work type
     Work key
     Composer name

Composer Composer name
     Work title
     Work type
     Work key
     Performance date
     Performance location
     Soloist
     Orchestra
     Conductor
     Record #
     Record speed
     Publisher name
     Track #

P5.3 Derive normalized relational schemata for each of the data structures for P3.4, P3.5, P3.6 and P3.7 of Chapter 3.

P5.4 Demonstrate that the relational synthesis technique always produces a set of relations which are in at least third normal form.

P5.5 Compare the concepts of multivalued dependency and fan trap.

Will multivalued dependencies ever arise in relational schemata generated by the synthesis technique? Hence, are the results of synthesis third or fourth normal form?

P5.6 Discuss the relevance of normalization as a data modelling technique, paying particular attention to the **disadvantages** of storing data in third normal form relations. Indicate what can be done to ameliorate these problems:

  a in the data model;

  b in the representation of the relations.

Would problems of these types arise in CODASYL (network) organization databases?

P5.7 Discuss the concepts of **optionality** and **missing data** in the context of the three relational schemata given below for the data structure shown. Hence, show how the presence or either, or both, of these properties could influence the choice between these schemata.

a A ($\underline{a}$, a', b-$R1$, b-$R2$, b-$R3$)
  B ($\underline{b}$, b')

b A ($\underline{a}$, a')
  $R1$ ($\underline{a}$, b)
  $R2$ ($\underline{a}$, b)
  $R3$ ($\underline{a}$, b)
  B ($\underline{b}$, b')

c A ($\underline{a}$, a')
  R ($\underline{R\#}$, $\underline{a}$, b)
  B ($\underline{b}$, b')

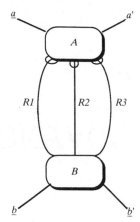

Would the discussion differ if the data structure were to be modelled using the CODASYL model?

6

ADVANCED DATA MODELS

This chapter can do little more than offer a few pointers to the topics which are of current concern in database research, and to provide appropriate references in the literature. It must be borne in mind that most of the references are to recent research publications which are not necessarily particularly easy to read. However, it should be possible for the reader of this text to make some headway with at least the introductory sections of most of the papers referenced.

6.1 DATA MODELLING

The dictionary definition of a model is a 'simplified description of a system to assist calculations and predictions' (Concise Oxford Dictionary). By a straightforward extension of this definition, a **data model** can be regarded as a simplified description of the real-world data which is required to perform some specified calculations and predictions. Although the nature of the calculations will vary greatly between different types of enterprise, the simplifying nature of a data model remains universal. Just as the data which are stored is merely a representation of the corresponding entities and relationships, so the data model itself is a representation of the real-world structures. The simplification implicit in the data model is the **abstraction** from the real world of those features which are either important or of interest. No data model is ever complete, since it can embody only a finite portion of the real world. What matters is that it must include a description of those parts of the real world which impinge on the enterprise that will use the database.

Much of this text has been concerned with various processes which address aspects of modelling. Since the model is expressed in terms of data structures intended to represent a part of the real world, the processes are often referred to generically as **data modelling**. Although the term data modelling has been used within this text for one specific stage of the process, that stage must be seen as only one of a number of modelling activities which are inherent in the process of deriving an appropriate database schema for some application.

The driving force for these activities has been a requirement actually to implement something. The three 'classical' data models, deduced in Chapter 4, were developed in the context of the types of structures which are feasible to implement. Hierarchies and networks were well established as computer data structures long before databases were invented, and the physical representation of a relation can be the even simpler structure of a table. Having derived a form for the data model, the justification for normalization has its basis in the implementation consequences of redundancy. In short, pragmatism and expediency, rather than theoretical considerations, have been the dominant concerns.

However, it has long been recognized that, as with any modelling process, data analysis and modelling can be developed from a formal basis. Indeed, as it was argued in Chapter 3, much of data analysis is completely independent of the ultimate implementation; this was the justification for the separation of the overall modelling process into two stages, referred to as 'data analysis' and 'data modelling'.

Established program design techniques, whether program driven or data driven, inevitably model data in terms of structures intended for implementation. Since early database systems were often regarded as little more than sophisticated file management facilities, the process of designing a database was often reduced to a question of choosing an appropriate physical representation for the required data. Thus, it is not surprising that data design was dominated by implementation considerations.

It was not really until the publication of Codd's proposal for the relational model in 1970 (Codd, 1970) that it was appreciated that there was a modelling process which could be separated from implementation. To some extent, this realization was reinforced by the ANSI/SPARC proposals for a three-level architecture, published in 1972, but that identification of the three levels of schema did little more than to introduce a distinction between 'logical' and 'physical' design. The types of data model used for the various levels of schema were usually identical to those which were to be used for the final implementation. If the implementation was to use a hierarchic structure, then the derivation of the conceptual schema would be performed in terms of hierarchic structures.

When Chen proposed his entity-relationship (E/R) modelling approach in 1976 (Chen, 1976), there was at last a modelling technique which dealt with an abstraction of the data which was to be represented, rather than with thinly disguised implementation structures. Although an entity-relationship data model could be mapped onto any one of the standard implementation models, the initial construction of the E/R model involved only consideration of the data which was to be represented, and not of the manner in which it was to be stored.

In the years that followed the introduction of entity-relationship modelling, there was an explosion of interest in the field of data modelling. Unfortunately, the 'novel' data models which were proposed very often seemed to be largely similar to each other, but at the same time mutually incompatible. In order to follow the research literature, it was necessary to expend considerable effort 'translating' concepts from one technique to another. For example, the term **entity type** in one technique would correspond to **object class** in another, or to **non-lexical object type** in a third. Each author appeared to be striving to show, not only that his particular method could cope with some difficulty hitherto unsolved, but also that it could handle every detail of everyone else's method – but using completely different terminology.

Nevertheless, a pattern did start to emerge of where interest was being concentrated. The principal areas were concerned both with data analysis and data modelling, as it has been defined in this book.

6.1.1 Relational theory

Some workers were exploring the theoretical consequences implicit in one or other of the classical data models. Since a theoretical basis was claimed for the relational model, it was this model which was the usual candidate for such discussion. Typical of such exercises was that reported by Kent (1981) and Fagin (1982), and in the correspondence which ensued. The point at issue was the interpretation of a relational schema comprising multiple relations, and in which one or more attribute names was common to more than one relation. Since it would be the intention in virtually all cases that the separate relations could be JOINed during queries, this would almost always happen.

The underlying assumption is of a single **universal relation**, from which all the schema relations are derived by projection alone. Since relations are, strictly, **mappings** between **domains**, the occurrence of an attribute name in more than one relation has implications sometimes overlooked by the schema designer. Specifically, it implies that each attribute with a given name should range over exactly the same domain, whereas in practice each would probably range over a different **subset** of the domain. That is, if any relation were projected over a single domain, then an underlying universal relation should imply that the set of values present in the resulting unary relation would be independent of the initial relation.

In practice, projections based on different relations within a given schema can often produce different results.

If a given attribute name were constrained to refer always to the same domain, then it would follow that two relations which comprised exactly the same attributes would be constrained always to be identical. However, two such relations could correspond to distinct roles between two entity types, and could contain very different data. Whilst this anomaly might not be important in practical implementations, it did place constraints on the development of the underlying relational theory.

6.1.2 Semantic hierarchies

Another area of interest was the range of constructs which formed the basis for data analysis. Chen's original model comprised only entities, attributes and relationships, although the last were somewhat more general than the simple binary relationships utilized in the approach demonstrated in this text. A particular weakness concerned sub-types, and hierarchies of such sub-types. Smith and Smith (1977) introduced the term **generalization** in their **semantic hierarchy model**, and thereby provided a formal basis for sub-types within an abstract data model. The semantic hierarchy model was subsequently extended by Brodie, when he

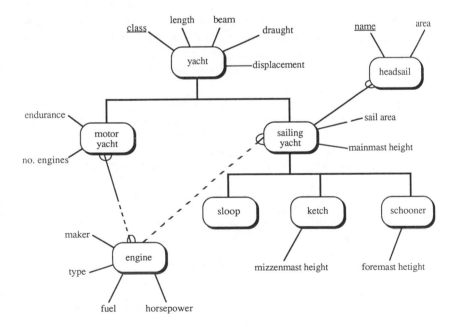

Fig. 6.1   Data structure for *yachts* example.

developed the approach to data modelling known as **active and passive component modelling** (ACM/PCM).

In the **extended semantic hierarchy model** (SHM+) (Brodie, 1981), the fundamental building block is an **object**, and objects are related by one of four types of structural abstractions, namely **classification, generalization, aggregation** and **association**. These operations are **abstractions** in the sense that details which are not relevant to the operation itself are suppressed.

Objects may vary considerably in complexity, from a single-attribute value to a complex structure of types and sub-types, and beyond. Each object is an **instance of** a particular **object class**, which has a particular set of properties. The structuring of the objects into object classes is termed **classification**. It is interesting to note that this is almost the reverse of the process of specifying an entity type, and then generating instances of the entity type, although the two processes are logically equivalent.

The relationships between entity types and their sub-types are represented specifically as **generalizations**. The entity type is regarded as a higher level, generic object, of which the various sub-types are *specializations*. For example, the object type *sailing yacht* shown in Fig. 6.1, could be regarded as a generalization of three categories, *sloop*, *ketch* and *schooner*. *Sloop* and *sailing yacht* are related by an *is_a* relationship. Since *sailing yacht* could in turn be regarded as a category of *yacht*, the generalization relationship is conceived as a hierarchy. SHM+ has its own diagram structure, using which the **generalization hierarchy** for yachts would be shown as in Fig. 6.2 as an SHM+ **object scheme**. Each category of object within the hierarchy **inherits** the properties of the generic object. Thus, all *motor yachts* and *sailing yachts* have a *length*, *beam*, *draught* etc., and all categories of *sailing yacht* have a *sail area* and a *mainmast height*.

Rather than retain the normal entity–attribute structure of earlier approaches, an **aggregation structure** is introduced which serves the same purpose. Thus, a *yacht* is considered to be an **aggregation** of the components *class*, *length*, *beam*, *draught* and *displacement*. Each of the components, such as *length*, is related to the aggregate object – *yacht* – by

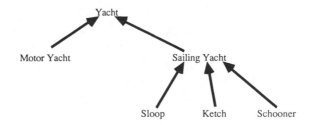

Fig. 6.2   Generalization hierarchy for *yachts*.

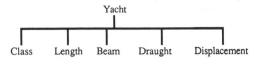

Fig. 6.3   Aggregation hierarchy for object class *yacht*.

a **part_of** relationship, so that *length* is part_of *yacht*. Since the aggregation abstraction is concerned with building higher-level objects from existing objects, without any concern for the internal structures of the component objects, it follows that the component object can have any structure of its own, of arbitrary complexity. The higher-level object **inherits** the properties of each of its components. Thus, the object *yacht* inherits the property of its component *length*, which is simply a value. If the component were a more complex object, such as *engine*, which had itself component values, then the object *yacht* would inherit those properties only. However, when specifying the aggregation, no account needs to be taken of the properties of *engine*, since aggregation is an abstraction. Figure 6.3 shows that part of the object scheme which defines the aggregations for *yacht*.

Since aggregation is analogous in structure to generalization, and also to a third abstraction termed **association**, used to model inter-entity groupings, the semantic hierarchy model features considerable internal consistency. Further, the three abstractions of aggregation, generalization and association are completely independent of any implementation considerations.

6.1.3   Semantic modelling

One criticism which was commonly levelled at the traditional data models was that, being concerned primarily with implementation, they were capable of embodying very little of the **semantics** or **meaning** associated with the data. For example, the attribute, or domain, names in a relational model do no more than identify the domains from which the values of particular attributes are drawn. Although the names used in a well designed schema might have some mnemonic significance, it would be quite possible to design a 'valid' schema in which the domains were labelled, say, *d1,d2,d3...* rather than *name, age, employee number....* From this potential deficiency in the relational model, there developed an interest in 'semantic' data models, through which it was hoped that rather more of the meaning, or semantics, of the data would be encapsulated in the database schema.

Semantic data models were developed both for data analysis and as extensions of implementations. Examples of the former include the models proposed by Hammer and McLeod (1981), Brodie (1981) and Verheijen and Van Bekkum (1982), and of the latter, extensions for the relational model described by Wong (1983) and in Codd (1979). In each case, the objective of the 'extended' model was to provide a technique through which the significance of the data could be recorded explicitly. For those semantic data models which are primarily design tools, the semantics are captured to a considerable extent as specific documentation of the schema, whereas the 'semantic' extensions to the relational model allow that information to be represented in the final implementation. Bubenko (1980) considers a number of data models, both implementation oriented and analysis oriented, and the degree to which they are capable of capturing the semantics of the data represented by a particular schema. One particular semantic data model, Hammer and McLeod's SDM is described in more detail in a later section.

6.1.4 Formal schema design

Once data modelling was recognized as a legitimate activity, interest grew in the formality of the process. Authors such as Zaniolo and Melkanoff (1982), and Carlson *et al.* (1982) addressed the details of formal dependency theory as it could be applied to schema derivation. Beeri and Kifer (1986) extended the formal approach to include both decomposition (normalization) and synthesis.

In recent years, a number of advanced texts have appeared, such as those by Tsichritzis and Lochovsky (1982) and Gray (1984b), which address the theoretical aspects of the data models as well as their practical application.

6.1.5 Conceptual modelling

Currently, interest is growing in the similarity between data modelling for database applications, knowledge representation in the context of artificial intelligence, and abstract data type specification in programming languages. The proceedings of a joint workshop between members of these three communities have been published by Springer-Verlag (Brodie *et al.*, 1984). Although much of the material is rather advanced, the overall flavour of the workshop is well described in the three introductory 'perspective' papers. It is through workshops such as this that the generic term **conceptual modelling** has arisen, embracing the modelling activities in each of the three areas.

For applications in which the data to be stored correspond to structured real-world objects, such as geographical features, the primitive data types offered by most implementation languages are far from adequate. For example, in a geographical or spatial database, fundamental data types might be *point* and *line*. However, such data must be represented as sets of numbers which define either a single point, the end-points of a line, or one end-point and the direction and length of a line. In addition, each attribute of a line is regarded as being essentially independent, whereas the line is characterized by the whole set of values. Clearly, some structured data types are appropriate for such applications. The concept of **abstract data type** can be borrowed from the programming language discipline. The design of a relational system in which domains can be of abstract data types is discussed by Osborn and Heaven (1986).

The **semantic network** is well established as a fundamental construct in the field of artificial intelligence and elsewhere. A semantic network is, essentially, any graphical structure in which information is conveyed by means of nodes and edges. Thus, for example, the data structure diagrams used throughout this text are examples of a particular type of semantic net, although they would not usually be described as such. The theoretical foundations and implications of this type of representation have received a great deal of attention, and Brodie *et al.* (1984) include several pointers to this work, whereas Griffith (1982) addresses the problems of representing semantic networks in non-graphical form.

6.1.6 Logic

First-order logic, or predicate calculus, forms the basis for the relational calculus. One of the principal advantages of calculus-based query languages is that they are essentially non-procedural, and free the user from considerations of how the query is to be evaluated. However, although relational theory includes some elements of propositional calculus, relations as implemented in most systems bear little resemblance to constructs of logic.

Semantic nets are closely related to the concepts of logic. Each arc of a network can be regarded as an independent predicate relating two nodes. For example, the predicate '*John teaches databases*' could evaluate either to true or false, depending on what *John* actually teaches. *John* and *databases* would correspond to two nodes in a semantic net, and the assertion that *John teaches databases* to an arc connecting two specific nodes which may or may not exist. Whilst a graphical form of this assertion is somewhat difficult to manipulate, the predicates which represent the semantic net are amenable to the processes of logic.

The relationship between logic and semantic nets is captured in approaches such as the **qualified binary relationship model** (Lavington and Jiang, 1985). The fundamental building block is a 'two-place predicate', which represents a single arc from a semantic net, as with the example above.

Logic languages, such as PROLOG (Kowalski, 1984) are now well established for combining sets of predicates to reason about some statement. The evaluation of a database query for a logic database consists of finding those **facts**, stored as predicates, which are known to the database and which satisfy the query. Such a process is an example of **rule-based** programming, an approach of growing importance, particularly in the fields of knowledge-based systems and deductive systems.

An example of a logic database is discussed briefly in a later section.

6.2 SOME ADVANCED MODELS

6.2.1 Binary and irreducible relational models

Boyce–Codd normal form has been presented in the last chapter as the usual target for normalization or synthesis. A schema in Boyce–Codd normal form contains little redundancy, and can also contain fewer relations than might be proposed for an initial skeleton model. Each relation represents either atomic facts or a set of related facts. However, two major criticisms can be levelled at a BCNF schema.

Firstly, its structure looks very much like an implementation. A tuple which contains several fields representing a set of related facts is not unlike a record, which is a structure devised for implementation. Even though there is a theoretical basis to the derivation of a relational schema, that theory applies to mappings between domains, rather than to record-like structures. It could be argued that a design technique which generates records masquerading as tuples has been 'hijacked' too far in the direction of implementation.

A second problem with minimal normalized schemata relates to incomplete data. Whilst a correctly normalized schema should be able to represent optionalities correctly without the need to introduce **null** values, the same may not be true for 'missing' data. If a tuple represents several facts, and the data for just one of them are currently missing, then it follows that the corresponding domain value in the tuple will be unknown. Since the remaining domain values are known, there is then a choice of whether to discard those facts which are known until the tuple can be completed, or to complete the tuple by inserting a 'null' value. Whilst, taken in isolation, a null value may be perfectly sensible, the meaning of nulls is less clear when relations are joined over a domain which contains nulls (Date, 1982).

Bearing in mind the points raised in the last chapter about the distinction between the **logical** conceptual schema and the **physical** internal schema, it possible to suggest an alternative approach which can overcome both of these objections.

Essentially, the relational model is concerned with mappings between two or more domains. Each domain corresponds to a particular (set of) attribute value(s) within the schema. Some of the attributes act as keys for the entity types in the schema, and so the mappings between the underlying domains correspond to relationships between entities. Conversely, the mappings between those domains and domains which do not correspond to key attributes represent the relationships between entities and their attributes.

Whatever the mapping, it is an atomic fact, and it is arguable that each such fact should be represented separately. If each mapping is represented by a separate relation, it follows that null values are not required. Each tuple contains an instance of a single mapping, so if one of the attribute values which represent that instance is missing, then the complete tuple can be omitted without losing information.

In addition, the schema is no longer oriented towards implementation, but is instead concerned with the pure facts which comprise the required data structure. Although such a schema would inevitably contain a larger number of relations than would a synthesized schema in third, or lower, normal form, there is no restriction placed on how it maps to the internal schema. For example, the internal schema could be in second normal form, and could contain null values. However, all manipulations would be performed in terms of the conceptual schema, comprising many more simple relations and no null values. The database software would be responsible for maintaining the mapping between the two schemata, and mapping queries appropriately.

Consider, for example, the *yacht* example of Fig. 6.1. In a BCNF schema, the *yacht* entity would be represented by a single relation, such as

YACHT (class, length, beam, draught, displacement)

This relation contains five distinct facts:

a that there is a particular *class* of yacht;
b that the *class* has a certain *length*;
c that the *class* has a certain *beam*;
d that the *class* has a certain *draught*;
e that the *class* has a certain *displacement*.

In a binary relation model, the entity type *yacht* would be represented by one unary and four binary relations:

YACHT_CLASS (class)
YACHT_LENGTH (class, length)
YACHT_BEAM (class, beam)
YACHT_DRAUGHT (class, draught)
YACHT_DISP (class, displacement)

If the history of the information about a certain new class of yacht were to proceed through stages where first the *class* were known; then, at a later date, the *length* and *beam*; then, later still, the *draught*; and finally the *displacement*, the two representations would have very different properties.

In the case of the normalized relation, the tuple corresponding to the new class of yacht would have to go through three stages in which it contained 'unknown' data:

(Sprayboat, NULL, NULL, NULL, NULL)
(Sprayboat, 34, 10.5, NULL, NULL)
(Sprayboat, 34, 10.5, 5.7, NULL)
(Sprayboat, 34, 10.5, 5.7, 7.5)

assuming that the new *sprayboat* class has a length and beam of *34* and *10.5* feet, respectively, a draught of *5.7* feet, and a displacement of *7.5* tons. However, the binary relation schema would require no null values. As each new fact became available, it would be represented by a new tuple being added to the appropriate relation.

Although the term **binary** relational model is used, the example demonstrates that it is likely that **unary** relations will also be required, since it may not be possible to guarantee that any given binary relation will contain a tuple with a particular key value. In fact, each binary relation represents a fact which is distinct from the existence of a particular entity; relying on projection of one of the binary relations to generate a list of entities would be to imply that the relation in question was representing **two** facts, which would be counter to the philosophy of the model.

The relations in a binary relational model are still relations, and they are still amenable to all of the relational operators, or to the relational calculus. Indeed, it is likely that many binary relations will need to be JOINed to satisfy a query, and that the result may not itself be binary. Nevertheless, the only relations which are logically present in the schema (but not necessarily present in the internal schema) represent only single facts.

It may be that it is not possible to represent all the required facts using binary relations alone. For example, the fully normalized schema developed for the *cars* database in Chapter 5 is **irreducible**, in the sense that it cannot be decomposed into smaller components without losing information. In particular, the relations

PERFORMANCE (model, engine, max speed)
BODY   (model, style, market)
CAR   (model, style, engine, price)

each represent a single (type of) fact. Although the relations are not binary, they do all contain only one attribute apart from their key. It is only because the keys are compound that the relations are not binary.

The **irreducible relational model** is an extension of the binary relational model, in which relations of degree greater than two are permitted if, and only if, they contain at most one non-key attribute, or one group of non-key attributes which together form the key of another relation. Apart from the rather obvious departure from purely binary relations, the irreducible relational model can claim to have all the same advantages as the binary relational model.

6.2.2 Functional data model

Functional data models are closely related to the irreducible models. The fundamental building block is again an atomic fact, which is represented not as a relation, but as a function. For example, for a yacht, there might be a function *length*, whose value *length (yacht)* would correspond to the length of a yacht. Three functional models which have appeared in the literature are FQL (Buneman and Frankel, 1979), FDM (Housel *et al.*, 1979) and DAPLEX (Shipman, 1981). The remainder of this section refers specifically to DAPLEX, although many of its features are to be found in other functional data models.

The primitives of a functional data model are **entities** and **functions**. Functions operate on an entity, and perform a **mapping** to another entity. There are no specific attribute values, since attributes are regarded merely as being instances of particular entity types such as INTEGER or STRING. Thus, the function *length* above performs a mapping from the entity type *yacht* to the (system supplied) 'entity type' INTEGER. The particular instance of INTEGER which is returned as the value of the function corresponds, in this case, to an attribute value describing the length of the yacht in question. Similarly, a function *class* might map from the *yacht* entity type to STRING, and its value would be a string representing the class of a particular yacht.

If the mapping is to a 'real' entity type, rather than to a data type, then the value of the function is an **instance** of the target entity type, and not a string (or other data value) corresponding to the identifier of the entity type. This is a fundamental distinction between the functional data model and the relational model, in which it is recognized implicitly that an entity occurrence can not be represented directly, but must be described in terms of its attributes. One of its attributes, normally the identifier, is used in such models for representing inter-entity relationships. However, (Gray, 1984a) has demonstrated that the functional mapping between entity types is analogous to the **set** mapping between record types imposed by CODASYL. In the latter case, obtaining the key of, say, the owner of a particular set is a two stage process: first, the record must be found, and then the relevant field accessed. Similarly, in the functional data model, a function to another entity returns an instance of the entity type; to obtain the identifier of that entity, a second function must be applied to map the entity to one of the data types.

For example, if the function *engine* maps from the *sailing yacht* entity type to the *engine* entity type, then *engine* (*sailing yacht*) will have as its value the instance of *engine* which is fitted to a particular sailing yacht. To obtain the identifier of the engine, it is then necessary to apply a second function, *type*, which maps from the *engine* entity type to the data type STRING.

Since the value of a function is an entity instance, it follows that an appropriate function can be applied directly to the result of a function. Thus, given *engine* (*sailing yacht*) and *type* (*engine*), it is possible to nest the function applications. The expression *type* (*engine* (*sailing yacht*)) would have as its value a STRING representing the type of the engine fitted to a particular sailing yacht. Nested function application, or functional composition, in this manner can make queries expressed in DAPLEX extremely concise.

There is no reason why a function in DAPLEX must be single valued. For example, most sailing yachts carry several headsails ('jibs'), and it would be possible to have a function *headsail* which mapped from a *sailing yacht* to a set of *headsails*. Again, the value of the function would be a set of *headsail* entities; further functions – such as *area* and *name*

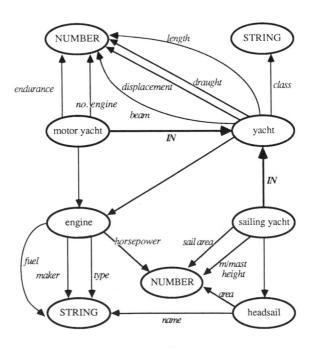

Fig. 6.4 A functional representation of the *yachts* schema.

would be required to determine the attributes of each headsail within the set.

A DAPLEX schema for part of the *yachts* database is shown in Fig. 6.4. Entity types are drawn in rounded boxes, and the arrows depict directed functions which map from one entity type to another. Each function must be named, since there may be several functions between any pair of entity types, either because there are multiple roles, or because the target entity type is an attribute domain, such as INTEGER. However, in many cases it is sufficient to use the name of the target entity type as the function name – for example, *engine (yacht)* or *headsail (sailing yacht)*. Although the primitive entity types NUMBER and STRING occur twice each within the structure, they do so purely for convenience; it makes it easier to avoid having lines which cross.

Only part of the data structure from Fig. 6.1 is shown, although it would be possible to include the remaining entity sub-types, linking them to the *sailing yacht* entity type by **in** functions. However, it should be noted that this graphical representation of sub-types, which is not due to Shipman, is not quite consistent with the remainder of the denotation. As drawn, it suggests that the **in** function is simply another DAPLEX function, whose result when applied to, say, a *sailing yacht* is an instance of *yacht*. In fact, DAPLEX has inherent sub-typing facilities, through which property inheritance is preserved, so that every instance of *sailing yacht* can have applied to it all the functions that are defined for *yacht*.

DAPLEX functions are directed. They are applied to a specific entity type, and map to a second entity type. Many database operations will require inverse functions, such as 'the set of *yachts* which are fitted with a particular *engine*', or, 'the *yacht* whose length is *43.6*'. DAPLEX allows such inverse functions to be defined, with obvious semantics. In most cases, the inverse of a single-value function is set-valued.

The DAPLEX query language is based on the notion of 'looping' through entity sets, selecting instances of the entities according to some specified predicate. The nesting of function applications within the query language allows queries to be read almost as if they are in English. For example,

FOR EACH *sailing yacht*
   SUCH THAT *length (sailing yacht)* > 30
   AND *maker (engine (sailing yacht))* = *'VOLVO'*
   PRINT *class (sailing yacht)*

could be read as,

For each *sailing yacht* such that the *length* of the *sailing yacht* is greater than *30*
and the *maker* of the *engine* of the *sailing yacht* is *'VOLVO'*,
print the *class* of the *sailing yacht*.

and the English version is a fair description of what would actually happen. It should be noted that the functions *length* and *class* can be applied directly to the entity type *sailing yacht*, because it is defined as a sub-type of *yacht*, for which the functions are actually defined.

6.2.3 Logic models

In a logic model, a database is represented as a set of **facts** and a set of **rules**. Facts are simply assertions, such as,

length (sprayboat, 34)
length (splasher, 32)
length (dripper, 21)

which bear remarkable resemblance to the primitives of either a functional model or an irreducible relational model. The rather terse notation for the facts is unnecessary, and they could be re-written as, for example,

a *sprayboat* has a *length* of *34*.

Such refinements have not always been adopted by proponents of logic languages for database implementation, so that logic languages have tended to remain enshrouded in the mists of formality.

Queries are formulated as assertions which contain **variables**. The logic system in effect searches exhaustively through its database of facts for values which can be substituted for the variables, and satisfy the assertion. For example, in,

dripper has *length* x ?

x is a variable. By searching the set of facts known to the system, the value which is found to substitute for x and satisfy the assertion is *21*. The answer to a query in general is the set of values for which the assertion is true.

The logic rules have a novel function, in that they allow various deductions to be made from the facts. For example, there could be a rule to distinguish the categories *motor yacht* and *sailing yacht* as follows:

a *yacht* is a *sailing yacht* if it has a *mast*

Taken in conjunction with some additional facts, such as,

the *mastheight* of a *sprayboat* is *38*
the *mastheight* of a *dripper* is *24*

then a query such as

y is a *sailing yacht*?

can be evaluated by considering each of the three possible yachts, and eliminating those which do not have masts: the result would be,

sprayboat
and *dripper*.

Clearly, logic programming has a lot to offer in the database field, since it provides a completely new approach to the specification and processing of queries. Indeed, research in knowledge-based systems and deductive systems are concentrating on rule-based approaches such as this.

However, it also suffers from two major drawbacks. Firstly, the number of facts necessary to represent even a modest sized database is, to say the least, daunting, and some sort of structuring is essential if query processing is to be performed with reasonable efficiency. The second problem lies in the (perceived) formality of the approach. Since logic is perceived as a mathematical abstraction, it has not received the attention from end-users which it perhaps deserves. Since it has not been widely adopted by end-users, it has remained somewhat mathematical. It is to be hoped that this vicious circle will be broken within the foreseeable future.

6.2.4 Semantic data models

Mathematical data models, including the relational model, tend to lose the 'meaning' of the data, since they represent only the data, and not its semantics. Indeed, great care is taken to derive a data structure in a context-free manner. The resulting schemata can often be somewhat alien to users, bearing little apparent relation to the intended applications.

A further disadvantage of abstracting the data structure from its context is that any **constraints** on the database must be imposed on the database externally; they cannot be incorporated in the schema.

Hammer and McLeod's **semantic data model** (SDM) (Hammer and McLeod, 1981) is one approach to solving this problem.

The general principles of SDM are that:

a a database is a collection of **entities** which correspond to real-world objects;

b the entities are organized into **classes** which are meaningful collections of entities;

c the classes within a database are not, in general, independent, but are related by **interclass connections**;

d entities have **attributes** which **i** describe their characteristics or **ii** relate them to other entities;

e attributes may be **derived**; and

f there are several ways of defining interclass connections and derivations.

The concepts of **entity** and **entity class** are not dissimilar from those of several other models, including Smith and Smith's semantic hierarchy model and even Chen's entity-relationship model. Attributes in SDM can have values which are themselves entities, in a manner which is not unlike the result of a DAPLEX function being an instance of an entity type. What is novel is the way in which the **interclass connections** are used to represent relationships, and the formalization of the description of each entity class.

The definition of an entity class includes a description not only of the entities which comprise the class, but also of any attributes or other properties which pertain to the class itself rather than to individual entities. The components of the entity class definition include:

a the NAME of the entity class;

b an (optional) verbal description of the class and its component entities;

c a definition of which entities are members of the class;

d a list of attributes, which may be multivalued, both for the individual entities and for the class as a whole; and

e a specification of which attributes serve as identifiers for the constituent entities.

Each entity class is either **base** or **non-base**. In the former case, the entities in the class have an existence in their own right, whereas entities in a non-base class are defined in terms of one or more other classes. The entities in base classes can be regarded as the primitives for the application. The members of each non-base class are defined in terms of an interclass connection, which can express either a sub-type relationship to another class, or a **grouping** of similar entities to form higher-level objects, such as grouping together certain *yachts* as *charter fleets*. This latter concept is analogous to an association hierarchy in SHM+. Neither type of interclass connection need refer to base classes, so that quite general generalization and association hierarchies can be supported.

One particular type of sub-type structure which is built in to SDM is termed a **name class**. Basically, each atomic domain is defined as a subclass of the primitive class, STRING. All data values which are used in communication with the 'real world' are termed SDM **names**, and must be drawn from some name class. In many ways, the definition of a name class is equivalent to the definition of a formal **domain** in the relational model.

When defining the attributes for a particular entity class, not only the name and domain of the attribute are defined, but also various constraints can be imposed. As with the definition of the entity class itself, it is possible also to supply a description of the attribute.

The **value class**, or domain, of an attribute is always an entity class, in the same way that DAPLEX functions always map onto an entity type. The existence of specific name classes, however, allows the value of an attribute to be a more traditional 'value'. Where the value of an attribute for members of an entity class is, in fact, an entity, a relationship is implied between that entity and the entity class being defined. As far as a user of the model is concerned, entities which are in effect attributes of a particular entity appear to be contained within that entity. Thus, the containing entity can inherit all the properties of the contained entity, in much the same way as in an aggregation hierarchy.

Each relationship of this type may be defined to have an **inverse**, meaning that each of the two entities appears as an attribute of the other. Since an entity appearing as an attribute of a second entity already contains the second by virtue of the inverse relationship, this is, of course, recursive – but the consequences will not be considered here!

In addition to asserting that the relationship is inverse, it is also possible to define whether an attribute is single- or multivalued; mandatory (a null value is not allowed); not changeable (once set to a non-null value, cannot be changed); exhaustive (every member of the value class must appear as an attribute for some entity – in effect, the inverse of 'mandatory'); and non-overlapping (each member of the value class is used at most once – in effect, the inverse of 'single-valued'). These restrictions, in essence, refer to the degree and optionality of the relationship which is being represented. Finally, a **derivation** may be defined for any attribute value. Such derivations might typically refer to set properties, although they need not. For example, the *maximum hull speed* of a yacht can be calculated as a function of the *length*, *beam* and *draught* of the yacht, and could be defined within an SDM schema as an attribute derived from those values.

The syntax of SDM permits relationships between entities to be defined in ways other than inclusion as attribute values, but these will not be discussed here. A full description will be found in Hammer and McLeod (1982), together with a comprehensive example and the full syntax for the model. An abbreviated syntax for an entity class definition, presented as a 'skeleton' description, is shown in Fig. 6.5, in which items enclosed in square brackets are optional.

Although SDM is defined in terms of a strict syntax, it is essentially a design tool rather than an implementation medium. This is largely because it has not yet been implemented, rather than that it could not be implemented. As an abstract data modelling technique, it can offer advantages in providing 'user centred views' naturally, since the recursive

ENTITY_CLASS_NAME

[description : ...]

[interclass connection : ...]

member attributes:

    Attribute_name
      value_class: ...
      [mandatory]
      [multivalued] [no overlap in values]
      [exhausts value class]
      [not changeable]
      [inverse : attribute_name]
      [match : attibute_name of ENTITY_CLASS on attribute_name]
      [derivation : ...]

[class attributes :

    attribute_name
      [description : ...]
      value_class : ...
      [derivation : ...]
]

[identifiers :
    attribute_name [+ attribute_name_2 + ...]
]

Fig. 6.5   Semantic data model — entity class definition.

inclusion of 'attribute' entities allows all the components of the data structure to be viewed in context. Further, the implicit constraints and relationships provide a more coherent view of the data than do the explicit relationship structures required in the traditional data models. Finally SDM can be used as a formal medium for the documentation and discussion of a database schema.

6.3 IMPLEMENTATION CONCERNS

The developments discussed so far in this chapter have been addressed to the problem of developing data modelling techniques with particular characteristics. In recent years, there has been some considerable interest in issues which are not confined to particular modelling techniques.

The proliferation of data modelling techniques has taken place against a background of an increasing number of database implementations. At the same time, advances have been made in computer communications, which make it possible for one database installation to communicate with virtually any other. However, given a variety of implementation models, such inter-database communication can be non-trivial.

Until recently, the principal implementation models have been based on the three 'classical' data models: hierarchic, CODASYL and relational. Initially, the hierarchic and CODASYL models were developed as database management systems, rather than as data models. Versions of the systems for different manufacturers' machines were developed largely by converting the software to run on the new machines. When the relational data model was proposed, as a theoretical model with no existing implementation, corresponding data models were abstracted from hierarchic and CODASYL systems. Given the model specifications, it was possible for new implementations to be developed based on one or other of the data models, but independent of the existing systems. The CODASYL standard is well defined, so that most implementations conform to it fairly closely. The hierarchic model has, in practice, been confined to the IBM user community using IMS, where it grew to be by far the most common database system in use anywhere. However, relational implementations have not always captured the complete essence of the relational model. Particularly following the advent of microcomputers, virtually every vendor seems to be offering a product which claims to be relational, but which may in fact be little more than a simple indexed file system. This particular problem was addressed by Codd himself in the 1981 ACM Turing Award Lecture (Codd, 1982).

In addition to systems based on one of the three established data models, there have been a large number of products which have served as database management systems. Some, such as ADABAS and TOTAL have ranked second only to IMS in popularity (see Kroenke (1977) for a brief tutorial on these two systems). However, for various reasons, the underlying data models have not been abstracted for such systems, probably because they are oriented too heavily towards implementation.

6.3.1 Canonical models

Given the three classical data models, each with their own considerable user community, and the development of implementations based on the irreducible relational models, functional model, semantic networks, and logic, communication between databases is becoming increasingly complex. It is not surprising that considerable effort has been addressed to the problem of translating queries from the data language for one data model into that for another. Parallel efforts have been directed towards integrating data models which are defined in terms of a variety of models.

The first mappings to be considered were the translation of queries expressed in CODASYL DML into a relational equivalent. Since the underlying data models have essentially the same expressive power, it was expected that it should be possible to regard databases expressed in the two models as being equivalent. However, the process of translating queries from one system to another proved to be non-trivial; see, for example, Katz and Wong (1982). The principal difficulty arises from the difference in philosophy of the two data manipulation languages. CODASYL DML is record based, with operations being performed record-at-a-time, and all iteration and recursion being expressed in a host language. Relational DMLs, on the other hand, are either based on set-at-time manipulations (algebra), or claim to be non-procedural (calculus). Despite this conflict, some relational interfaces are now appearing for CODASYL based systems such as IDMS.

A rather more straightforward mapping is possible between CODASYL and functional data models. For example, Gray (1984a) explores the relationship between DAPLEX and CODASYL, and how each type of schema can be treated in terms of the other.

The goal of building a **canonical** database system, which simultaneously supports a number of different data models, has been pursued by several workers. An example of such a system which has been implemented is PRECI (Deen, 1980, 1981). PRECI is based on the concept of a canonical data model with a number of 'local' schemata. Each local schema is essentially a view of the canonical schema, and expresses the data structure in terms of one of the classical data models, or indeed as an ADABAS, IMS or TOTAL schema. The concepts modelled in the canonical schema are entity type, entity relationship and usage constraints. The internal representation is, in fact, by a set of relations in fourth normal form, but an automatic mapping is provided for local schemata expressed in the CODASYL model. Pelagatti et al. (1985) have explored some of the theoretical problems which are encountered in this quest, and suggest that some new data model is required for the definition of the 'central schema', of which it would be possible to have both relational and CODASYL views.

Unfortunately, the problem of integrating schemata of different types is likely to be somewhat more complicated. Whilst it is possible that enthusiasts for several data models could exist within a single enterprise, it is more likely that the conflict between different data models would arise if attempts were made to integrate databases from different installations. Thus, the problem would not merely be one of an incompatibility of data models, but also one of **distribution** (see Chapter 7). Examples of two extremes of approach are the PROTEUS project (Atkinson *et al.*, 1983) based in a number of British universities, and MULTIBASE (Smith *et al.*, 1981), developed by CCA. The former extends the concept of a new data model for expressing an 'abstracted conceptual schema', with each 'conventional' schema being a view of the abstracted schema. All communication between the different databases is performed in terms of the abstracted schema, which also serves to unite all the separate schemata into a single logical whole. However, such a system requires that all of the databases must be defined from scratch as part of the abstracted schema, and it avoids the issue of integrating a number of databases which already exist. It is this approach which is taken by MULTIBASE, wherein the problems concern the integration of a number of schemata expressed in disparate data models. Again, an overall or 'global' model is defined, in which each pre-existing schema is mapped into the global model by means of an 'integration schema'; views – of any type – can then be defined on the global model.

Despite the considerable activity in this field, the problems are far from solved. Not the least of the outstanding problems is that there is seldom a unique way of representing any given data structure within a database, and yet all the equivalent representations must behave in the same way under the relevant mappings. It is likely that this will be an active research area for some time to come.

6.3.2 Modelling incomplete data

Another area which is attracting considerable research effort stems from the acceptance that the data which is being represented is itself not always complete. This problem has been considered briefly in earlier sections, and in particular with reference to the irreducible relational models. Interest is divided between the semantics of incomplete data – that is, what it actually means – and the interpretation of relational queries in databases which permit joins to be performed on fields containing null values.

Lipski (1979) suggests a mathematical interpretation of null values in the context of their underlying domain. The essence of the argument is that, even if nothing is known about a missing value, at least it is known that it must be drawn from the appropriate domain, which is in many cases finite and relatively small. Deductions can then be made on the basis of the set of all possible completions of the data, and thence, in principal, it may be possible to set bounds on the 'true' completion. Wong (1982) introduces an attempt to apply statistical theory to this type of process.

Codd himself proposed extensions to the relational algebra to accommodate the presence of null values (Codd, 1979), and the formal basis for these extensions has been investigated by such as Biskup (1983). However, the interpretation of the results of JOIN operations when either of the files involved in the join can contain null values is far from clear.

When comparing two tuples in the JOIN operation, if the JOIN field in one is null, it is not determined whether or not it should be joined to the other tuple. Since it is null, it is possible that its 'correct' value, if it were known, could result in the join of the two tuples, or it might not. The uncertainty is compounded if both JOIN fields contain nulls, since it cannot necessarily be assumed that two null values are either the same – or different! The same difficulty arises when enforcing the requirement that all tuples within a relation must be distinct, since two nulls might, or might not, be the same value. This latter point is usually overcome by insisting that no component of the primary key of a relation may be null – which is equivalent to saying that every entity must have a complete identifier. However, there is no equivalent solution possible for the problem of forming an average or total of the values of some attribute which can be null. These problems are discussed in detail in Date (1982, 1983a)

SUMMARY
Chapter 6

The three classical data models are by no means the end of the data modelling story. There is still considerable research activity in this area, both addressing the underlying assumptions of existing data models, such as the relational model, and proposing new types of data model.

The **irreducible** and **functional** data models express a data structure in terms of atomic facts rather than as record-like structures. **Semantic hierarchies** extend the data modelling primitives by introducing **generalization**, **association** and **aggregation**. **Semantic data models** attempt to capture not only the pure data, but also some of the meaning associated with it. A recent addition to the data modelling repertoire is based on **logic** programming in languages such as PROLOG.

The broad spectrum of data modelling ranging from artificial intelligence to programming languages is described by the term **conceptual modelling**. Given the variety of data models available, it is becoming increasingly important to be able to map from one type of model to another.

Incomplete or missing data can have interesting effects on the semantics of a database.

PROBLEMS
Chapter 6

It may be helpful to refer to some of the references before attempting to answer these problems.

P6.1 Compare and contrast the concepts of entity type, object class (SHM+) and entity class (SDM). To what extent do they represent the same fundamental concept but use different terminology?

P6.2 Both the binary relational model and the functional model are said to be irreducible. However, the natures of the respective query languages are very different. Devise some sample queries which can demonstrate the differences, and comment on your observations.

P6.3 Produce an SDM schema description for one of the problems from Chapter 3.

P6.4 Although an irreducible relational schema has some logical advantages over a schema in Boyce−Codd normal form, it also carries some implementation overheads. By considering the form of queries which could be addressed to an irreducible schema, discuss the relative merits and demerits of the two types of schema.

7

DATABASES IN PERSPECTIVE

It is very easy when discussing any subject to lose sight of its context within the real world. This is just as true for databases as it is for anything else. Just because the data model being used has a particular elegance, or the query language associated with that model permits the posing of wonderful esoteric *ad-hoc* queries, that is not in itself justification for the use of a database. What matters is whether or not the database serves the purpose for which it was intended — as far as the **users** are concerned.

Just as it is easy to forget the true justification for databases, it is also possible to imagine that, provided the data model is fully normalized, then all that needs to be done has been done. However, there are a number of other issues which must also be borne in mind, particularly if the database is to be released to real users.

Although the sole justification for a database is that it must satisfy the needs of its users, the existence of those very users can cause considerable problems. Inevitably their interest is in performing their own particular tasks, with the help of the database, with perhaps little consideration for the way in which their use of the database might interact with that of others. Worse, the users may not be well-versed in the niceties of data modelling and database construction. It can almost be guaranteed that at least one user will manage, somehow, to wreak havoc within the database — albeit, perhaps through ignorance rather than malice.

Such considerations imply that the story is far from over when the database system has been selected, and the data model designed. This chapter is intended to provide some pointers to the outstanding questions which must also be addressed. Space does not permit a detailed examination of these topics, but at least an outline of the concepts is presented.

7.1 WHAT PRICE DATABASES?

It has been an implicit assumption throughout the earlier part of this text that, once it has been established that data are to be shared between a number of applications, then a database is the answer. However, there are a number of arguments which should be considered both in favour of and against the use of databases rather than 'traditional' file processing techniques.

7.1.1 The case against

Not everything related to database systems augers in their favour. There are some distinct disadvantages to be weighed against the benefits.

Firstly, employing database technology can be rather like using a sledgehammer to crack a nut. For small, relatively straightforward applications, the complexity of a database system may not be truly justified if the same functionality could be provided by a simple file processing system. If the result of the data analysis and data modelling processes is a schema in which there are only one or two 'record' types (or segment types, or relations), it is unlikely that the power of a database system is really required. It must be borne in mind that the concepts of query languages and on-line processing are not restricted to the realm of databases — such sytems can be constructed fairly readily in most high-level languages.

The database management system itself is likely to be expensive. Whatever its cost, however, it is bound to be an **extra** cost compared with a file processing system, since it can almost be taken as read that any computer system will come equipped with an appropriate high-level language in which an application could be developed. It may be that the use of a database management system will mean that additional hardware, as well as additional software, will be required — yet another expense.

Even if data is to be shared, it may be the case that the sharing is not real. For example, one application may be quite content with the state of the world at the end of last week, whilst only the second requires up-to-the-minute information. In such a case, the former application could be satisfied readily by generating a weekly statement about the state of the world from the files used by the latter. There would be no need for either application to have access to data which was currently being used by the other.

Integrating a number of file processing applications into a single database also puts all the enterprise's eggs in one basket. Any failure to the database system puts all the enterprise's operations out of action, whereas a set of independent file processing applications, perhaps on separate machines, may be more tolerant to problems which arise within one application.

Finally, some of the points which will be introduced in the remainder of this chapter represent additional problems which can appear almost as a result of using database techniques.

It follows that use of a database should not be an automatic choice for every application which manipulates stored data – even if those data are to be shared.

7.1.2 The case in favour

Although some of the arguments against the use of databases are fairly strong, the case in favour of databases can be equally convincing. Even if the eventual decision is not to use a database system, there is a lot to be gained from adopting the database approach to the analysis of the problem.

The first point to be made is that all the problems which can arise as a result of using databases rather than file processing systems are recognized, at least in principle. Most reasonable implementations will actually go some way towards overcoming them. It may even be that, by considering them as part of the database design process, problems may be recognized which would otherwise have lain dormant until they erupted without warning to cause chaos and confusion.

One of the principal advantages of adopting the database approach is that all the problems are treated using a higher level of abstraction than might be the case for a single-user file application. Thus, a better overall picture can be obtained of the data processing requirements of the enterprise. Having obtained such an overall picture, the enterprise is then in a better position to decide whether or not a database is appropriate.

In particular, the potential complexity of database systems justifies the use of more formal data analysis and modelling techniques than might otherwise be employed. The use of such techniques is in itself a good reason for approaching an application with databases in mind – however tenuously.

Finally, the argument presented in Chapter 1 for the adoption of a database approach is still valid, and can be dominant. By integrating the data requirements of a number of applications, the need for duplicated data can be reduced. By eliminating such redundant duplication, not only can the physical storage requirements be reduced, but the problems of maintaining overall consistency can be eliminated.

On balance, the advantages of adopting a database approach can outweigh the disadvantages, even for single-user applications, for anything more than the most trivial of applications. However, perhaps the most relevant requirement is that these points should be actively considered when designing a data management system, rather than the decision being pre-empted by the prejudices — one way or the other — of the implementor, or the inertia of the data processing department.

7.2 THE DATABASE ENVIRONMENT

Although it bears repeating that the sole justification for a database system is its users, it is worth looking briefly at the cast of characters who provide the environment for the database.

7.2.1 The database administrator

Somebody has to design the database. The tasks of data analysis, data modelling and implementation generally fall to the person, or group of people, referred to as the **database administrator**, or **DBA**. For a small application, the DBA's job may only be a relatively small load. However, for a real-world sized enterprise, with a database whose conceptual schema includes perhaps a few hundred entity types, it is unlikely that a single person could exercise complete control over the database. In such cases, the DBA's job can occupy a substantial department.

The DBA's department must be responsible not only for the analysis and modelling of the data, but also for the selection of the database management system to be used, its implementation, and training both for the systems specialists and for the users. Perhaps one of the largest jobs is that of physically loading the data. There have been cases when an entire database project has foundered at this stage, simply because there were inadequate resources for the job.

Once the data is loaded, it must be maintained and kept up-to-date. Again, this task is the responsibility of the DBA, although the actual modifications to the data may be delegated to the user(s) who generate(s) the new data.

In addition, responsibility falls to the DBA for protecting the database against the threats outlined in the next section, and generally ensuring that the database can continue to serve its purpose whatever the users, and the world in general, happen to throw at it. That can be quite a challenge!

7.2.2 Users

Databases exist for users. Users can come in all shapes and sizes, from trainee programmers to data entry clerks or managing directors. Each user may have a specific application for the database, or (s)he may just require general access to the stored data. The queries posed by the users can be routine and repetitive, such as payroll processing or stock control, or they may be completely unpredictable and *ad-hoc*. The volume of data to be retrieved from the database can be measured in inches of lineprinter paper or in lines on a terminal. The data to be searched to generate those few lines on a terminal can range from a few records to the entire database.

Users may interact with the database using an interactive query language, or they may run established applications programs. When using the database, they may retrieve data, delete data, modify data or add new data. One thing which users would not normally be allowed to do would be to change the structure of the database, unless they have some private part of the database containing data which is not accessed by any other user.

Despite their variety, users tend to share one common attribute. Whatever their skill in computing generally, it seems to be a common phenomenon that database users develop tremendous skill in getting their systems tied in knots. It may simply be that, having access only to a sub-schema, a user may not be aware of the consequences of his actions as far as other users are concerned. Another explanation could be that databases are regarded as something special and mysterious, which is far beyond the understanding of mere mortals (!), so it is part of the folklore that users are **expected** to make a mess of things — so they do. Whichever explanation is appropriate, it is probably true that the greatest threat to an unprotected database is its own user community.

7.2.3 Abusers

Whilst users may cause problems for the database through ignorance, there are those who set out deliberately to hack their way around the system. The motive will vary between different systems; it may be simply to discover what information is being held, or it may be to alter that information, either to cause embarrassment or to feather someone's nest.

The characteristic which renders databases prone to this sort of attention is simply that the data is 'sitting there' permanently. Unlike filing cabinets, which are physically locked, and housed in a secure building when not in use, computer files are active for as long as the computer is switched on. With modern computers, many are left running 24 hours a day, even though no staff are actually accessing them outside normal working hours. To some, the presence of so much data on a machine presents a challenge. For others it is simply less risky to hack into a database system to change their salary, or bank balance, than it is to rob a bank.

Security has always been a problem with computer systems. The emergence of databases has just accentuated the problem.

7.2.4 Gremlins

This heading covers all those agents, humans or otherwise, which conspire to ensure that Murphy's laws apply to databases. 'If it can go wrong, it will' and 'Things always break at the least convenient times' are certainly aphorisms which can be applied to databases, just as they do to any branch of computing. It just seems that, with all the enterprise's data held in a single database, the scope for being able to go wrong at the least convenient time is greatly increased compared with a pre-database environment in which each data processing system is separate.

7.3 THREATS TO THE DATABASE

Protecting the database against the various threats which can arise is part of the DBA's job. A large part of the task is simply to recognize the sorts of problem which can arise. Many of these have been mentioned already, but it is worth collecting them together.

The simplest class of problem concerns failures either of the software or of the hardware. The consequence can be loss of or damage to all or part of the database. Although natural disasters, such as flooding, earthquake, or even power cuts, are in some senses a different type of threat, they often have the same type of effect.

Next, there are erroneous operations. These can range from loading incorrectly spelt data to erasing the contents of the entire database because the wrong option was specified for DELETE.

Finally, there is the large group of threats which come under the security classification. These include breaches of security which permit unauthorized access to data, or, more seriously, unauthorized modification of data. Also included is pure malicious damage, with whatever motive.

Working on the basis that nothing ever works perfectly all of the time, a two-pronged defence is required. First, checks and controls need to be implemented to reduce the likelihood of any particular failure. Then, extensive recovery procedures need to be in place ready for the eventuality of the checks and controls failing, or of the unextpected happening.

The demand for data in databases to be accurate, particularly when concerning individual people, is growing ever stronger. Many countries now have data protection legislation which imposes a duty on the user of any personal data to maintain its accuracy and to protect it from unauthorized disclosure. Thus, the job of the database administrator is likely to become even more important in the future.

7.3.1 Recovery

The process of recovery involves restoring a database to a state which is known to be correct, following some kind of failure. The techniques used are based on **redundancy**, in the sense that any given piece of information must be able to be reconstructed from other information available to the system. This does not mean that the database itself must contain duplicated data. Nor does it mean that the duplicated data must be kept up-to-date in step with the 'real' contents of the database. Either of these requirements would fly in the face of the goal of database systems to reduce redundancy, and hence the problems of maintaining consistency.

The most common way of ensuring sufficient redundancy to allow the database to be restored to a 'correct' state is for the contents of the database periodically to be **dumped** to, for example, tape. The dump is not maintained on-line, and may never be used if the system suffers no failures. However, in the event of a catastrophic failure, it is possible to reload the most recent version of the database dumped to tape, and carry on from there. Provided that it is known that the dumped version was itself correct, all that will have been lost are those operations performed since the last dump.

A refinement is to combine periodic dumps with a **log** of all the operations applied to the database. Following a failure, it may then be possible to 'roll forward' through the log from the point of the most recent dump to some time nearer to that of the failure. Such a log would have to contain details of all modifications to the database, whether changes to values, insertions or deletions. Prudent use of logs coupled with dumps can reduce the frequency with which it is necessary to take time-consuming dumps in order to provide adequate back-up.

The recovery process can be improved further if every update to the database is contained within a **transaction**. A transaction can be regarded as a unit of work, or recovery, which must either happen completely or not at all. There must be no possibility of a transaction being half completed, nor of it being applied to the database more than once, or lost from the system.

An example of a modification to a database might be the update of a personal bank account balance whilst withdrawing cash through an automatic teller machine ('Servicetill', 'Cashpoint', etc.). The changes which occur during the transaction are **a** the change in the current balance on the account, and **b** the change in current balance (i.e. cash) in the customer's hand. Bank customers might be rather upset if it were possible for the first change to occur without the second, whereas the bank might be less than pleased if the reverse were true. Thus, it is clearly important that either the complete transaction should happen, or that it should not take place at all. Further, it could be unfortunate if, during a roll-forward of logged transactions following a reload, the entire transaction were to happen again. Obviously, the 'old' bank balance, as reloaded, would have to be updated, but it would make no sense for the external part of the transaction – the issue of money from the teller machine – were also repeated. If, however, the transaction concerned a transfer of funds between two accounts, for both of which the balances had been reloaded, then both parts of the transaction would have to be re-done.

Although the use of dumps and logs, and organizing updates into transactions, can help with the task of recovery, the procedures required are not trivial.

7.3.2   Integrity

The integrity of a database comprises the accuracy, correctness, validity and consistency of the data. Whilst a database system can provide little protection against data errors which are made in the real world before the data are even loaded into the system, some protection can be built into a database to ensure that errors within the system are minimized.

Integrity is protected by imposing **constraints** on the values which may be stored in the database, or on the changes which are permitted for data already present. The constraints fall into two broad categories, **domain** rules and **relation** rules. The former refer to the suitability of any given value, whilst the latter address the suitability of a combination of data values, possibly within a single tuple, record or segment. Should a proposed update violate any integrity rule, then a **violation response** must be specified. The response may, by default, be rejection of the proposed update, but other responses, such as correction of the value, or aborting the entire transaction, are also possible.

Simple domain integrity rules are little more than definitions of the formal domain for each data item. Thus, any value submitted as a candidate value for a data item drawn on a particular domain, or set of possible values, must be an element of the domain. The domains can be defined either loosely (e.g. STRING), or tightly, (e.g. one of 20%, 35%, 50%), depending on the application.

Relation rules are simply rules which involve more than a single value. A number of distinctions are possible between different types of relation rule. For example, the rule may represent a **state constraint**, concerning static relationships between data values, or it may be a **transition constraint**, concerned with a comparison of the 'before' and 'after' states. For example, requiring that an employee's salary is always less than his manager's is a state constraint, whereas asserting that salaries must only ever increase would be a transition constraint.

A **record constraint** refers to the values comprising a single record (segment, tuple, etc.), whereas a **set constraint** may involve the values present in a number of records. If salary is age-related, then a record constraint could be defined if an employee record contained both age and salary. Alternatively, a set constraint might require that the total salary budget for a given department should not exceed a certain figure.

The constraint may have to be satisfied instantly, or it could be **deferred** to the end of the transaction, so that violations are permitted during the transaction. For example, if it is required that a project always has a team leader, and an employee cannot be a team leader for a non-existent project, it would be impossible to insert details of a new project and the appointment of its team leader unless the constraints need only be satisfied at the completion of the transaction inserting both sets of information.

Two particular integrity rules which apply to the relational data model are **entity integrity** and **referential integrity**. Entity integrity requires that the primary key of every relation is always non-null, and referential integrity that in every tuple of a relation which contains a 'foreign key' (a 'posted' identifier), the value of that foreign key must be equal to the primary key of some tuple in the 'foreign' relation; that is, all targets for the foreign key reference must exist. For example, if a relation *takes* has attributes *student* and *course*, representing the registration of students for courses, both attributes are foreign keys. Referential integrity requires that only the identifiers of students and course which already exist within the database may occur in the *takes* relation.

The problem with integrity constraints is often not specifying them within the database system, for which there is usually some high-level definition language provided, but deciding which constraints are required. As with domain rules, violation responses must be defined for each type of constraint.

7.3.3 Security

Problems of security are not specific to database applications, but arise also in the field of operating systems. The aim of security measures is to prevent unauthorized **disclosure**, **alteration** or **destruction** of either the data within the database or the database software itself.

The classical solutions to this problem are based on identification and authentication of each user, using password or similar systems, and matching his identity against a list of privileges. The privileges may be general for the database, or they may be **access rights** for particular items within the database. Before any transaction can be executed, the system must check that the user performing the transaction has the correct privileges for all of the operations in the transaction.

This type of system relies on the only access to the database being via the appropriate database software. If, however, the database is installed on a timesharing machine, unauthorized users may be able to gain access either to the database, or to the software, or even to the access control lists, via the ordinary operating system.

Alternatively, terminal lines might be tapped, particularly if data are transmitted over an ordinary, insecure, network such as the telephone system. Tapping can provide opportunities not only for unauthorized copying of data, but also for modification of queries, or even illegal access direct to the database system. Encryption can be some protection against this type of invasion, but it may not be foolproof.

7.4 CONCURRENCY

Integrity constraints can ensure that every individual transaction is 'correct', in the sense that, given a correct initial state of the database, the final state of the database will also be correct. However, this is only true if every transaction is executed in isolation. In a multi-user system, although each transaction might still be apparently correct, distinct transactions can interfere to produce incorrect results.

The most common problem is that known as **lost update**, in which two transactions are applying updates to the same data items, and only one appears to be effected, even though both transactions complete normally. If the transactions are concerned with booking a seat on an aeroplane, then each transaction might first check that a seat is available, and then after a pause (to confer with the customer), make a reservation. If two such transactions discover that a seat is free, both might decide to book the seat. However, neither would be aware that the other had also seen that there was a seat available. Each transaction would merely update the database to record the reservation. Whichever update was applied first would then be overwritten by the second, so that the first would be lost without trace.

In order to avoid this situation, a system of **locks** is generally used, according to some specified **protocols**. The general principle might be to prevent a second transaction looking at the reservation list for the aeroplane until the first transaction has completed. The second transaction would have to wait – perhaps a significant time – before it could proceed, at which point it might discover that there was no longer a seat available on the flight in question.

Whilst such a system might work for simple cases, such as the example outlined above, other problems can arise. For example, if two or more transactions are attempting to make updates to a number of records in a database, and each is prevented from accessing any record already in use by another transaction, then it is possible for a number of transactions to be in a mutually dependent wait state – each one waiting for the others. Such a situation is termed **deadlock**, and is almost as much of a problem for a database system as are lost updates.

Various protocols and locking schemes, and some approaches not based on locking, have been proposed to alleviate the concurrency problem. In general, there must be a compromise between maximizing the number of transactions that can run concurrently and minimizing the risk of deadlock. There is still considerable research activity in this area, particularly in relation to distributed databases, but the basic principles are now well established.

7.5 DISTRIBUTION

The discussion so far has assumed that the database is to be implemented on a single computer. However, as indicated in the last chapter, there is a growing interest in the distribution of databases over a number of communicating machines. This has, in part, been spurred by changes in the computer market, and, in particular, the growing availability of large minicomputers which are capable of running small databases for a fraction of the cost of a mainframe.

The advantages of distributed computing power have been recognized for some time, and it was inevitable that attempts should be made to distribute databases. The aim would be to retain the advantages of the database approach – shared data, reduced redundancy and better software – whilst avoiding the penalties of centralization – remoteness, inertia and expense.

A **distributed database system** is a database system running on a geographically distributed processing system which has data files attached to two or more processors, and on which the data elements or databases at different locations are interrelated. It would be expected that a database process running at one location could require data from another, but such remote access should be unseen by the user. As far as the user is concerned, the system should appear – from every location – as a single, integrated database.

Not surprisingly, distributing a database system introduces a number of new problems. Not least of these problems is determining where a particular data item is physically located, and ensuring that it is available for a particular process. Other problems arise in respect of maintaining consistency between data that are replicated between different sites, and controlling the interactions between concurrent processes based at different locations.

SUMMARY
Chapter 7

Deciding what data are to be stored in a database system is only part of the job. Whilst the processes of data analysis and data modelling are fundamental to the successful implementation of a database, there are a number of other implementation issues which must also be considered.

This chapter has introduced a number of topics which have been presented only in outline. These include recovery, integrity, security, concurrency and distribution. All of these are real problems which affect real systems, and those readers who intend actually to implement a database application are urged to consult an appropriate text for a complete treatment of these issues before embarking on a major implementation project.

Nevertheless, however good the implementation, in terms of robustness to the types of threat introduced in this chapter, what matters in the end is what information is actually stored in the database, and whether or not that matches the requirements of the users. Putting a system 'right if it uses the wrong concurrency protocols, or has insufficient security protection, may not be easy, but correcting an imprecise conceptual schema may require a complete return to the drawing board. Thus, the material presented in the earlier chapters of this text should be regarded as essential skills for any database professional.

8

FURTHER READING

Inevitably, there has been space in this text to give only a superficial introduction to some topics relating to databases or to data analysis. Whilst not intended to be comprehensive, this chapter gives a few pointers to further reading for some of the more important topics covered in the text.

CHAPTER 3

The data analysis techniques developed in this text are based on Chen's entity-relationship approach, described in Chen (1976).

Howe (1984), chapter 11, includes an extended discussion of connection traps.

Chapter 6 of this text contains some discussion of new approaches to data analysis.

CHAPTER 4

Each of the classical data models is discussed in considerable detail in a number of texts. Date (1982) chapters 15–22 gives a detailed description of IMS, which is abbreviated in Date (1986) chapter 22. The CODASYL model is discussed in Date (1982) chapters 23–26, Date (1986) chapter 23, Deen (1985) chapters 9 and 10 and Kroenke (1977) chapter 6, in addition to the original CODASYL database task group report CODASYL (1971).

Any of the four texts suggested for the CODASYL model also give an adequate treatment of the relational model, as would virtually any modern database text. However, Date (1986) is probably the most comprehensive. Codd (1970) is the paper which originally popularized the relational approach, and it is well worth reading to gain an appreciation of the history of the relational model. Codd's 1981 Turing Lecture (Codd, 1982) contains an interesting comparison of various types of 'relational' database system. The design and implementation of INGRES, which has an interface based on the relational calculus, has been well documented in the literature (Stonebraker *et al.*, 1976).

CHAPTER 5

The definitions of the first four normal forms are discussed in Codd (1972) and Fagin (1977). Codd (1972) discusses a proposal for what became known as Boyce–Codd normal form. In addition, most major database texts, such as Date (1986) or Deen (1985) include a considerable discussion of normalization. Unfortunately, there is rather less literature on the synthetic approach, but it is featured in a few texts, such as Howe (1984).

The problem of incomplete data is discussed further in Chapter 6, and also in Date (1982) and Date (1983a).

CHAPTER 6

As will have been apparent from the chapter itself, there is still considerable research activity in the area of data modelling. Papers in the area are published regularly in journals such as:

ACM-TODS (Association for Computing Machinery Transactions on Database Systems)
The Journal of the ACM
The British Computer Journal

Additional references will be found in published conference proceedings. There are a number of important series of database conferences, including:
International Conferences on Very large Databases (VLDB)
The ACM Special Interest Group on Management of Data (SIGMOD)
The British Computer Society British National Conference on Databases (BNCOD)

CHAPTER 7

Date (1983b) is widely accepted as one of the definitive texts for a treatment of topics such as recovery, integrity, security and concurrency, although they are covered more briefly in Deen (1985) and Date (1986).

Date (1983b) also contains a good presentation of the issues involved in distributed database systems. A good introduction is to be found in Davenport (1978).

REFERENCES

Note that *ACM-TODS* refers to the Association for Computing Machinery Transactions on Database Systems.

Atkinson, M.P., Gray, P.M.D., Johnson, R.G., Oxborrow, E.A., Shave, M.J.R., Stocker, P.M., *et al.* (1983). The PROTEUS distributed database system. *Proc. 3rd British National Conference on Databases (BNCOD-3)*, Leeds, July. Cambridge University Press.

Beeri, C. and Kifer, M. (1986). An integrated approach to logical design of relational database schemas. *ACM-TODS* **11** (2).

Biskup, J. (1983). A foundation of Codd's relational maybe-operations. *ACM-TODS* **8**, (4).

Brodie, M.L. (1981). On modelling behavioural semantics of databases. *Proc. 7th International Conference on Very Large Databases*, Cannes, France.

Brodie, M.L. Mylopoulos, J., and Schmidt, J.W. (Eds), (1984). *On Conceptual Modelling*. Springer-Verlag, Berlin.

Bubenko, J.A. *Data Models and their Semantics* (1980). Infotech State of the Art Report, Series 8, No. 4.

Buneman, O.P. and Frankel, R.E. (1979). FQL – A functional query language. *Proc. 1979 ACM SIGMOD International Conference on the Management of Data*, Boston, Mass.

Carlson, C.R., Arora, A.K. and Carlson, M.M. (1982). The application of functional dependency theory to relational databases. *The Computer Journal* **25** (1).

Chen, P.P.S. (1976). The entity relationship model: Towards a unified view of data. *ACM-TODS* **1** (1).

CODASYL (1971). *Data Base Task Group Report*. April 1971.

Codd, E.F. (1970). A relational model of data for large shared data banks. *Commun. ACM* **13** (6).

Codd, E.F. (1972). Further normalisation of the data base relational model. In *Database Systems*. Courant Computer Science Symposia Series, Vol. 6, Prentice-Hall.

Codd, E.F. (1979). Extending the database relational model to capture more meaning. *ACM-TODS* **4** (4).

Codd, E.F. (1982). Relational database: a practical foundation for productivity. *Commun. ACM* **25** (2).

Date, C.J. (1982). Null values in database management. *Proc. 2nd British National Conference on Databases (BNCOD-2)*, Bristol, July. Cambridge University Press.

Date, C.J. (1983)(a). The outer join. *Proc. 2nd International Conference on Databases (ICOD-2)*, Cambridge, Sept. Cambridge University Press.

Date, C.J. (1983)(b). *An Introduction to Database Systems*, Vol. II. Addison Wesley.

Date, C.J. (1986). *An Introduction to Database Systems*, Vol. I, 4th edn. Addison Wesley.

Davenport, R.A. (1978). Distributed or centralised database?, *The Computer Journal*, **21** (1).

Deen, S.M. (1980). A canonical schema for a generalised data model with local interfaces. *The Computer Journal* **23** (3).

Deen, S.M., Nikodem, D. and Vashista, A. (1981). The design of a canonical database system (PRECI). *The Computer Journal* **24** (3).

Deen, S.M. (1985). *Principles and Practice of Database Systems*. Macmillan.

Fagin, R. (1977). Multivalued dependencies and a new normal form for relational databases. *ACM-TODS* **2** (3).

Fagin, R., Menelzon, A.O. and Ullman, J.D. (1982). A simplified universal relation assumption and its properties. *ACM-TODS* **7** (3).

Gray, P.M.D. (1984)(a). The functional data model related to the CODASYL model. In *Databases – Role and Structure* (Stocker, P.M., Gray, P.M.D. and Atkinson, M.P., Eds). Cambridge University Press.

Gray, P.M.D. (1984)(b). *Logic, Algebra and Databases*, Ellis Horwood.

Griffith, R.L. (1982). Three principles of representation for semantic networks. *ACM-TODS* **7** (3).

Hammer, M. and McLeod, D. (1981). Database description with SDM: a semantic database model. *ACM-TODS* **6** (3).

Housel, B.C., Waddle, V. and Yao, S.B. (1979). The functional dependency model for logical database design. *Proc. 5th International Conference on Very Large Databases*, Rio de Janeiro, Brazil.

Howe, D.R. (1984). *Data Analysis for Database Design*, Arnold,

Katz, R.H. and Wong, E. (1982). Decompiling CODASYL DML into relational queries. *ACM-TODS* **7** (1).

Kent, W. (1981). Consequences of assuming a universal relation. *ACM-TODS* **6**(4).

Kowalski, R. (1984). Logic as a database language. *Proc. 3rd British National Conference on Databases (BNCOD-3)*, Leeds. Cambridge University Press.

Kroenke, D. (1977). *Database Processing*, 1st edn, Chapter 9. SRA.

Lavington, S.H. and Jiang, Y.J. (1985). The qualified binary relationship model. *Proc. 4th British National Conference on Databases (BNCOD-4)*, July. Cambridge University Press.

Lipski, W. (1979). On semantic issues connected with incomplete information databases. *ACM-TODS* **4** (3).

Manola, F. and Pirotte, A. (1983). An approach to multi-model database systems. *Proc. Second International Conference on Databases (ICOD-2)*, Cambridge. Cambridge University Press.

Osborn, S.L. and Heaven, T.E. (1986). The design of a relational database system with abstract data types for domains. *ACM-TODS* **11** (3).

Pelagatti, G., D'Appollonio, V., Fuggetta, F., Lazzarini, P. and Negri, M. (1985). The integration of the network and relational approaches in a DBMS. *Proc. 4th British National Conference on Databases (BNCOD-4)*, July 1985. Cambridge University Press.

Shipman, D.W. (1981). The functional data model and the data language DAPLEX. *ACM-TODS* **6** (1).

Smith, J.M, Bernstein, P.A., Dayal, U., Goodman, N., Landers, T., Lin, K.W.T. and Wong, E. (1981). Multibase – integrating heterogeneous distributed database systems. *Proc. National Computer Conference*.

Smith, J.M. and Smith, D.C.P. (1977). Database abstractions: Aggregation and generalisation. *ACM-TODS* **2** (2).

Stonebraker, M.R., Wong, E., Kreps, P. and Held, G.D. (1976). The design and implementation of INGRES. *ACM-TODS* **1** (3).

Tsichritzis, D.C. and Lochovsky, F.H. (1982). *Data Models*. Prentice-Hall.

Verheijen, G.M.A. and Van Bekkum, J. (1982). NIAM: an information analysis method. *Information Systems Design Methodologies: A Comparative Review* (Olle, T.W., Sol, H.G. and Verrijn-Stuart, A.A., Eds), North-Holland.

Wong, E. (1982). A statistical approach to incomplete information in database systems. *ACM-TODS* **7** (3).

Wong, E. (1983). Semantic enhancement through extended relational views. *Proc. 2nd International Conference on Databases*, Cambridge. Cambridge University Press.

Zaniolo, C. and Melkanoff, M.A. (1982). A formal approach to the definition and the design of conceptual schemata for database systems. *ACM-TODS* **7** (1).

INDEX